THE BLUE GARDEN

Recapturing an Iconic Newport Landscape

By ARLEYN A. LEVEE

Edited by Sarah Vance
2016, reprinted 2019

This publication was made possible by the generosity of
Dorrance H. Hamilton, whose commitment to share the Newport
story of Arthur Curtiss and Harriet Parsons James, the Olmsted Brothers
firm, and the Blue Garden is gratefully acknowledged by the author,
editor, the Blue Garden design and construction team, and the
Frederick Law Olmsted National Historic Site.

The Hamilton Family Charitable Trust
in association with D Giles Limited

© 2019 The Hamilton Family Charitable Trust

Published in 2019 by GILES, an imprint of D Giles Limited, in
association with the Hamilton Family Charitable Trust
D Giles Limited
66 High Street,
Lewes, BN7 1XG, UK
gilesltd.com

ISBN 978-1-911282-59-4

Designed by Bethany Johns
Typeset in Quiosco and Fakt
Index by Cynthia Savage
Copy edited by Susan Pennacchini

Printed in China

Cover illustrations:
Front: View across the Blue Garden to the south pergola,
© 2015 Millicent Harvey
Back: Hand-colored glass lantern slide #16541, July 1917, by
Frances Benjamin Johnston, Library of Congress, FBJ Collection

www.thebluegarden.org

CONTENTS

(above) The view in this late 1920s Aiglon aerial photograph is to the northeast toward Newport Harbor, over the expanse of some of the James property, said to be more than 125 acres. In the foreground is the circular amphitheater with tiers of rose plantings, backed by conical evergreens. Beyond and to the left is the Garage and Carriage House, built around a vast rock outcrop. In the middle is the mansion seen from the back, on Beacon Hill ridge. To the left of the mansion, the small circular Telescope House can be seen, with the Blue Garden on axis beyond it.

(left) This Aiglon aerial looks south with the main axis of the Blue Garden in the center, terminated at the northern end by the exedra and at the southern end by the elevated Telescope House on Beacon Hill ridge. This image reveals how the rocky outcrops define and give character to the various cultivated landscape areas and their structures, augmented by the evergreen plantings.

ACKNOWLEDGMENTS

Uncovering the history and personalities behind the creation, evolution and renewal of the Blue Garden has been an incredible project that has brought me into contact with many talented and generous people of vision and dedication. To have this opportunity to work with a remarkable patron, Dorrance Hamilton, and with Doug Reed and his team from Reed Hilderbrand, LLC, an extraordinary firm of creative landscape architects, has been an unparalleled learning experience. In particular, collaborating with landscape architects Sarah Vance and Joe James to extract from the documents the defining technical, aesthetic and cultural aspects of this story to guide their rehabilitation planning has enhanced the research process. Their thoughtful and dedicated pursuit of the most historically appropriate yet sustainable solution to the several design challenges resulted in a successful project of distinctive beauty. On the Newport site, it has been an educative experience to work with Peter Borden, project manager extraordinaire, who managed to balance myriad weighty tasks as he marshaled diverse operatives toward the garden's successful renewal.

Extracting the stories of Arthur Curtiss James and Harriet Parsons James and their Newport property has required research at several institutions where there have been many helpful people willing to dig beyond the obvious to find the forgotten file or photograph. The many hours spent at the archives of the Frederick Law Olmsted National Historic Site (FLONHS) in Brookline, Massachusetts, the main source of plans and photographs, have been made pleasurably productive thanks to all the help from Michele Clark, whose knowledge of the collection immeasurably eased the tasks. Anthony Reed, also of FLONHS, ably tackled some of the arcane curatorial questions. For the Olmsted correspondence relating to the several James projects and many other related Newport Olmsted commissions, Jeff Flanagan and the staff of the Manuscript Reading Room of the Library of Congress in Washington, D. C., were always helpful in finding files and sorting out the mysteries of their microfilm machines. Also in Washington, Joyce Connolly, museum specialist at the Smithsonian Institution, Archives of American Gardens, was extraordinarily diligent in pursuing slides, photographs and documentary material in this diverse collection, and extremely patient in instructing me in the use of their on-line resource.

Several university libraries were notable repositories for relevant material. At Amherst College, Margaret Dakin of the Archives and Special Collections was a most useful guide through their varied resources in the Arthur Curtiss James files. In Northampton, Massachusetts, Nanci Young at the Smith College archives helped with their alumnae information about Harriet Parsons and her sister Amelie. Elise Bernier-Feeley at the Hampshire Room for Local History of the Forbes Public Library, and Marie Panik from the archives at the Historic Northampton Museum and Education Center, patiently pursued my several requests to sort through Parsons family histories. In the Boston area, Lorna Condon of the Archives at Historic New England searched their collections for Newport material while the Frances Loeb Library of the Harvard University Graduate School of Design was an invaluable resource for early periodical articles about the James properties and more arcane documents which related to Newport work.

In New York, the archives at the New York Historical Society revealed some documents and portraits relating to Arthur Curtiss and Harriet Parsons James, while Columbia University Rare Book and Manuscript Library provided many files about Christodora House, a major philanthropic focus for Harriet James.

Finally, resources found at various Newport, Rhode Island repositories were invaluable as were the several librarians and curators who guided my searches. Paul Miller and the archive staff at the Preservation Society of Newport County were generous with their time and expertise. Marie Bernier and her colleagues at the Redwood Library, with its extraordinary collections, were so cooperative as we searched for yet another relevant photograph or book. At the Newport Historical Society, Bert Lippincott and the wonderful staff made much of Newport's history come alive with their vast knowledge of the sites, the families and the arcane historical "tidbits," in addition to their various photographic and documentary resources. Additionally, various individuals in Newport were generous with knowledge about this site and its original owners. In particular, Brian Stinson shared material from his research about Arthur Curtiss James that was most informative.

The tasks of editing the text, selecting the appropriate images to enhance the written words and reshaping a report into a volume to reach a broader audience have been made pleasurable and productive due to all the input of Sarah Vance. Throughout this project, she has been an amazing collaborator. Charles Birnbaum reviewed the manuscript with his discriminating eye, alert to tone, to nuance and to historical accuracy. His thoughtful suggestions were invaluable. My deepest gratitude, however, is reserved for my persevering and solicitous husband Newt Levee who, all through the research and writing, served as chief editor, fact-checker and literary critic, ensuring that the prose would contain clarity and a modicum of grace.

Yet, without the astute vision, the philanthropic commitment to sound preservation and the irresistible energy of Dorrance Hamilton to rescue the Blue Garden from its undeserved oblivion and provide for this magical space to be once again an enclave of beauty and a garden resource for Newport and beyond, this project would not have taken place. She mingles her determined dedication with humor and an inquiring enthusiasm that has provided a remarkable model for us all.

Received from T. W. Sears 3-3-14

3558- 207

FLOWER GARDEN FROM BEACON HILL.

(facing page) Watercolor illustration of the Blue Garden plan, date unknown, which clearly highlights the classical heritage of this axial design. This decorative plan was used in an article by John Taylor Boyd, Jr., in the *Architectural Record*, Vol. 44 of December 1918, entitled: "The Work of Olmsted Brothers."

(above) This late winter image, from March 1914, taken from Beacon Hill ridge, reveals the juxta-position of this Italianate classically inspired garden, serenely nestled within its walls and its young plantings, but surrounded by the expansive undeveloped boulder-encrusted moorland. The James's great appreciation for the Italian Renaissance and the Olmsted Brothers' con-summate skill combined to enable a remarkable landscape feat, the creation of such a space from the rugged terrain. This photograph was taken by landscape architect Thomas W. Sears, who had trained at Harvard and worked at the Olmsted firm until 1911.

9

PREFACE *by* CHARLES A. BIRNBAUM

"Newport by the sea, more famous than any other American summer resort, naturally possesses the greatest number of gardens on an elaborate scale," wrote Mac Griswold and Eleanor Weller in the 1992 book *The Golden Age of American Gardens.*

In their sweeping survey of exceptional Gilded Age places and their proud owners, Griswold and Weller specifically asked of the mansions that today still dot Bellevue and Naragansett Avenues, and Ocean Drive in Newport, "Where were the gardens that would hold all these flowers?" Historically, they noted, "The white elephants, as one may best call them, all cry and no wool, all house and no garden."

At the time of that book's publication, one of Newport's great icons, the Blue Garden, was disappearing behind an ever-expanding dense tangle of invasive trees, shrubs and rampant vines that were overtaking its failing stone walls, falling columns, decaying lattice fencing, and concealing its pools and rills. Long gone were the days when the elaborate garden's blue flowers, accented with white blossoms, were replaced two to three times during the summer months to ensure a continuous bloom.

Until recently, the Blue Garden was best known in faded memories and from vintage images such as the one on the cover of the second edition of *Newport in Flower*, first printed in 1979. Its author, Harriet Jackson Phelps, bemoaned, "The ensuing years have done much to cloud the splendor of Newport gardens in their great days, but they are still with us. Some are still carefully nurtured and tended, but even Nature cannot erase them entirely."

Like a lost symphony or manuscript waiting to be rediscovered, "Newport's horticultural past," Phelps wrote, "remains to be enjoyed and appreciated ... not of 'Paradise Lost,' but rather a glimpse of that 'Paradise' which may be regained."

Happily, we no longer need to refer to archival photographs to recall the Blue Garden's former glory. Landscape historian Arleyn Levee has produced a fascinating and carefully researched narrative about the garden's origins, development, heyday, decline and ultimate renaissance. Originally designed by Frederick Law Olmsted, Jr., and his firm, in collaboration with its patrons/ owners Arthur Curtiss and Harriet Parsons James, it has been brought back from near obliteration by its visionary patron, the philanthropist Dorrance H. Hamilton, who worked in concert with Reed Hilderbrand landscape architects. The Blue Garden has gone from being a nostalgic footnote in Newport's cultural and design history to an inspiring example of renewal. But this is also a story of commitment to thoughtful and thorough research in understanding the garden's evolution over time and what remains today, and holistic stewardship that balances environmental and horticultural values with sustainability goals and economic realities.

The Blue Garden: Recapturing an Iconic Newport Landscape skillfully interweaves the garden's design and social history with the stories of its founding patrons and the Olmsted landscape architecture firm. Among the many things we learn is that the historic design like the garden's renewal required a diverse team of experts. Historically, the Olmsted "team" included the resident man on the ground (John Greatorex), horticulturalists (Hans J. Koehler, Harold Hill Blossom), an expert to lay out the circulation network (Percy Reginal Jones) and someone to design architectural features in the landscape (Charles Robert Wait). This story can be told thanks in large part to several repositories that include the Olmsted archives at the Olmsted National Historic Site in Brookline, Massachusetts and the Library of Congress in Washington, D.C., as well as the Archives of American Gardens at the Smithsonian Institution.

What flows from this eloquent, nuanced and at times intimate narrative is more than just the story of a garden preservation effort, though the Blue Garden's return from near erasure is compelling. What we have is a timeless and inspiring account of the devoted patrons, skilled artisans and great designers whose unique collaboration produced and resurrected a masterpiece.

Charles A. Birnbaum, FASLA, FAAR, is President and CEO of
The Cultural Landscape Foundation in Washington, D.C.

Harriet Parsons James, depicted in this delicate triptych at the gates of her remarkable Blue Garden, epitomizes the elegance and grace for which she was known. The choice of this three-paneled art form by the artist, Mira Edgerly Korzybska, reflecting the cerulean beauty of flowers and sky, recognizes the classical Renaissance inspiration for this unique Newport garden.

Among the many notable gardens created by the Olmsted firm, the "Blue Garden," designed for Arthur Curtiss and Harriet Parsons James for their Newport estate, remains a unique expression of the art of landscape architecture. Blasted from the surrounding terrain of windswept jagged moors layered with enormous rocky extrusions, this garden room was shaped to elegant classical proportions and enlivened by an unusual horticultural palette requested by Harriet James: a monochromatic concentration of blues and purples.

In an era of architectural and landscape extravaganzas produced for the magnates of industry, each trying to outdo the other in ostentatious displays of wealth, the James estate, Beacon Hill House, was a study in discretion. While extensive in scale, reputed to be the largest in Newport in its era,[1] and lavish in the unusual amenities of house and grounds, the estate was marked by a careful modulation of natural site eccentricities melded with constructed architectural features. Thus, the Blue Garden, a space of considerable and level proportions, enough to accommodate hundreds of guests, was tucked in a created hollow on the northeast side below the high ridge of Beacon Hill. Though axial and formal in its layout of garden beds, pools and garden structures, this room was announced by neither a grand tree allée nor by a parade of sculptures as in many of its neighboring estates. Rather, hidden behind its textured border of guardian trees and shrubs, the Blue Garden was unobtrusively accessed by paths curving through man-made undulating meadows, around artfully placed plant groupings, keeping its horticultural riches out of incongruous conflict with the wilder irregular landscape beyond. It was a secret garden, a *hortus conclusus,* a historic landscape form replete with a full catalogue of allegorical and biblical allusions.

By its singular concentration on a palette of blues, however, the James garden expanded upon the usual metaphoric artistry of such a *hortus* as a classic sheltered and patterned space, serene in its seclusion, often enriched by water. This color, in all its various gradations of hue and intensity, highly prized throughout history, is rich in symbolism from numerous traditions: Egyptian, Byzantine, Persian, Judeo-Christian and Chinese, among others. The cultured taste and artistic sophistication of both clients and designers of this landscape, combined with the clients' considerable financial resources and the design professionals' comprehensive skills, enabled them to overcome the extreme challenges of the site. Instead of what might have been yet another notable estate landscape of Baroque pomposities, this nexus of cosmopolitan tastes resulted in a unique multi-layered creation of form and symbol, a triumph of architectural and horticultural prowess, yet expressed with subtle restraint.

The creation of the James estate in Newport, called Beacon Hill House for the ridge it encompassed, the highest elevation on Aquidneck Island, on which Native Americans and following generations of settlers lit their directing beacons, was a remarkable endeavor of respectful collaboration among various parties. Arthur Curtiss and Harriet James were clients of vast wealth, well-traveled and knowledgeable, with discriminating artistic and horticultural sensibilities, generously phil-anthropic, especially for social and educative causes, who treated their staff and their employed professionals with respect and courtesy. Moreover, they were "hands-on" clients, very engaged in the various aspects of the project. To advise initially on their newly acquired and growing Newport property, Mr. James turned in 1908 to the architectural firm of Howells & Stokes of New York (John Mead Howells and Isaac Newton Phelps Stokes, the latter a distant cousin of Arthur Curtiss). Howells then turned to Frederick Law Olmsted, Jr., scion of the father of the American landscape architectural profession and himself a visionary landscape architect and planner, whose own erudition and far-ranging interests were certainly a match for his Newport patrons.

There were numerous prior connections to link Olmsted, known

View along the main garden axis, along the long pool to the north pergola, 1914. Large planted pots, filled at this point with herbaceous plants, possibly agapanthus, line the grass paths, while the pool is sur-rounded by verbena or blue pansies, as noted in the original plant lists. The tennis court fence, to the left, is not yet fully screened.

A view of the south pergola, 1914. This photograph reveals the central blue pot sitting on the bench above the fountain "source"—a sea creature that spills water into a blue-tiled basin from which the rill connects to the pools. Blue amphorae and elaborate benches adorn the side terraces.

as Rick to his friends and family, to the James family and this project. In the first place, the Olmsted firm, under the direction of John Charles Olmsted, Rick's older half-brother, had in the early 1890s shaped the grounds of Onunda, the Madison, New Jersey estate of Daniel Willis James, father of Arthur Curtiss.[2] Additionally, although Rick was younger than the two architects Howells and Stokes, their studies at Harvard College had overlapped in the early 1890s, and they all doubtless moved in the same social circles. Anson Phelps Stokes, the father of the architect, was already a client of the senior Olmsted, who advised on his Miantinomi, Rhode Island property beginning in 1881.[3] By 1898, the retirement of the senior Olmsted put Rick and John Charles at the helm of their own firm of Olmsted Brothers. Among their long-term clients, beginning in 1906, was Isaac Newton Phelps Stokes, who was seeking landscape advice to shape his own Greenwich, Connecticut properties.[4]

Olmsted brought with him the skills of his firm, a diverse group of talented professionals and apprentices who could creatively implement Olmsted's plan, supervise complex site renovations, work with a bevy of other craftsmen and answer the demands of the clients' needs. Valued for the consummate skill with which they approached the architecture and art of landscape shaping, for the originality of their plans and appropriateness to house, setting and clients' desires, the firm was also known for its discretion. Their practice in Newport epitomized this trait. Beginning in the 1880s, the Olmsted firm had worked on numerous landscape commissions in Newport and surrounding areas, designing public spaces, residential subdivisions, institutions and private estates, many simultaneously. For their estate clients, many of great prominence, the firm managed to surround their mansions with landscapes of individual distinction without undue repetition of design modalities. For several of these clients, the firm also designed properties in other locales, again maintaining distinctive character.

While such discretion was critical for clients such as the Jameses, prominent cultural leaders in national and international circles, Rick's knowledge of successful landscape planning across the country enabled him to ensure a unique originality to his designs for Beacon Hill House with its Blue Garden. From the outset, it was clear that this would be a garden of great social exposure. In Newport, as at her various other properties, Harriet James was known for her grand parties, entertaining large numbers, whether a gathering of the international elite or the sailors from Fort Adams, whether for a charitable cause, a musicale, a garden club meeting or to present a debutante. While the Beacon Hill House landscape had numerous other "rooms" for events, the singularity of the Blue Garden made it a perpetual attraction, designed to provide gracious space and ever-changing horticultural interest for parties.

From its opening celebratory spectacle, "The Masque of the Blue Garden" of August 1913, a grand renaissance pageant for about 300 guests, followed by a feast of cuisine appropriate to Cosimo di Medici (portrayed by suitably costumed Arthur Curtiss James), events in this garden were covered in detail by newspapers and photogravure periodicals across the country. Professional architectural literature as well as popular magazines examined the unique interpretation of a classical design, the balanced articulation of spaces and sculptural elements, the interweaving of textures and color in the plantings, and skill and craftsmanship required to sustain such an art form. The garden's unique photogenic character was celebrated by noted photographers of the day, although sadly before the era of color film; these were black-and-white images or hand-colored glass slides which did not truly capture the iridescence of blue tonalities of garden and sky in the distinctive reflective light of Newport's waterfront environment.

From 1913 until the early 1930s, the Blue Garden social events were among the heralded features of Newport. With the development on the Beacon Hill House property of other specialized garden "rooms" — no longer designed by the Olmsted firm — the newsworthy landscape venues expanded. A circular amphitheater along the southwestern perimeter and a rose garden of considerable proportions along a south-facing terrace were established, which com-

View through the east gates into the garden, 1917. Mrs. James owned a pair of antique gates which she wanted to use. A similar pair was fabricated, both crafted to fit within the walls at the east and west entrances to the apse, reinforcing the idea that this was a private space.

peted for attention with the Blue Garden. As far-flung business and charitable interests and travel took the Jameses to diverse locales, as Depression-ravaged finances altered maintenance priorities, and as increasing ill health distracted them, the involvement of both Arthur and Harriet in the landscape of Beacon Hill House decreased. With their deaths in May and June 1941, within three weeks of each other, attention paid to maintain this labor-intensive property plummeted. The main estate, with its surrounding landscape of extraordinary garden features, was originally managed by the James Foundation.

Gifted to the Diocese of Providence, which used some structures for a school and convent but could not maintain such a large property, the estate decayed and the mansion burned. The Diocese then sold some of the property, which was subdivided without recognition of the once special garden spaces and their features. Slowly, the garden's sculptural elements disappeared; the structural features, the walls, shelters and pergolas of these once celebrated "rooms," eroded, subsumed under a nearly impenetrable blanket of untamed vegetation and invasive weeds. The architectural, artistic and landscape splendors of Beacon Hill House disappeared into the mists of memory.

It took the late Harriet Jackson Phelps, a woman of many talents, among them being the photographic editor of the Garden Club of America *Bulletin*, to serendipitously discover long-forgotten boxes of glass slides, which contained an extraordinary visual record of prominent gardens from across the nation as they existed in the 1920s–30s. Using these images, she embarked upon documenting Newport's horticultural heritage for her 1979 book *Newport in Flower*. With her curiosity piqued, she began a quest for "garden archeology" in Newport, wading through waist-high weeds on various sites to expose artifacts remaining from this once-grand heritage and to excite current landowners about their hidden endowment. From such debris, beginning in 1984, the tattered walls, pools and rills of the Blue Garden and the decaying trellis foundations of the Rose Garden pergolas slowly emerged.[5]

With the late twentieth-century resurgence of interest in historic landscapes, a new era of methodologies for research, for standards of restoration or rehabilitation and for devising sustainable futures for past landscape glories has emerged. More than simply recapturing the shapes of past elegance, contemporary practice seeks to understand how the layers of use and design altered a site; how decisions were made over time and by whom; what artistic and social values were applied to pattern a landscape; how much integrity remains; what can or should be rehabilitated and sustained; and how this work should be interpreted and stewarded toward a new future. These were among the many principles and concerns at play in deciding what elements of the extraordinary Blue Garden were retrieved and given a new life.

Looking northeast from the south pergola along the main axis of the Blue Garden, 1917. By this date, large pots along each side of the pools contain conical evergreens and rest on concrete plinths. Marble columns no longer surround the wellhead, and the large blue pot, formerly placed at the center of the south pergola, has been relocated to the center of the long pool.

The Newport Architectural Heritage

Each generation of settlers, from seventeenth-century religious refugees to twentieth-century vacationers, has left its mark upon the architectural and landscape environments of Newport. The resulting diversity of structures of all scales and materials, some on miniscule lots, others surrounded by acres of land, some on streets that are little more than lanes, others on broad avenues, and still others on the circuitous routes winding around the boulder-strewn moors, all combined to give this maritime city its richly "picturesque charm."[1] Newport's natural assets of a fortuitous location for commerce, access to natural resources, beneficial climate and its great scenic vistas attracted early colonists from diverse backgrounds to settle and prosper, proclaiming their success by building increasingly elaborate houses around the town, eventually moving further afield to develop substantial country seats with accompanying gardens. In their design, these properties reflected the European taste of their owners, many based on English country house models.

The post-Revolutionary War era saw significant alterations to the scale and shape of many of these properties, as estates of British sympathizers were appropriated and subdivided. For a while, new industrial and commercial endeavors blossomed, changing the agrarian landscape and the patterns of building to meet new needs and populations, all accelerated by the advent of the railroad. But in the economically turbulent decades after the War of 1812, business patterns changed and Newport went into a "state of arrested development."[2] Counteracting the commercial slough, however, was the increasing appeal of Newport for tourists affluent enough to afford a vacation away from the congested urban areas where they lived and worked. These visitors lodged first in rooming houses, then in hotels of

growing scale, and gradually began to build their own establishments, often on suburban lots well beyond the town's core. Included in this growing community were many cosmopolitan travelers of great means, coming from increasingly distant venues, who slowly coalesced into their own separate culture of the summer colony.[3]

Their chosen architecture, while still reflecting European precedents, progressively showed decorative elements and proportions that heralded the emergence of a distinctively American style. The English-inspired "cottage ornée" evolved into the array of patterns as guided by, among others, those nineteenth-century "apostles of taste," Alexander Jackson Davis, Andrew Jackson Downing, Robert Morris Copeland and Calvert Vaux. Downing, in particular, expanded the design realm from buildings alone into the landscapes that surrounded them.[4] Larger windows, piazzas and verandas, and a picturesque eccentricity of line and form, thrust outward from buildings' central masses to engage with landscape elements, to be embowered by trees or offset by lawns. For Downing, a tasteful manipulation of nature for beauty as well as utility, whether for the individual home or for an entire suburb, was a sign of the advancement of American culture, moving away from its pioneering roughness to a new sophistication.[5] With his popular writings and publishing endeavors, the reach of Downing's prescriptions for taste was considerable, and the growing summer colony in Newport in the 1840s and 1850s heard his message in shaping their new dwellings.

In the following decades, many of the new residents chose to demonstrate their wealth and power with buildings more monumental and formal in taste than picturesque and quaint. In the years bracketing the Civil War upheaval, professional architects imposed their myriad stylistic proclivities upon the Newport scene as the cottage ideal evolved into villas, which in turn

NEWPORT. R.I.

became mansions. Author and critic Cleveland Amory recorded with caustic wit the social implications of this evolution in his "Gresham's law of social resorts." Artists and writers, seeking scenery, are often first to discover places of special beauty, followed by professors and clergy looking for the simple life. They are succeeded by the "nice millionaires" also seeking simplicity, who are then followed by the "naughty millionaires" with social aspirations and tasteless materialism, which ruins simplicity for all.[6]

The influence of L'École des Beaux Arts, with its preoccupation with the grand manner

Bird's-eye map of Newport, Rhode Island, 1878. Note the density of small structures in the older core sections of Newport, in contrast to the southern end of the island and along the shoreline where sizable properties are evident.

There is sparse settlement to the west, except along the harbor. The rugged area of massive ledge outcroppings around the highest point on Aquidneck Island, known as Beacon Hill, remains undeveloped.

and academic historicity, added the French influence, somewhat counteracted by the English Queen Anne-inspired shingle style buildings.[7] The Philadelphia Centennial of 1876 contributed a developing nostalgia for the picturesque aspects of the earlier colonial aesthetic, while also expanding ideas into other foreign realms,

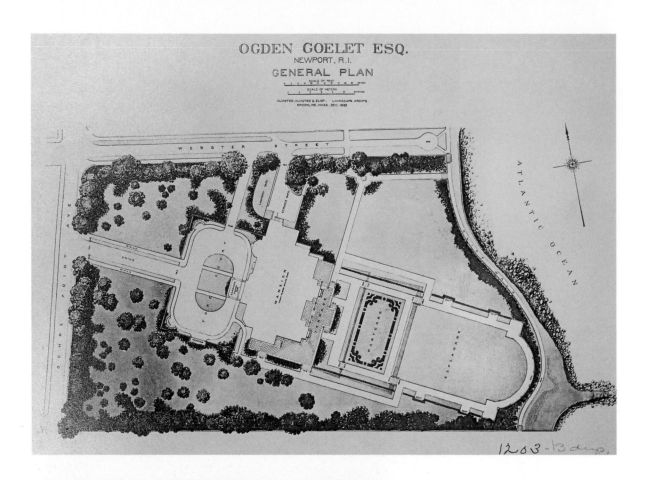

OGDEN GOELET ESQ.
NEWPORT, R.I.
GENERAL PLAN

Olmsted, Olmsted & Eliot, Landscape Archts.
Brookline, Mass. Dec. 1895

(above) Site plan for Ochre Court in Newport by Olmsted, Olmsted & Eliot, 1893, illustrates the influence of L'École des Beaux Arts. Opulent formality was imposed on the site without integration of any of the natural features into the plan. The building was designed by William Morris Hunt, who also designed The Breakers, in Newport, and Biltmore, the Vanderbilt mansion in Asheville, North Carolina.

(lower) Aerial photograph of Ochre Court, late 1920s. Note the uneasy juxtaposition of the formal walled spaces with the rugged ocean-side cliff. Today the mansion is the central administration building for Salve Regina University. The first floor rooms are used for concerts, student dances, lectures and special functions throughout the year.

as influenced by exhibits such as those from Japan. These diverse architectural expressions, eclectic in scale, materials and style, were equally eccentric in the way they related to their sites and the Newport environment. As wealth and desire for imperious opulence dictated designs for these domains, so often on plots inadequate to support such bulk, they became "stage sets," detached from the reality of place. No longer at work was the Downingesque balance integrating domestic architecture into its natural or carefully manipulated surroundings. Rather, as noted Yale Professor of Architecture Vincent Scully commented, the cold, barren limestone of Ochre Court dominated its undersized lot, reflecting a "preoccupation with the chastity of the drawing board" rather than an organic relationship to its scenic cliff-side location.[8]

Beyond the linear "super suburb" of Bellevue Avenue,[9] on more varied waterfront lots or set atop rocky crests within the moorland to the west, were other "cottages" or villas, which, while still sizable, tended toward less ponderously palatial architecture. Inventive in shape, picturesque or vernacular in detail, textured with diverse materials, these structures were better settled into their topographically irregular surroundings to take advantage of the notable scenic vistas. However, just as these dwellings, whether palace or cottage, reflected the wealth, social position and taste of their owners, the surrounding gardens and landscape settings with all their decorative accoutrements were likewise embodiments of status and sophistication. Owners looked to the emerging profession of landscape practitioners, whether gardeners or architects, to find creative and individualized solutions appropriately opulent or rustic.

The Olmsted Firm and the Newport Landscape

A distinctive American landscape sensibility was just emerging when Andrew Jackson Downing met his untimely death at age 36 in 1852. It was for Frederick Law Olmsted, Sr., a former journalist turned landscape practitioner, in partnership with Downing's former associate, English architect Calvert Vaux, to define over the next decades the parameters of a unique American profession with its own aesthetic, working in both the public and private realms. Olmsted, the more prolific writer and thinker, set forth principles of design for manipulating the land, based upon a profound respect for scenery and the natural environment. These he expanded into several fundamental tenets. Influenced by classic principles of art, with its interplay of foreground, middle and far ground, an Olmsted landscape also emphasized both aesthetic suitability to site, situation and appropriate style to avoid incongruous juxtapositions; and to service, promoting designs which met fundamental social needs and solved utilitarian problems. The well-considered landscape art was intended to provide restorative green environments for public use to offset urban congestion, and to grace residential and institutional settings with suitably scaled scenic surrounds.

With their successful park work in New York City, Brooklyn and Buffalo and their inventive residential subdivision design for Riverside, Illinois, Olmsted and Vaux were in high demand for all sorts of projects in the mid-to-late nineteenth-century decades. With the 1872 dissolution of their partnership, Olmsted proceeded to form his own firm and atelier, training succeeding generations of landscape architects. Moving his office to Brookline, Massachusetts, he was joined in this endeavor by his adopted son and nephew, John Charles Olmsted, who became his partner. Numerous talented young men, desirous of becoming landscape practitioners, apprenticed under their tutelage, some of them also becoming

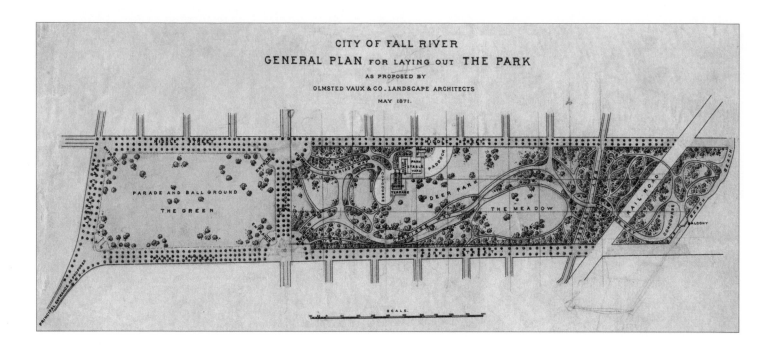

(above) General Plan for Laying Out the Park, City of Fall River, Massachusetts, May 1871, by Olmsted Vaux & Co. echoes the long rectangular shape of New York's Central Park, and likewise, is intersected by streets. Later named South Park, it ran from The Green, the plateau at the top of a hill, down the Deer Park and Meadow slopes, to a concourse at the shore of Mount Hope Bay. In 1903, Olmsted Brothers returned to redesign these park spaces for more active twentieth-century recreation, adding baseball fields and a swimming pool.

(below) Map for Laying Out the Property of the Newport Land Trust at Easton Point, July 12, 1887. Frederick Law and John Charles Olmsted worked together to divide the site into sizable plots, adapted to the terrain and connected by gracefully curving drives.

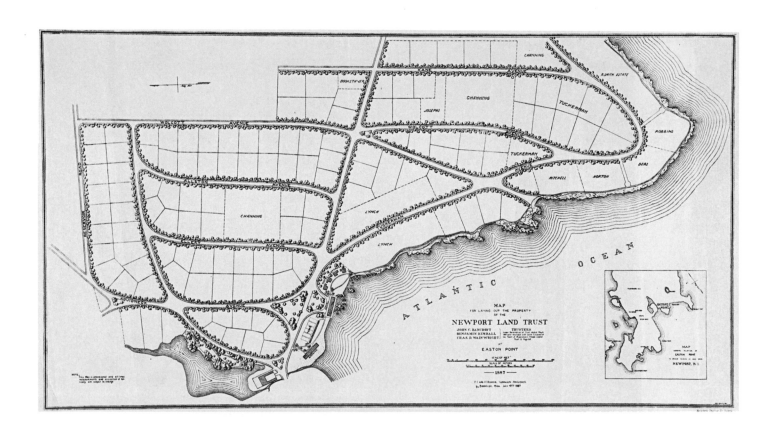

partners in the firm, such as Charles Eliot and Frederick Law Olmsted, Jr. This landscape firm, which began in 1857, continued under various Olmsted names until 1979, twenty-two years after the death of the younger Olmsted brother. In that timespan, the firm handled thousands of projects of all types, from coast to coast and in some foreign countries: public, private and institutional design; urban planning; shaping amenities for great scenic reservations, from national parks such as Yosemite, to state parks systems, such as in California, to large local natural areas. They designed parks and playgrounds, great estates and backyard gardens, campuses, cemeteries, industrial and exhibition grounds.

The work of the Olmsted firm in Newport began in the early 1880s, under the supervision of the senior Olmsted, just after he had moved from New York to Brookline, to begin planning the Boston park system. A decade earlier, in 1871, in nearby Fall River, Olmsted and his then partner Calvert Vaux had planned the first park for that city on the hillside overlooking Mt. Hope Bay, intended to provide a leisure meeting ground for the mill workers.[10] At that time, they had also consulted briefly with the city of Providence, Rhode Island, about its parks. Thus they had some familiarity with the locale, often traveling to the area from New York by the Fall River ferry line that connected to the local train.

Main entrance drive from Ocean Avenue to the J.R. Busk house, facing northwest, as photographed in September 1916. Mrs. James admired this drive with its thick evergreen plantings around the natural boulders, and suggested a similar treatment for the drives at Beacon Hill House.

In 1882, from his new Brookline office, Olmsted began planning residential grounds for Theodore M. Davis, John W. Ellis, Anson Phelps Stokes and other prominent new Newport residents. Additionally, he worked on the larger land holdings of the King-Glover-Bradley conglomerate, the Newport Land Trust and in the Easton's Beach area, subdividing some of these properties into graceful residential plots, adapted to the interesting terrain, while providing for good roads and some intended shared open space, always an important component of his residential subdivision designs.[11] By 1895, when the senior Olmsted retired from active practice,[12] the roster of Newport residential clients had grown to nearly twenty, including significant properties for notable New York financial and political leaders William Dorsheimer, Frederick W. Vanderbilt, J. R. Busk and Ogden Goelet.[13] Much of the work for these clients was carried out under the guidance of John Charles Olmsted and, later, Frederick Law Olmsted, Jr., working with chosen firm associates, thus setting a standard of landscape taste for the area. The Olmsted firm's relation-

Aerial photograph of Wildacre, late 1920s. The original plan was designed in 1901 by John Charles Olmsted for his uncle, banker A.H. Olmsted. Olmsted nestled the picturesque Irving Gill house and its landscape into a rocky site overlooking Price's Neck Cove, far to the west of the densely-settled Newport core.

ship with many of these clients would continue for decades, expanding or improving the designs according to changing needs and the tastes of the time.[14]

As the mansions became palatial and the dictates of garden fashion changed, the Olmsted language of landscape, formerly in a picturesque and naturalistic mode, became more articulated and structured, with defining walls, monumental ironwork, axial terraces and formal flower beds punctuated by sculptural foci and water features. Garden "rooms," delineated by changes in grade and separated by textured plant groupings, provided a succession of varied spaces to accommodate the social and recreational needs of this wealthy summer colony.

From the turn of the century through the 1920s, the Olmsted firm added another forty projects, though some were mere consultations. Many of these projects stemmed from the citywide examination and subsequent planning report which Frederick Law Olmsted, Jr., produced in August 1913 at the request of the Newport Improvement Association. He had been commissioned to review Newport's assets and problems, with particular emphasis upon improving transportation modes. As his father had thirty years earlier, the younger Olmsted noted that the city's prosperity was dependent upon its climate and upon its unique but fragile scenic advantages. The latter he divided into the assets of natural scenery—water vistas, rocky hillsides and open fields—and those of the "charming and picturesque expression" of human adaptations in the street scenery of the historic town. His recommendations covered three general areas: establishment of building codes to protect city character and accessibility; improvement of old and careful development of new streets and thoroughfares, and provision for adequate recreational opportunities, parks, playgrounds and seashore reservations, linked by parkways, to maintain the city as an attractive pleasure resort.[15]

The majority of commissions, however, continued to be residential, with some, like Wildacre for the senior Olmsted's half-brother, A. H. Olmsted; Harbour Court for John Nicholas Brown; Bonniecrest for Stuart Duncan; Hammersmith Farm for Hugh Auchincloss[16] and Beacon Hill House for Arthur Curtiss James, among many others, lasting decades and making unique and beautiful contributions to the garden vocabulary of American domestic design. Of the residential commissions in Newport and vicinity, the project for James, begun in 1908, was the largest, as measured both by the acreage covered and by the number of plans produced. In an active period of less than thirteen years, the team of Olmsted designers transformed the picturesque terrain on Aquidneck into a sophisticated series of differentiated spaces to surround and enhance the mansion. With comprehensive and visionary planning, working with and enhancing the natural scenery, they provided design solutions to the utilitarian challenges necessary to service a large estate with grace and efficiency. At the same time, they created a landscape environment of singular distinction and beauty to meet the expectations of their urbane and knowledgeable clients, Harriet and Arthur Curtiss James.

Arthur Curtiss James

Arthur Curtiss James was born on June 1, 1867 into a household of great privilege. The only child of Daniel Willis James and Ellen Curtiss James, he was descended from Anson Green Phelps, his great grandfather, a quintessential American entrepreneur who began with a small dry goods business in the early 1800s and parlayed this into an international metals trading company with interests in manufacturing, mines, lumber and railroads by the time of his death in 1853. Anson Phelps's partners in this vast and successful enterprise were his two sons-in-law, William E. Dodge and Daniel James.

Originally a close-knit family corporation, Phelps, Dodge & Co. expanded beyond its early nineteenth-century trade in importing English tin to iron and coal mining, to investments in Pennsylvania timber, and finally, to copper mining in the Arizona Territory, the latter a rugged pioneering outpost at that time. The copper proved a most profitable venture in the post-Civil War industrialization, with Phelps Dodge as an innovator of new uses and methods of handling the material. Railroad development was a logical consequence in order to get the goods to market. Daniel Willis James, son of Daniel James and father of Arthur Curtiss, became an important owner of the Northern Pacific and the Great Northern Lines, a feat that Arthur Curtiss would significantly advance. By 1931, the younger James had become the largest holder of railroad mileage in the United States, having acquired controlling interests in the Western Pacific and several other western lines.

All of these men, of New England Puritan stock, mixed their business acumen with strong Christian ideals, stressing that corollary to reaping the privileges of hard work were social duties to church and community. Thus, philanthropy

Daniel Willis James, in an undated photo, had large holdings in the Northern Pacific and Great Northern Railroad Lines, and in other businesses such as coal mining, Pennsylvania timber, and copper mines in the Arizona Territory.

directed toward education, religious charity and civic improvement was institutionalized in family and firm.[1] Shrewd businessmen, they provided the employees of their mining operations with sound housing, medical care and educational opportunities, but were as intolerant of union activities as other successful corporations of this era, with several notorious strike-breaking confrontations marring their philanthropic escutcheon.

Arthur Curtiss grew up in Manhattan and at an expansive summer estate in Madison, New Jersey. He graduated from Amherst College in 1889, where he was known to his friends as "Jake." Less than a year after graduation, he married Harriet Eddy Parsons, a student at nearby Smith College. He received an honorary Master's degree from Amherst in 1896.[2] After graduation he went to work at Phelps, Dodge & Co., learning the business from the bottom up, trained by his father, uncles and cousins, all engaged in their family-held diversified metals corporation. For banking, his family's association with J.P. Morgan provided him access to financial training at the grandest level. He also was tutored in railroads by his father's revered associate in the Northern Pacific and Great Northern Lines, the visionary James J. Hill, "the Empire Builder." Hill's entrepreneurial acumen and hard work were legendary, in a class with the Phelps-Dodge-James clan. His shrewd acquisition and development of railroads eventually linked the upper Midwest to Seattle. To increase usership of the lines, Hill nurtured industrial and agricultural endeavors nearby, bringing in Scandinavian and German homesteaders to populate his properties.[3]

For someone of such wealth, James kept a very low business profile, preferring instead to be noted in the press for his sailing feats and for his philanthropy. An enthusiastic sailor, he credited his initiation into this world to his boyhood reading of Lady Anna Brassey's *Voyage of the Sunbeam*, first published in 1878, which recorded the round-the-world journey in 1876–77 of her family and crew aboard a 159-foot, three-masted schooner. Beginning in 1893, James was given his opportunity for a similar adventure with the gift from his parents of the 133-foot, wooden-hull schooner, the *Coronet,* a vessel whose fame had been established on March 28, 1887 when it bested the *Dauntless* in a transatlantic challenge with Captain Christopher Crosby at the helm. Under the Captain's tutelage, James began a six-year apprenticeship in navigation and seamanship, which ultimately resulted in achieving a Sailing Master's Certificate in 1899, enabling him to take the helm of the sizable sailing vessels which would constitute his future collection.[4]

In 1896, James, together with his father, underwrote the costs for a six-month expedition aboard the *Coronet* to the northern islands of

Arthur Curtiss James, c. 1889, grew up as a privileged child in Manhattan, spending summers in Madison, New Jersey. He graduated from Amherst College and went to work in the family businesses, trained from the ground up by his father, uncles, and cousins.

Japan for Professor David Todd, his wife, writer Mabel Loomis Todd, and several scientists from the Amherst and Harvard Observatories, to photograph an August 9 solar eclipse and study the corona, using newly developed equipment. Additionally, he was to visit the indigenous Ainu tribal communities around Sapporo on the northern Japanese island of Hokkaido to study their customs and collect some curios for the American Museum of Natural History in New York, of which he was a generous patron. Mabel Todd was to do likewise for the Peabody Museum of Archeology and Ethnology at Harvard University in the communities around Esashi, the area selected for the eclipse camp, which was on the northern coast of Hokkaido.

Mrs. Todd's journal of this expedition, appearing first as articles in noted periodicals of the time, was published in 1898 as *Corona and Coronet*. An introductory chapter entitled "Deep Sea Yachting" was written by "Captain Arthur

Curtiss James," although he was still under the watchful eye of Sailing Master Crosby. In it, he revealed his enjoyment of such challenging sailing and adventurous foreign travel, combined with his commitment to use these experiences to further knowledge of currents, tides and winds for the U.S. Hydrographic Office.[5] This schooner, which was to be their abode for many months, came alive in Mabel's description as "… airy as a bird … of beauty indescribable" when its "cloud of canvas was spread to a brisk wind." She noted its commodious deck and living quarters; its carved mahogany saloon, amply furnished with piano, easy chairs, bookcases and a coal stove; its two staterooms and four other rooms to accommodate at least twelve guests. It carried a crew of ten plus a sailing master, two mates, a cook with two assistants and two stewards.[6]

The *Coronet* left New York in December 1895, with only the crew and Captain Crosby at the helm, to sail around Cape Horn through often turbulent weather, to meet the travelers in the sheltered harbor of Sausalito, California. The rest of the party left New York on April 6, 1896, traveling by rail in James Hill's commodious private car, the "A-1" along the Great Northern route from Chicago to Seattle and then down the coast to San Francisco, arriving there on April 16, 1896. They had traversed many tracks that would be part of the James holdings thirty years later. On April 25, with all available deck and cabin space occupied by scientific equipment, they set sail for Yokohama, stopping first in Hawaii on May 11, for two weeks of social events and exploration of the islands' institutions, features and vegetation. James was to write an article in 1897 for the *North American Review* supporting the cause of annexation, extolling the beauty, resources and strategic position of the islands. From Hawaii, their southwesterly course was frequently slow and warm until trade winds arose to speed the journey, reaching the busy Japanese harbor on June 22, 1896.[7]

After a week in Yokohama and Tokyo, being entertained by friends and dignitaries, visiting the sights and artisans' studios of the area and arranging for permissions for their further travels, the scientists with all the equipment went north by various means to Esashi to set up their eclipse camp. The Jameses and the others of the "unscientific contingent," as they had dubbed themselves, continued their touring, now around Kobe and Kyoto, eventually going south to the picturesque Inland Sea with a Mr. Okita as interpreter. Rather than testing *Coronet*'s agility among the narrow passages and quaint bays of this area, without steam power and in the chancy weather of the typhoon season, they went by a rented steamer.[8] They returned by way of Osaka, going inland to explore the temples in Nara, accessed along a grand avenue of majestic ancient *Cryptomeria*. Deciding on August 1 not to join the eclipse party on Hokkaido, this group then traveled for the next month to the hot springs of Miyanoshita; to hike in the picturesque countryside around Hakone; and to examine the ancient temples in Nikko and the beauties of Lake Chuzenji. By the end of August, the eclipse groups had returned after marginal photographic success in capturing the corona due to persistent clouds.

The *Coronet* set sail for home on September 2, 1896, this time charting their month-long voyage through the Northern Pacific along the great circle route, at what James called "the worst time of year" due to the typhoons. Their course brought them through gales followed by calms, through heavy seas with nearby waterspouts, and obliterating fog as they approached San Francisco on October 1. In Mabel Todd's words, "No longer could the faithful owner and Captain of the *Coronet* be gayly [sic] termed a summer yachtsman; he had fairly earned his title of skilled and experienced deep-sea navigator…"[9]

With his newly refined skills and seaworthy experience, with his new certificate as a Sailing

Master, in 1899 James supervised the design and launch of his next sailing vessel, the *Aloha I*, a 130-foot brigantine with auxiliary steam power, which made her maiden voyage in 1900, carrying the Jameses and friends across the wintery North Atlantic to tour the Mediterranean for five months. James became the commodore of the Seawanhaka-Corinthian Yacht Club in Oyster Bay, New York from 1902 to 1907.[10] Although they made yearly voyages to England, Scotland, Scandinavia or the West Indies, the *Aloha I* was not sufficient to fulfill Arthur's "Round the World dream." As he noted, "advancing years and the desire for additional creature comforts" resulted in the 1910 launch of the *Aloha II*, to great fanfare as one of the largest of the American-built yachts of its day. Steam-powered and steel-hulled, this 219-foot, three-masted, square-rigged barkentine was fitted with every luxury and a crew of thirty-eight, including a stewardess. He had become the commodore of the prestigious New York Yacht Club from 1909 to 1910, and *Aloha II* became its flagship. Before the Government took her over for temporary service during World War I, she made numerous trips across the Atlantic.[11]

In 1921–22, James finally realized his dream to circumnavigate the globe in a yacht, leaving New York on September 15, 1921. Their course took them through the Panama Canal to Hawaii; to Japan and the Far East; to various ports-of-call in Southeast Asia; around India to Aden; through the Suez Canal; crossing the Mediterranean to Marseilles for their homeward journey, arriving in Newport on June 1, 1922. Besides the Jameses, the traveling party consisted of Florence Sullivan, "Fluff," one of Harriet's companions, also involved with Y.W.C.A. work; William Matheson, a friend, Florida neighbor and fellow industrialist, specializing in chemical dyes; Andrew P. Alvord, an Amherst friend and frequent sailor; and Karl Vogel, a doctor and assistant Professor of Clinical Pathology at Columbia University, who kept the log which became the 1922 publication, *Aloha Around the World*.[12] Throughout the 1920s and 30s, Harriet and Arthur, with their many guests, cruised the seas for months at a time on the commodious *Aloha II* until the late 1930s, when ill health prevented James from taking the helm, depriving him of a task from which he had derived so much pleasure.

The yacht *Aloha II*, steam-powered and steel-hulled, was a 219-foot, three-masted square-rigged barkentine, fitted with every luxury, and manned by a crew of thirty-eight. In 1921-1922, the Jameses and a party of friends circumnavigated the globe on the *Aloha II*, a journey that took nine months.

Inheriting a considerable fortune in 1907 with the death of his father,[13] Arthur Curtiss became more public in his philanthropy, carrying out his father's many charitable bequests and guiding his widowed mother in her choice of charities. Following his father's long-time interests in the Children's Aid Society, the Union Theological Seminary, tenement improvement groups and in other educational and welfare organizations, James distributed donations in the six figures for program and building funds. His mother, prior to her death in 1916 and in bequests under her will, augmented these gifts from her own fortune, with particular emphasis on religious and educational institutions for immigrants and minorities. But, for the most part, the James family philanthropy was deliberately unheralded, with James threatening to cancel gifts if they were publicized.[14]

Also after his father's death, James began to acquire significant personal and business properties. He sold many of his father's New York real estate investments, buying others, including a luxury apartment house at 81st Street and Fifth Avenue, called "the House of Gold Knobs."[15] In 1908, he began his Newport real estate purchases, first with the acquisition of Belvoir, the former John Glover estate, which he quickly augmented with additional adjoining acreage. By 1915, he had quietly purchased several nearby parcels, either developing them himself or selling them to friends, thus creating a community of colleagues around his mansion. This was a practice he was to continue through the 1920s.[16] After his mother's death in 1916, he sold Onunda, the family's Madison, New Jersey country estate, to a distant cousin, Marcellus H. Dodge, and his wife Geraldine Rockefeller Dodge.[17] To accommodate his father's prized Guernsey herd which he transported to Newport, James developed some of his abutting land holdings into an architecturally unique farm to "devote some of his vast acreage ... to some practical use," a mark of prevailing attitudes during these war years.[18] For this task, in

1915 he hired innovative architect Grosvenor Atterbury and his associate, Stowe Phelps, a distant James relation, to create, amid the rocky outcroppings, a picturesque farmstead, Surprise Valley Farm, evocative of the Italo-Swiss countryside. Atterbury, a talented artist and architect, had developed a practice that emphasized both decorative beauty and utility in his creations. Atterbury was also to design Vedimar and Zee Rust, two of the nearby guesthouses that James developed.[19]

In New York, James family donations enabled the Union Theological Seminary to build a new campus on Morningside Heights. James thus acquired the school's former site at 69th Street and Park Avenue, part of which he transformed, beginning in 1914, into a four-story English Renaissance-style marble mansion, designed by Boston architects Allen & Collens, who had designed the Seminary buildings. Furnished with valuable art, Renaissance tapestries, antique furniture and a Skinner organ in its two-storied grand salon, this house became a showplace for their New York social life. As he had done in Newport, James also purchased nearby properties to protect this investment, selling these, with building restrictions, often to colleagues.[20]

Rounding out their residential properties was a prime twenty-acre site on the Bay in Coconut Grove, Florida, which James purchased in 1913 from his friend and frequent sailing companion, William J. Matheson. Named Four Way Lodge for its unusual airy one-story design, this sizable Spanish-style house with loggia was surrounded by an expanse of lawn, fruit groves and gardens, with a boat canal and a much-heralded stately avenue of royal palms. During the season, these grounds were frequently used for large social events, musicales or various charity fundraisers.[21] A houseboat, the *Lanai*, augmented the Florida accommodations.

What is particularly notable about these several almost simultaneous acquisitions and

Four Way Lodge, the James Florida home, was on a prime 20-acre site on the Bay in Coconut Grove. It was named for its unusual one-story design and loggia that was surrounded by fruit groves and gardens. As with the other James homes, the grounds were used for extensive entertaining, and for charity fundraisers.

developments is a pervasive artistic sensitivity to architecture and site. While grand in their scale and in many of their details, these buildings demonstrated restrained opulence and appropriateness to setting which characterized the classic taste of Arthur and Harriet James. The sophistication of their architectural appreciation was demonstrated by the talented professionals they chose; some, like Allen & Collens, were used on several other personal and philanthropic projects. The numerous contractors, craftsmen and artists were also used repeatedly for work or for events over time at the various properties. Likewise, the personnel at the James business establishments and at the properties, including the yacht, tended to remain as loyal employees for decades, an indication of the mutual respect which developed in the employer-employee relationships.

The First World War and the postwar years added some new civic and philanthropic responsibilities to the usual social and fundraising engagements at the Metropolitan Opera, the New York Philharmonic and at various museums. Prominent yachtsmen received naval preparedness training, lending their vessels and crews for coastal defense or working with commissions to ensure efficient operations at the ports.[22] Benefits raised funds for war relief, to support the Red Cross to buy ambulances and other necessities for the Front.[23] James joined his Dodge cousins, who had long been involved with missionary schools in the Middle East, with

large donations to aid the Armenians after the Turkish genocide and to develop educational and other institutions in this area so drastically restructured after the 1919 Treaty of Versailles.[24] For his aid in resuscitating Italian cultural treasures, he became a Commendatore of the Crown of Italy; for his services in restoring the Library of Louvain University in Belgium, he was awarded the Cross of the Officer de l'Order de Léopold II. He likewise joined other civic leaders with donations for building American cemeteries in France and for an American church on the Quai d'Orsay in Paris.[25]

Beginning around 1926, Arthur Curtiss James emerged from his usual self-imposed business anonymity into the newspaper limelight with his astute railroad purchases to create a new western rail alignment to reach California.[26] His profile as one of the country's richest men—a Wall Street outsider and "never a railroad man" —suddenly became front-page news with articles nationwide detailing the power struggles and shifting financial alliances among the railroad-holding interests.[27] Arthur Curtiss James, as noted by a *Time* article, was called the "Achilles in this canto of the railroad epic ... Bearded, eye-glassed, urbane, he is known for different things to different people ..." as a socialite, yachtsman, Phelps Dodge Vice-President, orchid fancier and owner of "more railroad stocks than anyone else in the country."[28] Through a series of astute maneuvers, James and his cohorts had gained

Arthur Curtiss James driving the golden spike that linked Western and Northern railroad lines at Bieber, California, November 10, 1931. The event was followed by a freight train filled with products from the Northwest, headed to San Francisco.

control over several smaller operations to finally realize a railroader's dream of that era, the second transcontinental link between the Western and Northern lines, breaking through the Cascade Mountains to reach northern California. James drove the symbolic golden spike in "an old-time cowtown of Bieber, CA" on November 10, 1931. This event was followed by a lumbering freight train filled with products from the Northwest, headed for San Francisco. With the extent of this newly linked system and with recently developed refrigerated cars, perishable items could now reach far-flung destinations, promoting development in formerly under-served areas.[29]

Arthur Curtiss James had achieved and bested James J. Hill's dream for another transcontinental route, one that would also link the Northwest and Southwest. But as prescient as the James vision for this linked system was, this was a very different era from the earlier age of empire builders. New government regulations and concern over monopolies and other powerful transportation lobbies hobbled the task of upgrading infrastructure and running a successful railroad enterprise profitably. In an article for the

Saturday Evening Post, James wrote "A Plea for Our Railroads," in which he fervently argued for recognition of the critical importance of railroads to the national prosperity, especially in the worsening conditions of 1932. Next to farming, railroads were the second largest industry in the country, affecting not only all markets but also a large investor base. Consolidation of lines was vital for efficiency and to lower rates that would allow rails to compete with other carrier systems, which were subsidized by the government. Rails needed to make some profits so they could make capital reinvestments for the future. As sagacious as his message was, however, it was not heard in the face of the country's worsening economic panic.[30]

For James, the second transcontinental route had been achieved at considerable cost, both financially and personally. In the deepening economic depression, there were fewer products to move to market and fewer markets to absorb them. Even as the spike was being hammered, James' rail holdings had lost about 71% of their value. The son of conservative financiers, it must have been galling when some of his railroad lines, at the edge of bankruptcy, could not meet mortgage payments in 1934. While his personal wealth was still extraordinary—large ownership in Phelps, Dodge & Co. and ancillary holding companies, among other investments—he had sincerely believed that prosperous development would follow the rail linkage, bettering the lives of people in formerly underserved areas. This was not to happen in his lifetime. As he wrote in 1934 to his classmate and friend William P. Bigelow, a professor at Amherst, while he was bullish on America, he was not bullish on world conditions in general and no longer trusted the security of investments, life insurance, trust funds, etc., which had been thought to provide for economic stability. In 1939, he resigned his hard-won chairmanship of the Western Pacific line. The following year, the Interstate Commerce Commission dissolved the old trusteeships and restructured the holdings.[31]

The stress of a decade of intense railroad negotiations and the glare of the subsequent publicity had taken a toll on his health and that of his wife. While he frequently escaped to sea on his beloved *Aloha II* throughout this period, from the mid-1930s these voyages became fewer, with James taking Cunard Lines for his European explorations.[32] He suffered two serious heart attacks between fall 1935 and spring 1936 which left him considerably weakened and under nursing care. His illness so interfered with his mobility that in 1937 the unthinkable became reality. The *Aloha* was broken up and sold, marking the end of this era of James' yachtsmanship.[33] James died of pneumonia on June 5, 1941, following by three weeks the death of Harriet, his wife of fifty years. With a still vast fortune and no direct heirs, his will ordered numerous specific bequests to institutions, extended family and employees. After these bequests were made, all the remaining properties were to be sold and assets liquidated. A series of significant auctions were held in fall 1941 by the Parke-Bernet Galleries in New York, including one held at the Park Avenue mansion in December to sell off its furnishings, which netted nearly $46,000. All monies were to go into the James Foundation to be distributed to educational, religious and charitable organizations as the Trustees saw fit over a 25-year period, at the end of which time the Foundation itself was to be terminated.[34] Thus the extraordinary Newport estate, with its unique Blue Garden, was subject to the eccentricities of this decision with no specific provision made for a future.

Harriet Parsons James

Born in Northampton, Massachusetts on September 6, 1867, Harriet Eddy Parsons, daughter of Sydenham C. Parsons and Harriet E. Morton,

Christodora House was a settlement house that provided shelter, health care and training for an ethnically diverse population of immigrant families on New York's Lower East Side. Their varied programs placed a special emphasis on skill training and educational opportunities in the arts.

came from a family of four daughters with a distinguished lineage. Her father's English ancestor, Coronet Joseph Parsons, was one of the founders of the Northampton plantation in 1642, while her mother's ancestor had immigrated to Hingham, Massachusetts in 1637. Sydenham Parsons, a druggist by trade, was a well-respected member of the community. Active in the Congregational Church and a Sunday school teacher, he was an organizer for the Young Men's Christian Association (Y.M.C.A.) and a strong temperance advocate. Some members of the Northampton community, angered by his views, physically attacked him. Shortly thereafter, he died mysteriously, a possible suicide, perhaps hastened also by business losses related to the great Northampton bank robbery of 1876, which left many businessmen in the area at financial risk. His death was followed a week later by that of his father, Samuel Parsons, leaving behind a devastated family. To date, no documents have been found to shed light on how this widow and her four daughters managed over the years.[35]

An attractive young woman, known for her vocal and literary talents, Harriet, known as "Hetty" to her friends and family, followed her older sister, Amelia "Amie" Olmstead Parsons, to Smith College to study music, then a three-year course.[36] Enrolled in the class of 1892, Harriet left early to marry Arthur Curtiss James, an 1889 graduate of Amherst. The wedding on the evening of April 23, 1890, at the First Church was an event of greater splendor than Northampton was used to. The church, decorated by New York florists, was filled with fashionable and socially prominent guests, many of whom came on a special train. These included the former First Lady, Mrs. Frances Cleveland, a special friend of the officiating Reverend Dr. Parkhurst from New York and the James and Dodge families. "A brilliant reception" for 300 was given at the bride's Henshaw Avenue home, transformed by flowers, an orchestra and a special caterer. This house had been purchased by Daniel Willis James as a wedding present for his new daughter-in-law, to keep this property in the family. Initially, the young couple was to reside in New York with his parents, at the newly renovated third floor of the James mansion at 39th Street and Park Avenue.[37]

Early social references usually place Harriet accompanying her mother-in-law, Ellen James, to luncheons and flower shows, etc., learning the world of charities that the James family underwrote, eventually having her own status at these events. She soon became the president of Christodora House in New York, originally a settlement house which provided shelter and training for poor immigrant women. Though its roots were Christian, it served a diverse Lower East Side population with its large groups of European Jewish and later Italian immigrants. This was a charity to which she would give generously of her time and money throughout her life, eventually

financing a new sixteen-story building in 1928.[38] Ellen James also had an interest in horticulture and was a frequent flower show prize-winner, with the help of her New Jersey estate manager. It is possible that some of Harriet's abiding interest in plants and landscapes was stimulated by her mother-in-law. Certainly, this interest had been passed on to Arthur Curtiss, who was an avid orchid collector.[39]

By 1894, Harriet had learned to share her new husband's passion for the world of sailing, becoming well attuned to the rules, the etiquette and the signals of life at sea. In his newly acquired schooner, the *Coronet,* they set off from Brooklyn in a February 1894 snowstorm with friends, including Harriet's sister Maud, to explore the West Indies. From accounts in the log, later published as *Coronet Memories*, Harriet acclimated to the rough seas with good humor, joining "Jake" and their companions to explore the features on the various islands. In subsequent years various other cruises followed, to the Canadian coast and back to the West Indies.[40]

For the six-month Amherst expedition to Hawaii and Japan in 1896 to study the solar eclipse, Harriet kept a detailed journal for her in-laws, Daniel and Ellen James, which was sent back to New York from various stops along the lengthy route of their travels. She noted her pleasure in writing this travelogue, telling them to "read between the lines for those messages which come from our hearts and cannot be written."[41] She was an articulate raconteur, providing them with a vicarious travel experience by her richly detailed account of places, events, people and scenery, which included her interest in the varied plant palette they were encountering. Her descriptions were sensitive to the nuance and subtlety of the changing social customs and cultures in the diverse locales that they visited. Moreover, she seemed to maintain grace and humor, even in the most trying conditions, being flexible enough to "roll" with the seas and circumstances, and yet to "roll" up her sleeves to

The James party on the terrace at Taormina, Sicily, 1900, on the maiden voyage of the *Aloha I*. Harriet James is foreground left with the parasol; Arthur Curtiss James at right.

pitch in to the various labors required, particularly to aid the eclipse scientists. Not only were the gracious living quarters and deck space of the *Coronet* truncated by all the equipment stashed everywhere, but many hours on the outward journey had to be spent by all hands fashioning specialized apparatus for recording the event. Likewise, there were times, particularly in Japan, when the planned arrangements had to be radically changed: adapting to a rented Japanese steamer where space was minute, ceilings were too low to stand up and beds were hard mats; or to local trains or rural hotels where accommodations were minimal.[42]

Harriet shared with Arthur a profound pleasure in the adventure of these new experiences, noting her pride in his developing navigational skill with the *Coronet* in difficult weather and in his careful management of the complicated land arrangements and permissions required for travel at this time in Japan. Under challenging circumstances, she remained a gracious hostess to the dignitaries entertained on board the *Coronet* when in port, and tactful when greeting the curious onlookers who dogged their passage around the Japanese countryside where Western visitors were unusual.[43] Together with Mabel Todd, she enriched their on-board time with music, whether madrigals, shanties or hymns for Sunday church services. They arranged skits and readings from the well-stocked library; lectures on the nature of eclipses and on the heavenly constellations, changing along the course of their route; and became chess masters using an ingenious board constructed on a pillow with pins as chessmen. Weather permitting, they exercised on deck, doing gymnastics with the ropes and walking the circuit, noting that sixty-one loops equaled a mile.[44]

Throughout their explorations in both Hawaii and Japan, Harriet's descriptions of the scenery of these volcanic islands—the interesting

The James mansion at 39 East 69th Street, New York, c. 1920. Decorated with Renaissance tapestries, antique furniture and a Skinner organ in its two-story salon, this was a notable venue for parties, musicales, and lectures.

topography and vistas, the lushly varied plant palette, the unique beauty of ancient temples and the picturesque serenity of the rural communities—revealed an eye attuned to landscape beauty. But she also looked behind the façades to comment on the inequity and poverty of the "real Japan."[45] Like so many other Western tourists of this period, these travelers were also interested in the unique artistry of Japanese craft, the cloisonné and porcelain, the intricate embroidery and delicate silks, some of which they collected along with more vernacular curios, such as Ainu bearskins. This journey proved a formative experience for the aesthetic sensibilities of both Arthur and Harriet, instilling in them an abiding interest in Hawaii and a deep respect for the restraint and delicacy of Japanese art and culture.[46]

The maiden voyage of the new James yacht, the *Aloha I*, in the spring and summer of 1900, took Arthur and Harriet, her sister Maud, and other friends through the Mediterranean, from Gibraltar to Constantinople, to the Greek Islands and then to Venice; around Italy, along the Riviera to Marseilles. From Marseilles a month-long overland trip took them to the Paris Exposition and then on to England. Although the illustrated journal for this trip, as published, was co-authored by friends, Dr. Vanderpoel Adriance and Peter Alvord, many of the observations reflect Harriet's interests as expressed in the earlier *Coronet* accountings, emphasizing an appreciation for landscape scenery. Moreover, the authors were in admiration of Harriet's sailing prowess, her adaptability to unexpected circumstances and her enthusiastic interest in the diverse cultures.[47]

By the launch of the second *Aloha* in 1910, Harriet was affectionately recognized as "their admiral" by members of the New York Yacht Club. No doubt her taste was at work in the artful Norse carvings and other unique decorations that characterized this vessel's luxurious cabins.[48] Certainly, in the development of their various properties, in the architectural choices, the furnishings and artwork, and in the surrounding landscapes, both Harriet and Arthur were very

involved clients, with strong opinions, discriminating eyes and a flair for the distinctive; and with the resources to indulge their taste and desires.

Harriet applied her artistic sensibilities to her hospitality as well. A notable hostess, she was legendary for the range of unusual programs she devised for the entertainment of her guests. Her connections to the world of art and music, and her philanthropic support for cultural institutions, gave her access to leading artists. Their New York mansion, at Park Avenue and 69th Street, with its grand spaces and its central organ, was the venue for frequent remarkable gatherings, whether parties, musicales or lectures. Among the latter was a 1923 event at which Polish author Joseph Conrad, on his only American visit, gave a reading from his 1915 work *Victory* before 200 people at their home.[49] Among the performers who came to Beacon Hill House in Newport were dancers Ted Shawn, Ruth St. Denis and their pupil, Martha Graham; British actress Estelle Winwood; actors from the *Comédie Française*; all types of musicians; Japanese acrobats; garden photographer Frances Benjamin Johnston and other expert lecturers on many topics.[50]

To entertain with elaborate fetes was certainly the Newport style in both the pre- and postwar periods. As one reporter noted, such parties were a "staple entertainment at the James Newport villa ... before Cecil B. De Mille made his first movie."[51] For their productions, Harriet consulted Joseph Lindon Smith, an artist, producer and friend. He wrote, costumed, choreographed and performed in the 1913 spectacle, "The Masque of the Blue Garden." In later years, he produced "Gardens in Poetry and Color" as a wartime Red Cross fund-raiser, and helped Harriet introduce her newest Beacon Hill House garden "room" in 1925 by staging "A Summer Night in the Rose Garden." He even traveled to Northampton to entertain the families of Amherst trustees at her behest.[52] Additionally, he was responsible for decorative elements at Surprise Valley Farm. Many of the arts and crafts buildings, designed by Grosvenor Atterbury,

Arthur Curtiss James believed that the corollary to reaping the rewards of hard work and good fortune was duty to church and community. He was quietly generous to a broad range of cultural and educational institutions. Harriet Parsons James pursued her philanthropic interests, traversing the country to speak to groups about the conditions of women around the world.

were enhanced by highly colored and whimsical bas-reliefs, identifying the building's function.[53]

The photographs and portraits of Harriet Parsons James show an attractive woman with an open smile, a regal presence and an elegant yet understated style. Thoughtful and hard-working in her preparations, she took a lively and hands-on interest in the many cultural and philanthropic endeavors which engaged her. More than purely monetary contributions, she committed time to comprehending the particular problems and needs of the various organizations. Her many acts of personal generosity, often distorted through the public lens of newspaper coverage,

reveal a depth of discriminating thoughtfulness for people, whether family or strangers. At one level, she could memorialize Daniel Willis James with the donation to the Cathedral of St. John the Divine of a rare illuminated Gothic litany book inscribed "... in grateful appreciation of the noble life and character of my beloved father-in-law ... April 15, 1832–September 13, 1907," a treasure which would increase the value of the church's collections.[54] At another, she would provide frequent entertainment and social events for the sailors at nearby Fort Adams in Newport to ensure that there was some fun in their structured military lives.

She was devoted to her family. Very early in their marriage, Arthur and Harriet had anonymously endowed the Sydenham C. Parsons chair in history at Smith in memory of her father with a donation of $75,000. In later years and in her will, she augmented this endowment by $50,000 and continued with donations to other

Northampton institutions: the Hill Hospital Chapel, the Dickinson Memorial Hospital, the First Congregational Church, and the Northampton Y.M.C.A. of which her father had been president. The Henshaw Avenue home was left as a life estate with endowment for her widowed younger sister, Maud Larson, but was eventually to become the Clark Institute for the Deaf upon Maud's death.[55]

Harriet was devoted to her older sister Amie, who had married Harvard graduate and New York banker E. Hayward Ferry, and especially to their daughter, Harriet. The Ferrys became Newport neighbors at Edgehill, one of the many James properties, and were frequent guests and traveling companions, with young Harriet acting as her aunt's personal assistant for several years. The social program for the Jameses in Newport included parties and dances for the younger generation as well as grand charity balls. With the younger Harriet's marriage to Howard de Forest Manice, the James family circle expanded to include the young Manice children. At her death, Harriet James made significant bequests to both her sister and her niece.

The public face of Harriet James' philanthropy was more than simply hosting fundraisers and writing checks. She took an active role in the management of many of the charities she supported, working with the Children's Aid Society, Christodora House and United Neighborhood Housing to improve housing and educational opportunities, particularly for immigrant and minority women. Responding to the postwar needs, particularly in Europe and the Middle East, she became an ardent public spokeswoman for the Red Cross and the Y.W.C.A., particularly as the latter moved beyond its Anglo-Saxon ideology to embrace a more diverse world-view. Harriet put her own international travel experience to work for the organization. She used the eight-month world cruise in 1921–22 on the *Aloha II* to learn about Y.W.C.A. activities across the globe. She returned to head a half-million dollar fundraising campaign. Called the "leading woman globe trotter," she traversed the U.S., often in the Jameses' private railroad car, speaking to groups about the conditions of women around the world. Noting the need to expand services into more countries, such as Russia, she noted, "The very best American ideals are being passed on to the women of India, Japan and China and at the same time the best that is the heritage of their own lands is retained."[56] In the mid-1920s, she coordinated her speaking engagements to the upper Midwest with her husband's trips to negotiate for the railroad mergers. Linking the Y.W.C.A. work to the League of Nations outreach, she noted the continuing need for friendship and racial understanding for women worldwide. By 1929, in a speech as chair of the World Service Council of the Y.W.C.A., she observed, "I consider it one of the greatest missionary movements of all civilization that has brought the women of privilege to lend their moral and financial support to the women who have to earn their own living ..."[57]

Maintaining this pace of active charity work, in addition to her extraordinary social schedule, to which was added the stress of her husband's railroad manipulations, took its toll. She was not in attendance in 1931 when Arthur hammered in the golden spike, reputed to be at home recovering from a nervous breakdown.[58] Throughout the 1930s her newspaper coverage was so reduced that the Cholly Knickerbocker gossip column wondered, "Mrs. Arthur Curtiss James' illness is still a mystery to society."[59] She died of a heart attack in their New York home in May 1941. Three weeks later, her husband succumbed to pneumonia, exacerbated by his deteriorating heart condition.

Architects: *Howells & Stokes*

In choosing the design team for his newly acquired Newport property, Arthur Curtiss James, who could have selected any one of the nation's premier architectural firms, chose instead the young firm of John Mead Howells and Isaac Newton Phelps Stokes in New York City. These two classmates at both Harvard College, Class of 1891, and at L'École des Beaux Arts in Paris, had begun practice together upon their return from France in 1897. Howells was the son of the "Dean of American Letters" and editor of the *Atlantic Monthly*, William Dean Howells, and a nephew of architect Rutherford Mead of McKim, Mead & White. Stokes, son of banker Anson Phelps Stokes and distant cousin of Arthur Curtiss James, was also a legatee of the Phelps, Dodge mineral fortune.[1] At the time of their employment by James, they had already created some projects of significance. They had won the competition for the University Settlement House on the Lower East Side of Manhattan, and for Woodbridge Hall, constructed in 1901 for the Yale Bicentennial—the money donated by his aunts, Olivia and Caroline Phelps Stokes, with the stipulation that they design the building.[2] They had also achieved acclaim in their design

of St. Paul's Chapel at Columbia University, 1905, which reflected their respect for historical forms and construction methods. This chapel was part of the Columbia University campus development being planned under the general supervision of McKim, Mead & White. In this project, they were working alongside Frederick Law Olmsted, Jr., who had been engaged to enhance the campus land-scape, work which his father had begun in 1893.[3]

These architects developed a practice with a concentration on public and academic projects. Stokes was an ardent advocate for well-designed low-income housing, becoming a member of the New York State Housing Commission that passed the landmark 1901 tenement legislation establishing basic housing design regulations. Along with colleague Jacob Riis, he supported comprehensive planning for slum removal, pro-vision of more open space and healthy housing conditions. At the same time, in addition to their university work, Howells & Stokes developed a successful practice in commercial buildings, offices and apartments in New York and other cities, in a style that combined historical aesthetics and modern building methods. They were respon-sible for projects such as the Stock Exchange building in Baltimore, Maryland, the Bonwit Teller store on Fifth Avenue and buildings for the

Arthur Curtiss James selected architects John Mead Howells (left), a nephew of architect Rutherford Mead of McKim, Mead & White, and Isaac Newton Phelps Stokes (right), a distant cousin. Classmates at Harvard College and at L'École des Beaux Arts, both men had created significant projects early in their careers.

American Geographical Society, among others. When this partnership dissolved in 1917, Howells continued much of the institutional design, while Stokes turned to other endeavors. Stokes maintained the Phelps family tradition as a progressive social reformer, supporting, like his James cousins, a broad range of philanthropic efforts for minority and immigrant education. He worked energetically to design better building methods for healthy low-cost housing with surrounding open space, believing that professional municipal planning was critical to improve living conditions and working opportunities. To achieve best results, however, such planning should be a collaboration of private enterprise and federal programs. These interests brought him into the professional spheres of like-minded colleagues, such as Frederick Law Olmsted, Jr., a leader in the burgeoning discipline of urban planning, and architect Grosvenor Atterbury, with his interest in affordable modular units.

Beyond his housing reform, Stokes was an ardent preservationist. At a time when New York City was undergoing rapid transformation, he fought to save many New York architectural icons, believing that urban modernization should be informed by historical precedents. To this end, he was engaged for decades in collecting an encyclopedic range of original historic texts, maps and images, documenting New York's evolution from geologic past to the twentieth century. This was the basis of his exhaustive six-volume study, *The Iconography of Manhattan Island*, which detailed the development of the city and its architecture. While this study made Stokes an invaluable consultant for the 1939 Works Progress Administration *Guide to New York City*, it also diminished his professional practice and once-substantial assets. At the end of his life in 1944, he was relatively penniless; however, he left a considerable intellectual legacy, exemplifying a historical record of a place and its times.[4]

Landscape Architects: *Frederick Law Olmsted, Jr. and Olmsted Brothers*

For the development of the property, Arthur Curtiss James indeed hired the nation's leading landscape firm, Olmsted Brothers. Rather than choosing John Charles Olmsted, who had supervised the work on Onunda, the New Jersey country estate of Daniel Willis and Ellen Curtiss James, he followed Howells' suggestion and chose the younger brother, Frederick Law Olmsted, Jr.

By 1908, Rick Olmsted's accomplishments were already legion. Raised in a household that was also his legendary father's working office, he had grown up surrounded by the myriad design and intellectual endeavors which impassioned the senior Olmsted. From childhood, Rick had been trained to think comprehensively, to evaluate

Frederick Law Olmsted, Jr., known as Rick, was a convincing spokesman for the social and design ideas he inherited from his father, Olmsted, Sr., yet was able to adapt them to the changing conditions of public and private concerns that developed with twentieth-century modernization.

the environment, both natural and built, and the social impulses that shaped it. He had been inculcated with a passionate respect for nature and natural scenery, with a profound understanding of landscape design as an art form to be in harmony with nature, and with a mission for public service, to improve urban and suburban conditions using environmental planning as the tool. Multitalented, broadly educated, well-organized and energetic, Rick Olmsted was a convincing spokesman for the social and design ideas he had inherited, yet able to adapt them to the changing conditions of twentieth-century demands.

While still an undergraduate student at Harvard College, he had worked on the 1893 World's Columbian Exposition in Chicago, which his father was planning with the leaders of the design professions. Upon graduation in 1894, he had supervised planting at Biltmore, the palatial mansion and estate of George W. Vanderbilt II in Asheville, North Carolina. With his older brother and others, he was instrumental in setting up the American Society of Landscape Architects in 1899; at the same time, he was appointed the Charles Eliot Professor of Landscape Architecture at Harvard to develop a formal training program for this profession, which he soon expanded to include the study of the nascent associated discipline of city planning.[5]

In 1901, as an acknowledged leader in the profession of landscape architecture at age 30, Rick Olmsted was appointed to the prestigious Senate Park Commission, the so-called McMillan Commission, to recast the original eighteenth-century concept for Washington, D.C. into a visionary plan for the city's renewal, to make a capital architecturally worthy of a world leader. Together with his older distinguished colleagues on the Commission, planner Daniel Burnham, architect Charles McKim and sculptor Augustus St. Gaudens—the triumvirate with whom he had served when working on the Columbian Exposition—this group embarked, with journalist Charles Moore as secretary, on a three-month tour of European capitals, to study and measure notable architecture, civic monuments and their landscape settings as inspiration for adaptation to the American soil. Olmsted thus became well-versed in the aesthetic attributes of Europe's cultural models, as well as in various ventures into comprehensive urban planning which were then underway in countries such as Germany.

Development of Washington, D.C., to fulfill the McMillan Commission recommendations would continue for decades, with Rick Olmsted as a leading consultant. In addition to his teaching responsibilities at Harvard, beginning in 1904 he was engaged with shaping a park system for Baltimore as well as planning several high-end suburbs for that city. Designing attractive well-planned residential suburbs became a considerable part of his practice, with such commissions as the innovative Forest Hills Gardens, New York; the complex multi-community planning for the peninsula of Palos Verdes, California; and resort enclaves such as Mountain Lake, Florida; Yeaman's Hall, South Carolina; Fisher's Island, New York; and Tucker's Town, Bermuda. Rick produced major planning analyses for other cities across the country—Utica, New York; Pittsburgh, Pennsylvania; Boulder, Colorado; Newport, Rhode Island, to name a few—as well as numerous individual commissions for estate and institutional design. Although park design continued as an important component of his roster, with Fort Tryon Park on the upper Manhattan escarpment being a unique accomplishment, his focus gradually shifted toward planning for vast natural areas to preserve America's great landscape features—the Colorado River basin, the Everglades, the California mountain and forest landscapes.[6]

Rick Olmsted was to keep up this extraordinary pace of productive accomplishment for his entire professional life until his retirement in 1950, engaged in active design, knowledgeable consulting or working with multiple state and federal agencies. His designs encompassed

John Charles Olmsted, in addition to managing his own projects, set up the organizational procedures that enabled the Olmsted Brothers firm to track the plans, photographs and correspondence of its numerous national and international projects. These documents now comprise the archives at Fairsted, Frederick Law Olmsted National Historic Site, the former home and office of the firm in Brookline, Massachusetts.

several stylistic modes—informed by the site and program—from controlled axial formality to curvilinear spaces of textured plantings, from great urban schemes to small garden plots, from vast reservations to schoolyard playgrounds.

To achieve such extensive, complex and geographically widespread accomplishments, Olmsted relied upon a well-managed office of talented colleagues and assistants, many of whom had been trained in the Harvard landscape architecture program. John Charles Olmsted had set up the organizational procedures that enabled the Olmsted Brothers office to track far-flung projects, keeping a record of voluminous job-related correspondence, numerous photographs and plans. Until his death in 1920, John Charles, like Rick, was usually out of the Brookline office, traveling to projects across the country, taking with him varied assistants to manage aspects of the jobs according to the skills needed, whether in design, horticulture, engineering or architecture. These assistants were expected to adroitly handle prestigious clients, provide explanatory reports and correspondence, as well as supervise complex construction with the myriad of landscape and architectural details for projects of all types.

The various documents from the Jameses' Newport project record the numerous assistants who collaborated with Rick Olmsted to draft plans or manage parts of this large multi-faceted commission for this important client.[7] His associate partners, James Frederick Dawson and Percival Gallagher, often stepped in to consult, especially when Rick was away on travel. In addition to John Greatorex, selected by Rick to be site construction supervisor, several Olmsted assistants are of special significance, shouldering major creative and development responsibilities for the Blue Garden and the Beacon Hill House landscape: Percy R. Jones, Charles R. Wait, Hans J. Koehler and Harold Hill Blossom.

Landscape Architectural Assistants:
John H. Greatorex

In 1909, Rick Olmsted recommended hiring John Greatorex to be the resident man on the ground, to coordinate the daily work of the contractors and consultants installing the site infrastructure. It was common practice of the Olmsted firm to assign a site manager to oversee their large and complex projects, such as that for the Newport property. Sometimes they used a member of the firm's staff to temporarily take up residence in an area to supervise a project; otherwise they had a coterie of young men whose skills they had observed in the course of their national practice, and who were usually eager to work on an Olmsted project. With numerous projects of all types spread from coast to coast in this pre-war period, the Olmsted firm could not spare an assistant, so sought a manager elsewhere.

Greatorex, an English gardener, had worked for three years for Louis Comfort Tiffany, most probably at Laurelton Hall, his extensive Long Island estate.[8] Although this was not a property on which the Olmsted firm had worked, Laurelton Hall was surrounded by Olmsted projects for clients of great note who had discovered the beauties of Long Island's North Shore. On the abutting estate of Henry de Forest, Rick Olmsted was involved in 1907 with coordinating roads and a bridge toward the Tiffany land, which may have given him the opportunity to meet Greatorex.[9] Tiffany, a disciple of English horticulturalist William Robinson, had planned much of his own landscape, which included many ancillary buildings in addition to the mansion. The Tiffany estate was reputed to have been characterized by extensive layers of native species, trees, shrubs and perennials, planted in naturalized drifts with special attention to a harmonious color palette, as would befit an artist such as Tiffany.[10]

On the Olmsted Brothers payroll until 1911, Greatorex was to ensure that the landscape features at the Beacon Hill property were protected during the utility work, that any early wall building or land shaping was done to suitably aesthetic standards and at reasonable cost. After 1911, he went onto the James payroll at an increased salary, but he was to continue to work under the supervision of the Olmsted firm to coordinate site construction details and implementation of the plan. A hard worker with a "good eye" and excellent management and horticultural skills, according to one of the Olmsted supervising designers, Greatorex proved his mettle in implementing the numerous tasks.[11] As estate manager for Beacon Hill House, he was given residence in the gate lodge, from where he presided over a very complex operation to keep this large estate with its ever-growing list of component parts in prime condition and ready to host a continuing cycle of elaborate social events. Maintaining the diverse specialized garden spaces—a vast vegetable, rose and cutting garden, multiple greenhouses, a tennis court, extensive meadows and planted moors, all with elaborate horticultural requirements and complicated by Mrs. James, who continued to rearrange or augment the plantings—challenged his skills and that of his crew.[12] By 1920, he sought the Olmsted firm's support, particularly with regard to "... weeding and detailed readjustment of the planting," looking for on-site support from Olmsted horticulturalist Hans Koehler to advise on removals or rearrangements to overcome the "messy appearance."[13] John Greatorex died in Newport on July 9, 1929, leaving a widow and son, his loss mourned by Arthur Curtiss James as that of "a most efficient and valued friend."[14]

Percy Reginald Jones

Known as "Pa Jones" to his co-workers, and as "Reg" to his wife, this tall, lanky Englishman came to the Olmsted firm in 1886 as a draftsman after working at the architectural firm of Shepley, Rutan and Coolidge in Boston. Hard-working and skilled, he remained at the Olmsted firm for the rest of his career until the early 1930s, when the Depression conditions and his poor eyesight curtailed his active role. He expanded beyond drafting responsibilities to manage a wide range of projects as a principal assistant. He accompanied John Charles Olmsted on his various trips to cities to review the work in progress, drafting on-the-spot plan changes to achieve a better fit between the site and the intended design. As John Charles' health deteriorated after 1917, Jones coordinated the tasks for his myriad clients. At the end of his career, he was involved with the vast California project on the Palos Verdes peninsula. Here, at the behest of the major investors, J. P. Morgan bankers, particularly John Vanderlip, in the early 1920s, the Olmsted firm was transforming the steep slopes of this coastal scenery into several distinct residential communities of picturesque character. These villages, spread over a 25-square-mile area, were being planned with all amenities necessary to modern living, public transportation links to Los Angeles, educational and other public services. Additionally, given the spectacular hilly terrain with its ocean vistas and beaches, varied recreational opportunities were planned to take advantage of scenery and beneficial climate.

Jones began working on the James estate project shortly after Rick Olmsted's initial visit in 1908. From the outset, he began the preliminary studies to fit the needed amenities, drives, buildings, etc., to the challenging ground. He coordinated the various subcontractors and other Olmsted assistants, overseeing the surveys; the grading and utility work; road, path, wall and

trellis building; soil improvement and planting. He was Rick Olmsted's general ombudsman with Mr. and Mrs. James, translating the plans, transmitting their questions and desired changes, and drafting new plans as needed. As a fellow Englishman, he had a good working rapport with Greatorex, both of them committed to making the Beacon Hill House estate a showplace of horticulture and design.[15]

Charles Robert Wait

Charles Wait, "Chick" to his friends, received a degree from Harvard College in 1903 and in architecture from Harvard University in 1904. He was awarded a Nelson Robinson Traveling Fellowship, which enabled him to travel through Europe during 1905–06 and which required him

Charles Robert Wait (right). Although he trained as an architect at Harvard University, he was interested in landscape planning and skilled at integrating structures into the land. In his many years of work with Olmsted Brothers, he designed buildings and garden structures for a range of projects.

Percy Reginald Jones (left) was Rick Olmsted's general ombudsman with the Jameses, translating their changes into revised plans, in addition to supervising subcontractors responsible for site improvements.

to make measured drawings of selected buildings or landscapes. A slide of an undated measured drawing of the Villa Lante, the Renaissance Italian garden in Bagnaia, Italy, ascribed to Charles Wait, is extant at the Frances Loeb Library at Harvard, which speaks to his early interest in the architecture of the landscape.[16] Upon returning to Boston, Wait was employed by Olmsted Brothers, beginning in 1908 and remaining until 1920, as an in-house architect with a particular sensitivity to landscape values. Reaching beyond his architectural training, Wait developed an understanding of landforms and the symbiotic integration of structure into the terrain. He gained a specialized comprehension of the spatial composition of the landscape, defined by plant groupings and contours as much as by built elements. During his tenure at Olmsted Brothers, Wait designed buildings and garden structures for a range of projects, from public parks to cemeteries; from college campuses to large private estates. Establishing an independent architectural practice after 1920, he continued to consult with Olmsted Brothers through the 1950s, especially on the exclusive Mountain Lake resort community in Lake Wales, Florida. Here, Wait's friendship with the developer, Frederick Ruth, brought him over thirty commissions for new homes or renovations, often accompanied by elaborate gardens designed by the Olmsted firm on which he frequently collaborated.[17]

While Wait's initial work for the James property was architectural, working with Howells & Stokes to design the boathouse, the greenhouse and the unique Telescope House, he also was involved with many early landscape decisions regarding wall and light locations, steps and path construction. By February 1910, he had begun to sketch an Italianate plan for a formal garden layout ending in a curved apse, although it was unclear at this time where this could be located in the irregular topography.[18] By February 1912, this garden concept had been

Hans J. Koehler's horticultural skills involved finding diverse plant material that could survive the sea winds and rocky slopes at Beacon Hill House and naturalize into the terrain.

enlarged, refined and given a site location where blasting would create the space to accommodate it. Over the next year, Wait continued to draft plan refinements, developing the pergola ideas and altering the planting bed proportions. Several times he had to passionately defend his concept when Mrs. James suggested additions of inappropriate sculptural objects or alterations injurious to the carefully balanced proportions.[19] He dealt with details of tile production, patterns and coloring; with all of the cast stone objects— rills, basins, edgings, pots—with the water system and ironwork. While Rick Olmsted was doubtless the master hand at work in the development of the Blue Garden, Charles Wait, as a very talented assistant, had a major role in setting the aesthetics and proportions for the unique design, which was then enhanced by the firm's talented plantsmen.[20]

Hans J. Koehler

Koehler, of German heritage, entered the employ of the Olmsted firm in September 1896, and was put to work on the Boston parks, particularly at Franklin Park. His horticultural skills, special knowledge of trees and artistic ability to harmoniously adapt natural conditions for human use made him invaluable in analyzing woodland health and improving growing conditions in the numerous parks which the Olmsted firm was designing across the country. His broad experience with shrubs and herbaceous plant material and his ability to use them in imaginative groupings gave him a unique appeal for estate practice. Thus, in three decades working with Olmsted Brothers, either as an employee or as a consultant, he helped to texture public and private spaces from coast to coast, most notably changing the barren original landscape at the Bok Tower park in Florida into a lush tropical sanctuary, or developing the unusual heather garden overlooking the Hudson River in Fort Tryon Park, New York.

For Koehler, the landscape challenges on the James estate involved finding diverse materials which could survive the sea winds and rocky terrain, and grouping them in various manners according to their place and purpose, but everywhere so that they looked natural and settled. In some locations, ericaceous material and wildflowers were planted in swaths to cover the ground like a naturally occurring moor. In others, specimen trees and more formal combinations were used to provide focal points along the drives and paths or in defining vistas. In still others, trees and shrubs were interwoven to make a densely textured screen—at the boundaries, around the tennis court and especially around the Blue Garden. Koehler worked closely with Charles Wait under the supervisory eye of

Harold Hill Blossom's specialty was perennials and annuals, making him well-suited to advise on the textured groupings of plants around and in the Blue Garden.

Olmsted partner Percival Gallagher, also a master horticulturalist, to develop lists of perennials and annuals to meet Mrs. James' exacting desires for the Blue Garden and on a tree-shrub palette to enclose the garden and its approaches. Koehler would return in 1921 to advise Mrs. James on the development of a rose garden which was then to be located around a new amphitheater-like space to the west of a Gate Lodge which had been built at the entrance drive from Brenton Road.[21]

Harold Hill Blossom

A 1902 graduate of Amherst College, "Hal" Blossom continued his education, becoming in 1907 the first graduate of the newly formed Masters in Landscape Architecture program at Harvard University, under the direction of Rick Olmsted, who became his friend and employer.

Additionally, James Frederick Dawson, another Olmsted partner, was his brother-in-law. Personable, well-mannered and intelligent, in his early years at Olmsted Brothers he became a site supervisor of design and planting for many of the grand estates under construction at that time, particularly those on Long Island, New York, such as Henry de Forest's Nethermuir and Harold Pratt's Welwyn.[22] A skilled engineer, he was also knowledgeable about plant material, with a special mastery of artfully textured, yet seemingly natural combinations, particularly of herbaceous material. As a firm representative, he supervised planting at the 1909 Alaska-Yukon-Pacific Exposition in Seattle, an Olmsted-designed event renowned for its horticultural splendors that thrived in the beneficial Northwest climate. Returning east, he was assigned to various Newport estates to develop their planted borders. Among these projects were those for Harbour Court for John Nicholas Brown, for the property of Harold Brown[23] and for the Beacon Hill House estate for the Jameses.

Blossom took over as the Olmsted planting supervisor at the James estate in May 1912, when work on the Blue Garden plant selections was becoming critical. He coordinated with Koehler on the greater landscape's horticultural effects, but since his specialty was perennials and annuals, he was well-suited to advise on the textured groupings to maintain the desired floriferous presence during the season. With his artist's eye and sense of color, he was a skillful collaborator with Charles Wait on the numerous architectural and tile issues still to be resolved to prepare the garden for its debut.

Blossom left Olmsted Brothers in 1919 to open his own design office in Boston with two associates, also Harvard graduates, Guy H. Lee and Hallam Movius who had been working independently. Their practice was centered mainly in the greater New England area, with many of their clients among the region's social elite desiring designs for their country places in Boston's developing periphery. Blossom continued to advise the Browns at Harbour Court in Newport, his work there awarded the 1923 Gold Medal of Honor in Landscape Architecture from the Architectural League of New York for Excellence in Design. During the 1920s he taught design at the Lowthorpe School in Groton, Massachusetts, and at the Cambridge School in Cambridge, Massachusetts, both providing education and training in landscape design, particularly for women, to meet the growing interest. His work was acknowledged in many of the noted periodicals of the time, praised for its consummate horticultural artistry, its sensitivity to site and use, and for the effect of luxuriant yet restful simplicity that he achieved. Blossom died in 1936, still in his mid-fifties, leaving a notable legacy of beautifully designed private estates.[24]

Belvoir, the house on Beacon Hill originally owned by businessman John Glover, was designed by the office of McKim, Mead & White in the 1880s. The home, with a stable and 28 acres, was purchased by the Jameses for $125,000 in 1906.

Acquisition of the Property

With all of their sailing and social connections, Newport was a most appropriate venue for a summer season "cottage" for Arthur Curtiss James and Harriet Parsons James. It is unclear exactly when they first ventured to the colony, but in 1908 they were recorded as renters of "one of the Pinard cottages."[1] By the time they left this summer rental to go to Onunda, their Madison, New Jersey country place, James had already purchased the former Glover property on Beacon Hill, now called Belvoir. This property was referred to as one of the "handsomest estates on the market." The rectangular stone dwelling and stables, designed by the firm of McKim, Mead & White,[2] had passed through several prominent renters and owners since it had been constructed for John H. Glover in 1888. Set on the high ridge of Beacon Hill, it was surrounded by a minimally improved landscape consisting

of acres of moor and scenic granitic outcrops, with very few neighbors.[3]

The challenging irregular land west of Newport center where Belvoir was located was originally owned by various members of the King, Glover and Bradley families. After much controversy, these owners hired Frederick Law Olmsted, Sr., to improve accessibility so that their properties could be developed. Beginning his work in 1884, Olmsted planned for curvilinear roads around the rugged terrain to create graceful routes for "pleasure drivers" who might also be seeking new properties. His plan laid out proposed house sites with winding drives "to secure the largest advantages of scenery for each."[4] He continued,

The eminencies [sic] and seaward slopes are wind swept and now treeless, but bear an abundance of varied and very interesting forms of low vegetation, and owing to their

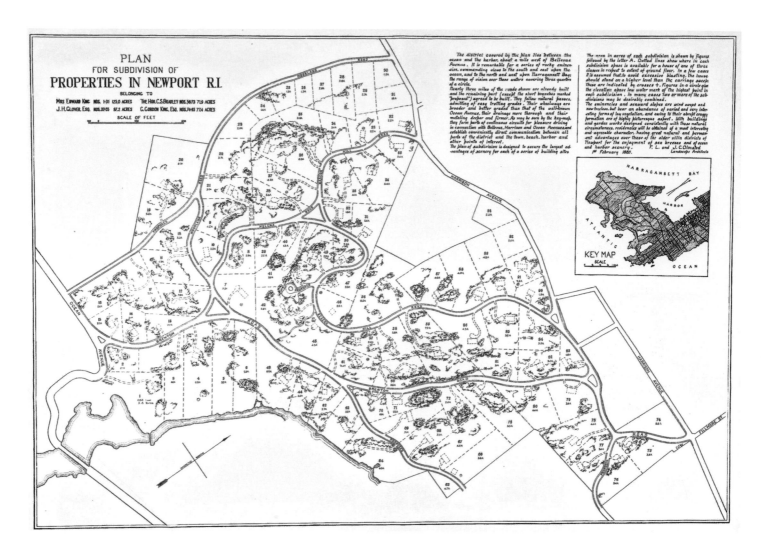

Plan for the Subdivision of Properties in Newport, Rhode Island, belonging to Mrs. Edward King, J.H. Glover, the Hon. C.S. Bradley and G. Gordon King. The property consisted of 361 acres in the general area of Beacon Hill and Hammersmith Farm. In their February 1,

1885 design statement, Frederick Law Olmsted, Sr. and John Charles Olmsted described the rocky "eminencies" which they shaped into varied house sites with commanding views over the ocean and Narragansett Bay.

abrupt craggy formation are of highly pictur-esque aspect. With buildings and garden works designed consistently with these natural circumstances, residencies [sic] will be ob-tained of a most interesting and agreeable character, having great natural and perma-nent advantages over those of the older villa districts of Newport for the enjoyment of sea breezes and of ocean and harbor scenery.[5]

By the late 1890s Glover's health had dete-riorated, so he rented his Belvoir estate to a succession of individuals such as Anson Phelps

Stokes, William K. Vanderbilt and J. Edwards Addicks. In 1900, Addicks acquired Glover's property for $80,000. By 1906, it was under the ownership of the Savings Bank of Newport, having been purchased at a mortgage sale. James reportedly paid $125,000 for the twenty-eight-acre property, consisting of house, stable, some drives, but few landscape improvements except for a lily pond. He immediately set architects Howells & Stokes to work analyzing the existing house for remodeling. A surveyor was engaged to chart over thirty-five acres, which included the estate and additional property purchased by James. At the architects' request, by September 22, 1908, Rick Olmsted was in Newport to evalu-ate the grounds, commenting at that time on how poorly the roads developed under his father's plan fitted to the land.[6]

The initial work on the property dealt with boundary adjustment, entrance and service roads, location for garage and stables, and infrastructure development. Neither James nor Olmsted were pleased with the sharp arc of Beacon Hill Road, which was not yet public. At that time, the bend of the road intruded significantly into what should have been a more gracious foreground for the mansion, also making for a problematic intersection between the road and the existing estate drive. To improve the road curve and distance it from the house, James agreed to buy more land. At the cost of nearly $2,000 an acre and negotiations with twelve abutting landowners, an agreement on the new road shape with gentler curves was finally achieved in 1910. The newly built, well-drained Beacon Hill Road, lined with trees, was opened to traffic in May 1910.[7] Given the irregular rocky terrain, road building and other construction would involve careful blasting to avoid destroying the existing vegetation. Joseph Cotton, an experienced civil engineer, who had worked for the senior Olmsted on the original subdivision layout and road grading, was hired to make an accurate survey so this work could be started. During the summer of 1909 the Jameses occupied their new home to assess the property and its future usage.

Throughout this period, the clients and their professional advisors were engaged in complicated discussions on major design issues. Among these decisions were the following: whether to renovate the old house or build a new one—the old house was ultimately deemed too small; whether to have one or two drives—they chose two approach roads plus a service drive;[8] where to locate a new garage-stable—they decided to place this behind the immense rock outcropping where the original stable had been; where to locate a gardener's lodge—they decided on the Brenton Road entrance; where to place one or two tennis courts, a possible tea house and other ancillary structures; and finally, where to locate a vegetable garden and a flower garden and how extensive should they be. Treatment for the entrances and perimeter walls had to await the final development of a redesigned Beacon Hill Road.

James chose a contractor with whom he had worked on previous projects, Whitney-Steen Company of New York, who brought along associated companies to work on the water and other utilities. Together with Howells & Stokes and Rick Olmsted, they developed a division of responsibilities and working procedures to manage this complex project. To oversee the early landscape work, the Olmsted firm hired John Greatorex, to be "inspector and head gardener … as our representative." Initially, he was placed on the Olmsted Brothers payroll at $80.00 a month,[9] with duties to supervise the soil preparation, seeding and planting and any other work that might "influence the appearance of the final result." As the clients' and the firm's appreciation of his wide-ranging skills grew, his duties were increased to include construction supervision for wall and road building, utility installation, and development of the vegetable garden complex.[10]

Harriet James had definite ideas about aspects of the landscape. She admired the drive curving around boulders that the senior Olmsted had designed for the Busk house[11] as being "more interesting and attractive" as a main approach. After a Newport meeting on September 8, 1909, Rick Olmsted, who was also an accomplished sailor, accompanied them on their return trip to New York aboard the *Aloha I*, discussing gardens, plant choices, desired colors and a timetable. Mrs. James wanted "a pretty vegetable garden with flower borders for cutting and rose arbors with pink and red flowers." Mr. James listed the vegetables and fruits he desired. Around the house and by a water basin intended in that area, Mrs. James wanted yellow, blue and white, with very specific plant recommendations.[12] She was impatient to have a garden for the next summer, and wanted a picture of what it would look like. For the latter, in 1909, the firm contacted George Walter Dawson, brother of Olmsted partner James Frederick Dawson, who taught painting at the University of Pennsylvania, specializing in watercolors of landscapes and flowers. He agreed to prepare rendered illustrations of the proposed garden scenery as indicated by the plans. These paintings, delivered in February 1910, were to her liking.[13]

Beginning in the fall of 1909, blasting for the installation of water pipes, sewage systems, electric and telephone conduits was in process. The complex issues of establishing suitable grades for the future house and gate lodge, for anticipated landscape features and for boundary walls, while keeping the natural character of the land, made progress slow. Establishing a plateau on which to build a new and expanded house with accompanying terraces, while creating no impediments to the surrounding views, made for a challenging interplay between architect and landscape architect.[14] Moreover, Commodore James had an antique telescope collection for which he wanted a Telescope House placed on the ridge, from which he could watch the yacht races. Harriet James, in turn, wanted a garden overlook. On a site so completely in flux, deciding who was to design these various structures

and amenities, where to locate them and how to settle them into the slopes without too much clutter, was a source of much discussion. An article in the *Newport Daily News* of June 1910 described the complex construction activities on the site at that time, emphasizing in particular the skillful stonework by artisans for both the house and retaining walls.[15]

Early Planting Considerations

Simultaneously with the infrastructure development, critical work was begun to "clothe" these disrupted slopes with groupings of trees, shrubs and groundcovers so that the new vegetation could adapt to the wind, fog and salt spray and begin to naturalize. Early topographic studies of the property indicated that Glover had left much of the ledge bare, with random groupings of trees and shrubs by the house, on the lower southeastern slope and by the Beacon Hill Road entrance.[16] In March 1910, Greatorex and Hans Koehler, the Olmsted horticulturalist, visited other Newport properties, many designed by the firm, to see how various plants, evergreens in particular, fared in the south-southwestern sea-spray laden winds. Koehler noted that where there was some protection, they were hardy, but where exposed, they "existed in all stages of … decrepitude …"[17] From these explorations and detailed site investigations,

BEACON HILL HOUSE
NEWPORT, R. I.

(left) Beacon Hill House by John Mead Howells and Isaac Newton Phelps Stokes, completed in 1911. The fort-like massive fieldstone walls were constructed over enormous ledge outcroppings to create a level lawn terrace of significant proportions.

(facing page) General Plan of Estate, Plan No. 188, dated 1911. The mansion, carriage house, gate and several garden areas are carefully delineated. The plant massings along the perimeter walls, around the rock outcroppings and along the drives are contrasted with the large open lawn areas, creating distinct character zones and spatial flow throughout the property. Not evident here are the extreme topographic changes that required the Olmsted firm's sophisticated skill to locate the structures and lay out the drives.

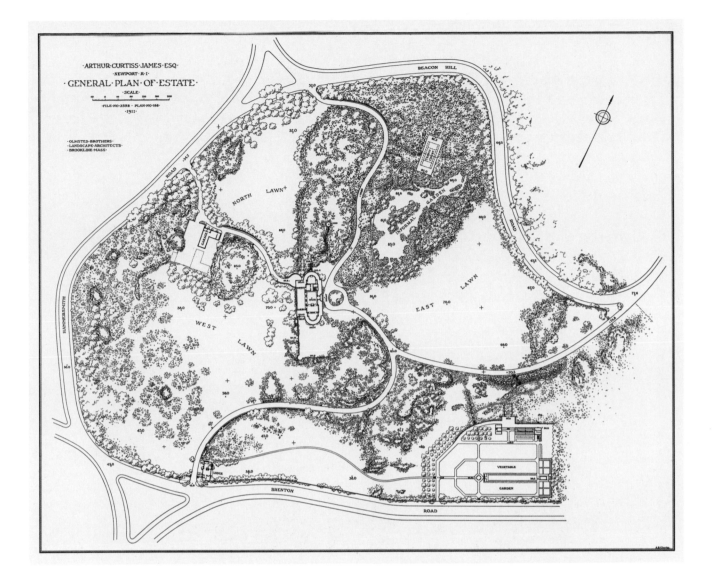

Koehler presented his recommendations in late March 1910, for $16,000 worth of plant material for spring-summer planting, including several specimens to "give a somewhat finished and matured effect at once." He suggested treating the entrance lodge with a "touch of formality" with elms and low conifers, planting the verges of the approach roads with low perennials and shrubs, and carpeting many of the rocky slopes with bearberry and sedum. Along the property's perimeter, he recommended mixed plantings, mostly around fifteen-feet tall, to provide privacy while framing views into the estate.[18]

Praising many of these suggestions, James balked at the expense, fearing that these ideas might be too detracting from the "wild and rocky character of the ground itself." Instead, he requested a simpler planting plan that he could

implement over time.[19] However, the planted masses as conceived by Koehler, combined with the developing structural and infrastructure planning, were incorporated into a General Plan of the Estate, produced by the Olmsted firm in June 1910. This plan encompassed the vision for the whole estate, the spatial flow among the architectural elements, the drives and the landscape forms within perimeter walls. This plan proposed a graceful interweaving of open lawns to planted masses to rocky outcroppings, surrounding the mansion with varied outlooks and differentiated garden "rooms" while respectful of the native terrain.[20]

During late spring and summer of 1910, deciduous trees—beech, birch, linden, maples, oaks; evergreens—cedars, firs, hemlocks, junipers, pines, spruce and large shrubs—viburnums, alders—along with diverse groundcovers, were installed at several locations on the grounds, as suggested by this General Plan.[21] But by August 1910, having spent over $100,000 on the still unfinished grounds, with an estimated $43,000 of work remaining to be done on the grounds for landscape features and plantings, James asked the Olmsted firm for updated estimates. Finishing the roads and walks with essential lighting; completing the walls; building a terrace south of the house, a tennis court and the structures in the vegetable garden and installing

meadows, lawns and some of the plant groupings were tasks still to be done by the end of 1910. John Greatorex was about to go on the estate payroll, so James hoped to do more of the work with in-house staff.[22]

Suggestion for Main Entrance Gates, Plan No. 203, June 20, 1910, shows a plan and section of entry gates and walls which were built according to this drawing. They have been preserved to this day as part of the existing neighborhood, and are examples of the extraordinary craftsmanship that went into building the original project.

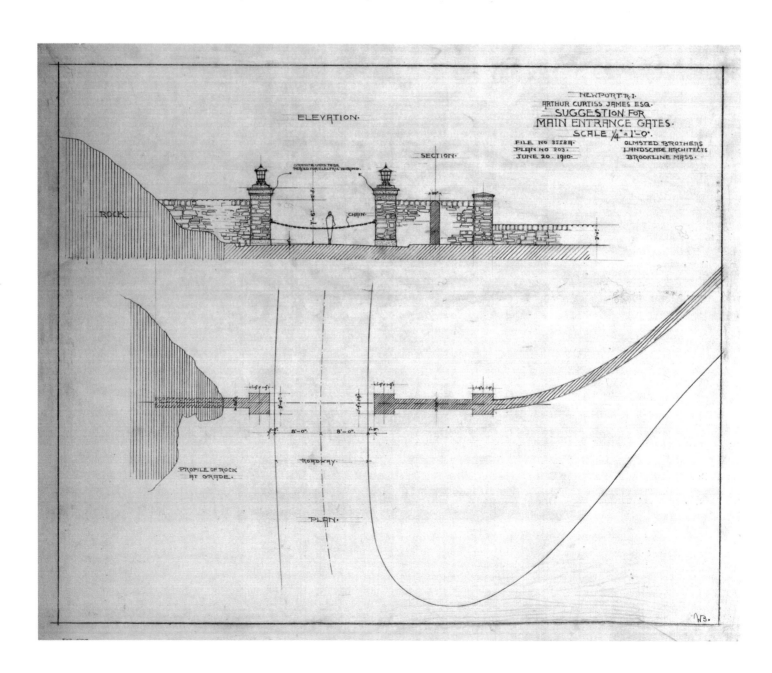

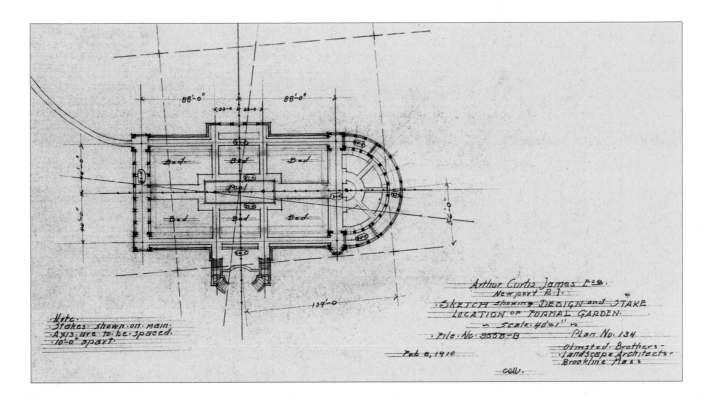

Considering a Formal Garden

Still unresolved at this point in 1910 was the issue of a flower garden and how formal it should be, a topic which continually emerged in discussions and correspondence between the clients and the Olmsted firm. Although an elaborate flower-cutting garden, conceived on very formal lines, with rose arbors, garden shelters, a lily pond and a *tapis vert*, was under construction in the vegetable garden area, this did not seem enough for Mrs. James. The Olmsted firm was concerned that to create a formal garden somewhere else on the estate would be incongruous with the rugged land forms and injurious to the overall plan to protect and enhance the natural environment. Their design intention was to provide a rich layer of flowering herbaceous material as understory to their tree and shrub groupings through which curving paths were designed to meander. Although initially Harriet James acquiesced in these ideas, she was clearly conflicted on this topic and wavered over her decisions.

Beginning in September 1909, Olmsted designers produced numerous sketches, labeled formal garden studies, but these plans do not survive.[23] In a November 1909 plan that is extant,

A preliminary sketch for the future Blue Garden, entitled Design and Stake Location of Formal Garden, Plan No. 134, February 8, 1910, by Charles Wait. Note the formal double staircase at the bottom of the plan. Without a north arrow on this sketch, and with no supporting correspondence, it is difficult to understand exactly where this area was to be located on the property.

a rectangular area was sketched northeast of the house, not far off Beacon Hill Road, although the final shape of this road curve was still in flux as James negotiated more land purchases.[24] By February 1910, Charles Wait had produced a formal axial sketch, a rectangular arrangement terminating in an area with semi-circular ends, this latter shape echoing that of the James mansion under construction. In this oval area, a central pool was surrounded by flowerbeds. This was simply a sketch on plain paper, not located on any of the developing plans for the whole property.[25]

At a May 1910 progress meeting, Harriet James wavered again, stating that, "she did not want a formal garden and had never contemplated such a thing." Rather she "wanted all the natural beauty preserved as much as possible." Her suggested plant palette included gorse, broom, heather and wild roses, to give a "Scotch air to

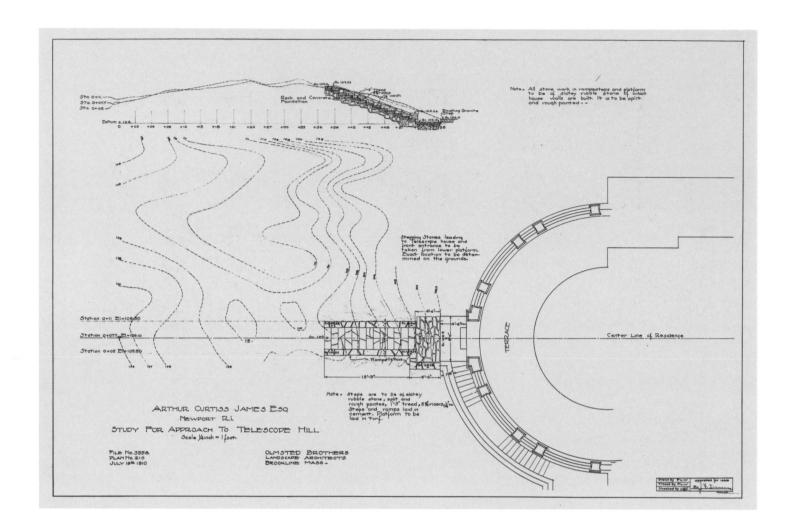

ARTHUR CURTISS JAMES ESQ
NEWPORT R.I.
STUDY FOR APPROACH TO TELESCOPE HILL
Scale 1/4 inch = 1 foot

FILE No.3556
PLAN No. 210
JULY 19th 1910

OLMSTED BROTHERS
LANDSCAPE ARCHITECTS
BROOKLINE MASS.

(above) Study for Approach to Telescope Hill, Plan No. 210, July 19, 1910. The plan shows the terrace of the main house and the relationship of the steps that connect it to the Telescope House. The bottom of the steps, aligned with the center of the house, is at elevation 102.4, and the top of steps is 109.33, the approximate high point of the site.

(left) View at the west end of the house, July 1915, photograph by Harold Blossom. The Telescope House at the right is reached by stone steps that were indicated in Plan No. 210 above, enhanced by evergreen plant groupings. Note also the metal steps to reach the viewing platform on the roof of this shelter.

the place," fearing that rhododendrons might be "too sophisticated" for the moors.[26] Therefore, the June 1910 General Plan of the Estate showed only an area of irregular plant groupings, south of the tennis court, marked "Informal Garden." This location is approximately where the Blue Garden was later to be placed. But as Jones would note in an office memorandum a month later, after meeting with the clients,

> *Mr. and Mrs. James expect something wonderful in this [flower] garden and are looking forward to its being the gem of the whole place … It is up to somebody to lay himself out on that garden business and do the very best he can and we must remember that Mrs. James wants it all ready by the time she comes to Newport next spring or rather summer.*[27]

Before leaving for a European cruise on their new yacht *Aloha II*, the Jameses met with Charles Wait and Hans Koehler to review planting plans. Whatever sketch plan Wait presented for the informal garden—not specified in the documents—was disappointing to Mrs. James, who said "that is landscape gardening, not my idea of a picking garden." Mr. James also objected to the roadside-planting plan, saying it looked too much like a Boston park, not wild enough for the site. A house-warming party was planned for February 22, 1911, and all the planting was to be in place by the following June. [28]

Still to be finalized were the plans for the visually prominent Telescope House, for its setting and for paths to connect it to house and garden. Early sketches of this structure showed an awkward treatment, more like a teahouse, with stone stairs leading down to the mansion terrace. In earlier discussions between Rick Olmsted and architect I. N. Phelps Stokes, they had agreed that, given its position on the rock summit so close to the house, it needed delicate architectural handling. James wanted it to be in harmony with the land when viewed from Ocean Avenue. Olmsted's idea was that it should be a "strong,

light, carefully designed and nicely finished structural skeleton of metal: a thing somewhat suggestive of the top of a lighthouse." What was finally constructed reflected this concept, although in stone, and was to play a major role for the Blue Garden.[29]

The Second Phase of Work 1911

To comply with the Jameses' request, in March 1911, Koehler presented an analysis of planting for the estate. His accompanying planting plan[30] was an extraordinarily detailed overview of the entire property, noting work completed in 1910; plantings and removals to be done in 1911 and recommendations for future plantings. Included in this plan was the planted elaboration for the formally designed vegetable and cutting garden, now developed along cross axes with various pools, lawns, shelters and garden structures. He provided recommendations for an orchard of standard and espaliered fruit trees and fruiting shrubs in great assortment; for varieties of roses to be trained along the walks on garlands; for shrub beds of viburnum, philadelphus, spiraea, native junipers and other shrubs to enclose the garden's borders, all underplanted with drifts of flowering herbaceous material. The long vegetable beds were to be edged with dwarf boxwood. For a sophisticated client, well-versed in Renaissance art, Koehler's vegetable-cutting garden plan blended elements of the early Persian garden with its axial linearity and floral tapestries; of the Medieval "flowery mede," and of the fifteenth-century orchard gardens, "gardens of pleasure" filled with fruits and blossoms, so romanticized in art, literature and troubadours' ballads.[31]

Likewise, the rolling terrain of the estate was subject to the same elaborate planting recommendations. With instructions to maintain any interesting native growth, paths and road verges were to be clothed with large drifts of shrubs. Mountain laurel, azaleas, hollies of various types, viburnum, clethra, broom, among

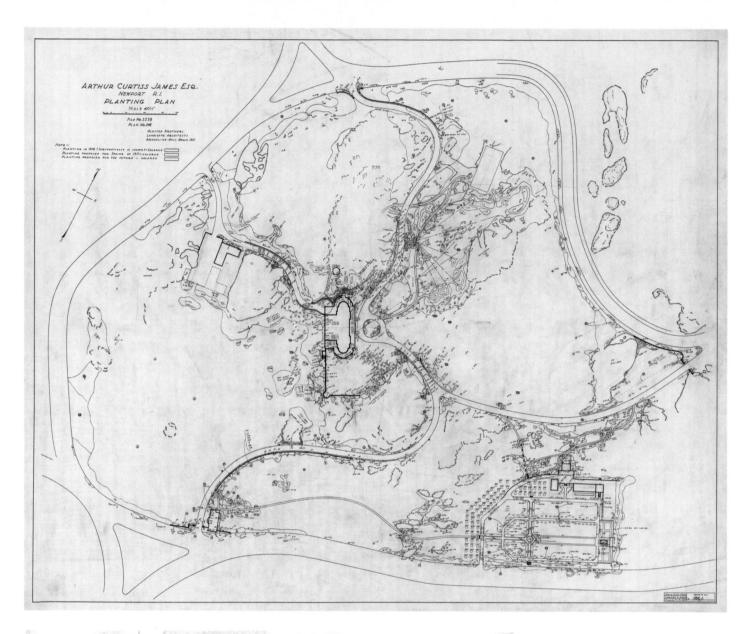

ARTHUR CURTISS JAMES ESQ.
NEWPORT R.I.
PLANTING PLAN

NOTES:-

A.   Plant in spring 1911.

B Remove in spring 1911 the plants set here in 1910.

C.   More completely clothe the rock by dividing existing plants and replanting. Plant the Bearberry, designated by number, on top of the ledge, not at the base. Add soil if necessary.

D.   Remove sod borders.

E.   Remove all exotic shrubs at base of cliff and leave all native shrubs.

F.   Interlock the various existing groups in a more natural manner all along this wall.

G.   Approximate limit of existing wild growth.

H.   Some of the shrubs in this area can be used for the planting of 1911 and later.

I.   Allow wild shrubbery to come in.

J.   Remove alders standing among low growth, Leave rambling paths through this low growth and seed them down to grass. Hard outline along meadow should be softened by rooting out a few plants.

K.   Remove everything in this vicinity except the group composed of gray birch and cherry and the one composed of cornel and elder.

L.   Weed and encourage existing Rosa lucida and Rubus canadensis.

M.   Leave irregular trail in old roadway.

N.   Make bay in plantation of Rosa lucida.

O.   Make this planting outline less artificial.

P.   Plant the juniper so that it will not seriously interfere with the bearberry.

Q.   Remove the common barberry plants along here.

R.   Remove Norway maple.

S.   Plant in vicinity of steps as ground cover.

T.   Cut passage through the branches of the two trees.

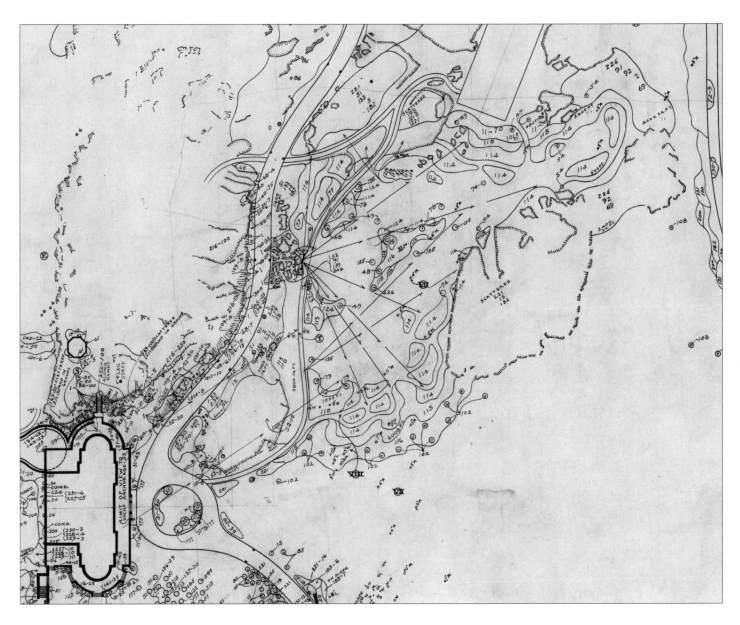

1. Juniperus virginiana, 119 plants,
   Red Cedar.
2. Viburnum dentatum, 174 plants, 4' apart,
   Arrowwood.
3. 8 Beds, 204 plants, 7' apart,
   Pinus austriaca, 104 plants,
   Austrian Pine.
   Pinus sylvestris, 100 plants,
   Scotch Pine.
4. Beds, plants, 7' apart,
   Pinus austriaca
   Austrian Pine.
   Pinus sylvestris,
   Scotch Pine.
   Pinus strobus,
   White Pine.
   Pseudotsuga douglassi,
   Douglas Spruce.
5. Beds plants, 8' apart;
   Tilia europea,
   European Linden,
   Fagus sylvatica,
   European Beech.
   Acer platanoides,
   Norway Maple.
   Quercus palustris,
   Pin Oak.
6. Tsuga canadensis, plants, 5' apart,
   Hemlock.
7. Cedrus atlantica glauca,
   Blue Cedar.
8. Abies veitchii,
   Veitch's Spruce.
9. Rosa lucida, 1220 plants, 2' apart,
   Dwarf Wild Rose.

Quantities given refer only to plants to be used this spring or in the future. Quantities used in the planting last spring are not given in this list nor on the plan accompanying same, although the kinds used last spring are embraced in this list and upon the plan accompanying same.

(above) Detail from Plan No. 248 depicting the area to the northeast of the mansion. In this area below the ridge, amid the various boulders, the Olmsted firm originally intended an informal flower garden with large drifts of perennials and annuals, surrounded by evergreen groupings, as noted on the detail of the planting list (left). Such a planting, they felt, would not be incongruous with the rugged terrain. They gave careful attention to the development of view corridors as noted on the plan detail. Instead, this area was to be reshaped in 1912 by dynamite to provide the level space for the Blue Garden.

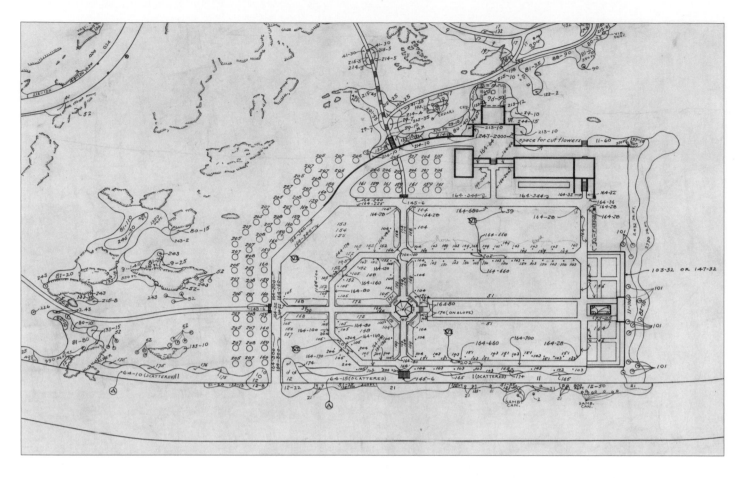

James, - 12.

201. Rosa setigera, 170 plants, 3' apart,
    Prairie Rose.
202. Parsley, Box edging to be planted on this space.
203. Sweet Allyssum, " " " " " " "
204. Espalier Plums, 9 plants,
205. Standard Apples,
    *Yellow Transparent. 1 plant
    8 Standard apples were planted Spring 1910.
206. Standard Cherries,
    *Bigarreau Napoleon, 2 plants,
    *Bigarreau Windsor 2 plants,
    *Black Heart, 1 plant
    *Black Tartarian, 1 plant
    *Gov. Wood. 1 plant.
    * May Duke. 1 plant
207. Standard Peaches,
    *Belgrade, 3 plants,
    *Early Canada, 3 plants,
    *Cumberland, 3 plants,
    *Downing, 3 plants,
    *Hale's Early, 3 plants,
    *Waterloo, 2 plants,
    *Imperatrice Eugenie, 1 plant,
    4 Standard Peaches were planted spring 1910.
208. Standard Plums,
    *Beauty of Naples, 1 plant,
    *Bradshaw, 1 plant,
    *Imperial Gage, 1 plant,
    *Yellow Egg, 1 plants,
    *Abundance, 1 plant,
    *Early Favourite, 1 plant,
    *Reine Claude, 1 plant,
    *Jefferson, 1 plant,
    *These varieties to be discussed with Mr. Greatorex.
209. Not used.
210. Calluna vulgaris, 58 plants, 2' apart,
    Scotch Heather.
211. Campanula rotundifolia, 4126 plants, 1' apart,
    Scotch Hairbell.
212. Erica vagans, 50 plants, 1½' apart
    Cornish Heath
213. Ligustrum regelianum, 45 plants, 3½' apart,
    Regel's Privet.
214. Euonymus obovatus, 116 plants, 2½' apart,
    Prostrate Burningbush.
215. Myrica cerifera, 210 plants, 2½' apart,
    Bayberry.
216. Arctostaphyllus u-va-ursi, 6000 plants, 1½' apart,
    Bearberry.
217. Ceanothus americanus, 50 plants, 2' apart,
    New Jersey Tea.   (low form), 50 plants, 3' apart

(above) Elaborated on Plan No. 248 was planting for the vegetable and flower garden complex with its greenhouses and barns. This garden area was designed in a classical manner, with the planting beds along a main and cross axes, punctuated by decorative shelters and pools. The paths were lined with rose standards, some trained as garlands.

(left) Along the western edge of the complex an orchard of mixed fruits was planted, some of the trees treated as espaliers, as noted in the planting list detail.

(facing page, above) View over Vegetable Garden, July 1915, photograph by Harold Blossom. Visible in this image are some of the farm buildings and greenhouses in the foreground. Beyond is a large patterned garden, laid out along a long lawn axis, a *tapis vert,* punctuated by urns and terminated by shelters and ponds. Paths, either parallel or at cross axis, are defined by edging and roses, trained on pillars and as garlands. The western edge of the garden, at the right in the image, is defined by an orchard.

(facing page, below) Study for Garden Group, Plan No. 231, March 1910, by Charles Wait, illustrating the stable, plant house, greenhouse, and potting shed, with the layout of the buildings that define the yard and the relationship of buildings to grade.

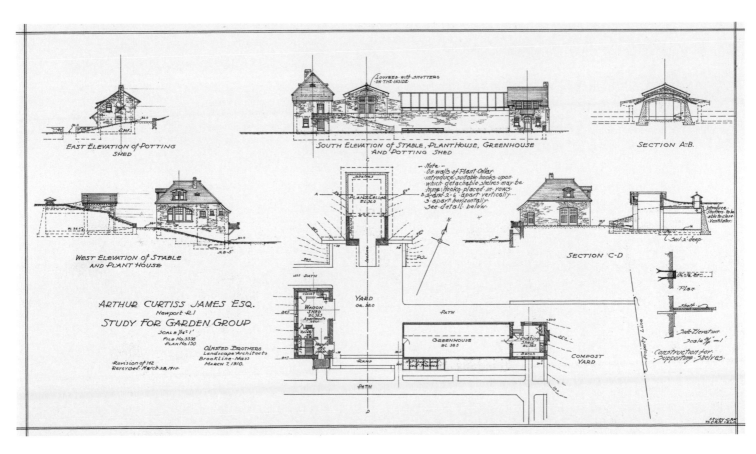

EAST ELEVATION OF POTTING SHED

SOUTH ELEVATION OF STABLE, PLANT HOUSE, GREENHOUSE AND POTTING SHED

SECTION A-B

WEST ELEVATION OF STABLE AND PLANT HOUSE

SECTION C-D

ARTHUR CURTISS JAMES ESQ.
Newport R.I
STUDY FOR GARDEN GROUP
SCALE ⅛"=1'
FILE No.332
PLAN No.130

OLMSTED BROTHERS
Landscape Architects
Brookline Mass
March 7, 1910.

Revision of 142
Rereised March 28, 1910.

others, were intended to give year-round textural interest. These were recommended in vast groupings, with ferns, yuccas, and other flowering material at the ground level. Trees, in great diversity, both deciduous and evergreen, were placed for the most judicious effect among these shrub beds and throughout the grounds. The larger slopes, named the North, West and East Lawns, were left in turf or meadow, punctuated by an occasional copse or groups of ground-hugging shrubs or heathers around the many boulders.

Around the mansion, with an elevated lawn terrace on its south side surrounded by a low wall, Koehler proposed an enclosure of shrubs, with trees carefully placed so as not to interfere with the views. In the style of William Robinson, he edged this lawn with drifts of perennials, such as baby's breath, delphinium, heuchera, and clumps of heather, anchored by small-leaved Japanese holly, low junipers and pines. He blanketed the ridge to the northwest on the path to the Telescope House and flagpole with ground pines and juniper, heather and heath, harebells and other Scottish plants.

In this detailed planting plan, large irregular drifts, abounding with flowering material artfully interspersed with tree and shrub groupings, were intended to be used architecturally to shape and embellish the spatial flow throughout the estate. Koehler was still responding to the notion that in this rugged and picturesque environment, plantings should follow a naturalistic pattern rather than the structure of a formal garden. Therefore, in the hollow to the northeast near the proposed tennis court, in the area designated as "Informal Garden," he provided for large perennial masses among the rocky outcroppings, carefully considered for selected vistas as indicated on the plan. Harriet James' desired formal flower garden was not yet a part of his horticultural planning.

Overall, Mr. James was again disturbed by the amount of work suggested by this plan and by the estimated costs to implement it. After diplomatically thanking the Olmsted firm for "your most careful and most satisfactory solution of this difficult problem in Newport," James stated that at the moment they would only focus upon the spring shrub plantings.[32] Thus, between March and September 1911, the number of letters and plans produced by the Olmsted office was considerably reduced. Using his on-site staff, headed by Greatorex, James attempted to complete the various unfinished projects, both architectural and in the landscape.

Beacon Hill House opened for "the Season" in 1911 to great acclaim, receiving a laudatory review from the New York Times for the commanding "views of city, country and sea" and "its magnificent grounds." In July, a grand musicale for 150 guests, the elite of the Social Register, inaugurated the mansion. In the great hall, William Hammond performed on the new organ while costumed dancers executed pas de deux from various ballets. Numerous teas, receptions and charity events followed throughout the summer and early fall months.[33]

In September 1911, James again contacted Olmsted, this time to plan for his intended boathouse, dock and access road. To achieve the latter, James was buying a strip of land from Stuart Duncan, a Midwest banker and new neighbor, who had recently purchased a property along the water. James suggested that Olmsted consult with Duncan about doing some landscape planning for his new property.[34] Working with Howells & Stokes and various marine engineers over the next year, the firm guided the planning and construction of a picturesque stone boat landing and floats for James, in a very limited space carved out of ledge at the water's edge. The access was through a narrow strip of Duncan land, bordered on the opposite side by the Clarke-Burden property, on which the Olmsted firm had consulted in 1893.[35] Elderly Mrs. Clarke was unwilling to give up her existing wall, even though when surveyed it was discovered to be beyond her property line.

Planning for this shorefront feature, at which James could moor the launch for the Aloha II, his 219-foot yacht, within sight of his landlocked mansion, proved to be more problematic than simply that of limited access. The rocky terrain complicated installation of utilities in this narrow space. Choice of materials for buildings, walls and drive surface, scale of structures, amount of blasting, construction of floats, all involved numerous consultations. Even though some of the structures had been built by May 1912, there were still issues to be resolved over the wall and ledge treatment along the drive. Trying to reason with Mrs. Clarke elicited her response, "I trust you will not annoy me further on this subject ..." To resolve the challenge of turning around an automobile in such limited space at the end of the drive, they ingeniously built a large turntable such as would be used to turn railroad engines.[36] However, the narrow tunnel-like drive displeased James, who agreed to a constructed archway over the road and entrance piers to give some architectural definition to an otherwise cramped space.[37]

During a September 1911 inspection of the Beacon Hill House grounds at the clients' request, Rick Olmsted was not pleased with what he observed. Without Olmsted supervision, plant substitutions had been made, changing the proposed effect. Greatorex, while an excellent site manager, had not fully understood the artistic intention of the Olmsted plans, which was to have plantings with a distinctive beauty, based on refined choices and details. They had wanted "to concentrate certain kinds of effects in certain locations and to put a deliberate and calculated restraint upon the use in other localities ..." Olmsted recommended that closer consultation in the future between firm and client would ensure the desired outcome of a distinctive landscape for Beacon Hill House as a unified composition, made up of several distinct zones or rooms. In that regard, the Olmsted firm was asked once again to address the design of the formal garden in the area between the house and tennis court, now according to new ideas that Harriet James had for her Blue Garden.[38]

View down the narrow road between Harrison Avenue and the James boathouse, July 1915. Note the James yacht, *Aloha II*, visible beyond the boathouse.

Evolution of an Idea

Without the existence of personal records or correspondence, assessing what influenced Harriet Parsons James in her decision to have a Blue Garden becomes speculative. Though she was reputed to have had a significant horticultural library, which she would read in her conservatory decorated with Gustavino tiles and Della Robbia ceramics, no list of her books remains. Examination of the Parke-Benet catalogues of Jameses' holdings, auctioned off after their deaths in late 1941, reveals very few garden volumes among the many first editions.[1] In the records of their trips that exist prior to the development of the Blue Garden, no special place is notably characterized by this color.

However, Harriet and Arthur Curtiss James were sophisticated patrons of the arts and world travelers who would have been exposed and responsive to many cultural and artistic influences. Beyond the obvious associations of blue tonalities with sea and sky, clearly important to a yachtsman, blue is a regal color of historic importance. In ancient Egypt, it was associated with pharaohs and precious jewels; in Mesopotamia, lapis was revered for jewelry and art; and in Byzantium early churches and mosques were tiled with blue. Ancient Celts painted themselves blue for fierceness. From the twelfth century through the Renaissance, blue had a religious significance associated with the robes of the Virgin Mary, therefore, with holiness or virtue. The Jameses, as worldwide museum patrons and collectors, would have been well-versed in the symbolic implications of this color, as depicted in art in all media, in illuminated manuscripts, in Della Robbia tiles, in Far Eastern porcelains and in Persian rugs.

Interest in color theory and a painterly

THE RECEPTION ROOM AND MORNING ROOM OF MR. JAMES' RESIDENCE.
Howells & Stokes, Architects.
Builders: The Whitney Co.
Electrical Contractors: Blackall & Baldwin Co.
Heating and Ventilating Engineers: The Merrill Co.
Interior Marble: Batterson & Eisele.
3558-201

(left) The Conservatory or Palm Room at Beacon Hill House was decorated with Gustavino tiles and Della Robbia ceramics.

(facing page) Planting Study for Part of Informal Garden, Plan No. 278, December 30, 1911. Since the first sketch, Plan No. 134 in 1910, the garden has been relocated below and to the north of the house. The garden is beginning to take its classical form, and includes the north pergola, as outlined on this sketch. It is augmented by suggested plant groupings located among the boulders. To the north, a rectangle is outlined, indicating the location of the tennis court.

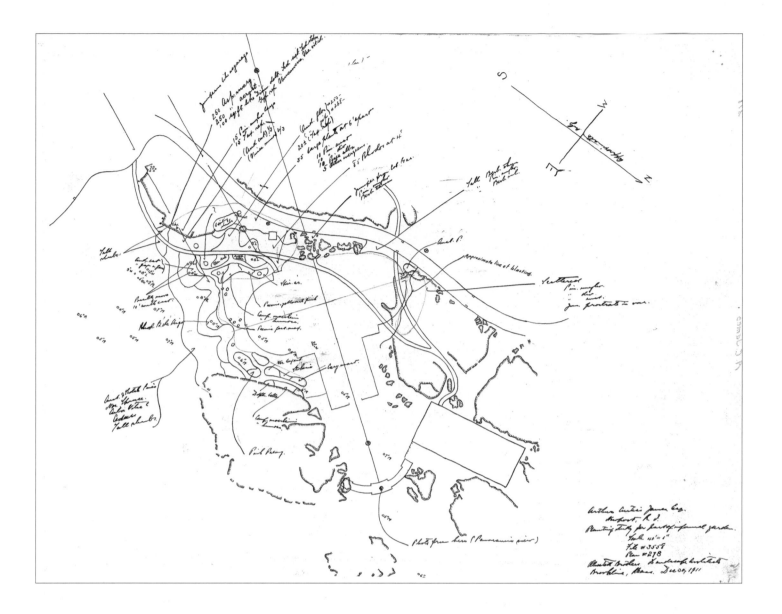

palette in landscape planting was of great currency in the pre-World War I period, influenced by the writings of English gardener Gertrude Jekyll and others. Learning from the romantic, impressionistic manner in which English landscape painter J. M. W. Turner infused his work with color and ethereal light, Jekyll, likewise, used color sequences as a compositional principle to heighten the emotional impact and sense of perspective. Although she explored ideas of monochromatic gardens, she cautioned against doctrinaire rigidity, "Surely the business of the blue garden is to be beautiful as well as to be blue … an experienced colourist knows that the blues will be more telling … by juxtaposition of rightly placed complementary colour." Jekyll's collaboration with architect Edward Luytens added a structured classical dimension to her influential horticul-

tural advice. Harriet James would have been familiar with Jekyll's books and, no doubt, would have visited gardens designed by her on numerous trips to England.[2]

More than all these intellectual theories, this may have been a color of choice for Mrs. James for personal reasons. Certainly after the fame of the Blue Garden had spread, the social pages would take special notice of her couture, so often noted for its shades of blue. As one *Miami Herald* reporter noted, blue was a color Harriet James loved because it matched the color of her eyes.[3]

Whatever she read or saw, by September 1911, Harriet James had developed definite ideas of what she wanted her flower garden to be, "blues and purples, no *reds*."[4] A *New York Tribune* article of July 1911 had described a garden, a "riotous

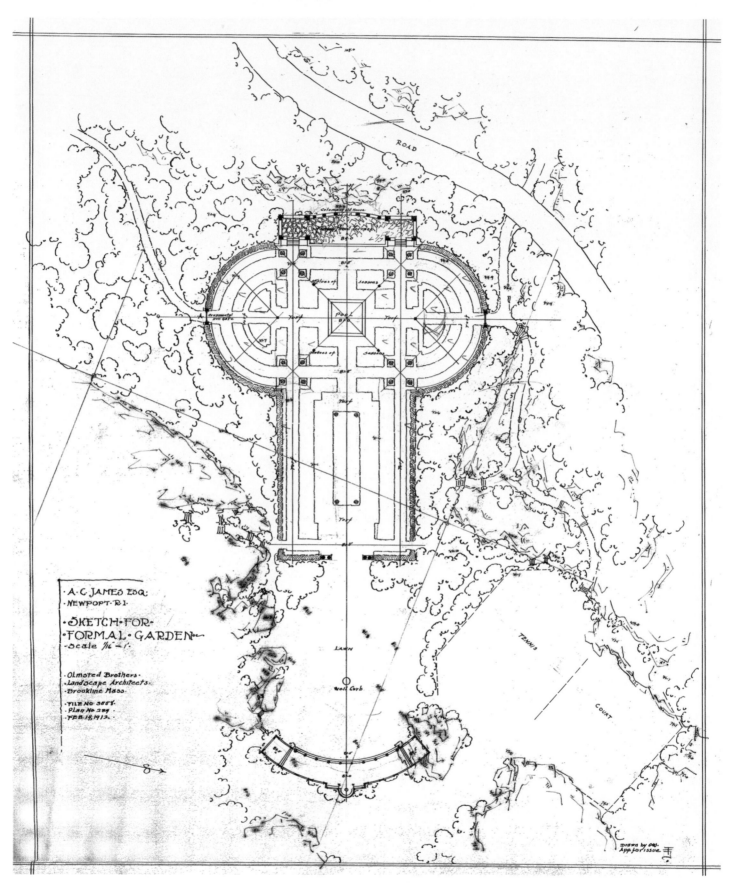

Sketch for Formal Garden, Plan No. 284, February 14, 1912. Although called a sketch, this plan provided greater detail than the earlier plans of the garden layout and architecture, with spot elevations indicated on the inside and outside of the garden. The massing of plant groupings surrounding the garden is indicated along with paths and steps to accommodate the change in topography. The area to become the long pool is treated as a planting bed, and the southeast pergola is in its originally planned position, before it was pushed further south at Mrs. James' request. It is noteworthy that the north pergola is drawn in a fashion similar to a pergola installed in the 1920s rather than the one that was originally built.

mass of blue" containing both cultivated and wild flowers, belonging to a wealthy woman on Long Island—both exact location and personage unspecified. The owner was said to have been inspired by "Queen Margherita's famous garden" in Europe. To date, no such blue garden has been identified; but certainly, if such a garden was in vogue for the European traveler of that era, Harriet James would have visited it.[5]

At his September 1911 meeting in Newport, Rick Olmsted was given a plan entitled, "Study for Garden worked out by Greatorex under Mrs. James' direction"—no longer extant. Over the following months, these garden ideas were advanced further by the Olmsted firm. By early December, Charles Wait presented a "Diagram on axis of Formal Garden as proposed by Mrs. James,"—also no longer extant—which pleased both clients.[6] Further developed during December, Wait's ideas located this garden on the northeast slope below the ridge where the house was located, now aligned on the axis of the Telescope House. As outlined on a December 30 sketch plan, "Planting Study for Part of Informal Garden," drafted by Koehler, an improved version of Wait's earlier concept for a formal garden outline from February 1910 was now introduced, superimposed upon the suggested plantings. His new ideas outlined an expanded cruciform shape, with the cross axis, now moved to the end of the long axis—it had been in the middle in the earlier sketch—terminating the space with a large oval rather than the earlier apse.[7] This revised outline, located on a plan in the vicinity formerly labeled "Informal Garden," was in a boulder-filled area that would require considerable blasting to clear a reasonably sized level plateau for such an enclosed space.[8]

Two months later, in February 1912, Wait had refined the garden design in a new plan drafted with greater attention to detailed elements. This "Formal Garden Study"[9] developed the interplay of axes, of volumes and voids, of defined linear and curving geometries. The cruciform shape was now clearly delineated by walls, which Wait

considered "highly essential to the ultimate success of the garden as a whole." These walls were to be backed by an evergreen hedge, for which *Ilex crenata* was recommended for its year-round foliage. Up against the rocky outcrop of the Beacon Hill ridge, an elevated pergola was to be the southwestern terminus, with square ends and a slightly curved center. From this vantage point there was to be an uninterrupted vista along the garden's long axis "allowing one to appreciate the long shadows as they play across the plot of the garden and the numerous surrounding points of interest."[10] Within the enclosing walls, articulated planting beds and paths echoed the garden's form, with a square pool at the center of the cross axis between the apses in front of the southern pergola. Beyond the entry to the walled garden, an open lawn area, a *plaisance*[11] was planned to contrast with the structured linearity of the planting beds, to be terminated at the northeastern end of the axis by another elevated pergola, this one curved to echo the arcs of the southern apses.[12] This was a classic landscape form, inventively used by an architect with landscape sensibilities, and clearly reminiscent of shapes and textures Wait would have appreciated on his European travels.

Paths, curving amid the thick plant groupings and the picturesque boulders, connected the house and tennis court to the gated entrances at the center of the apses. Koehler augmented Wait's garden scheme with plans proposing a richly textured multi-layering of irregular plantings to surround the garden, in a manner very reflective of English landscape gardener William Robinson.[13] These were to combine deciduous shrubs—forsythia, spiraea, viburnums—with broad-leaved and coniferous evergreens—rhododendron, mahonia, American holly, inkberry, among others—to "relieve the coldness and somberness in winter," which was Harriet James' stated desire.[14] Complicating Wait's carefully calibrated scheme were various sculptural objects that the Jameses had acquired on their travels, which she desired to be integrated into

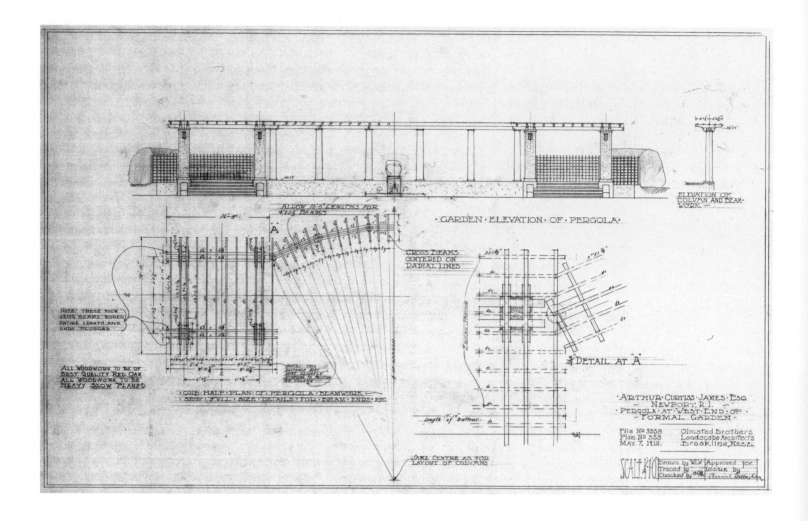

the plan: diverse columns, an antique gate, figures of the Seasons, various vases and a wellhead.[15] Concerning the planting, Mrs. James reiterated her desired color scheme of "blue and blue purple — no magenta purple — with some yellow and white. Wants no pinks or reds." Purple rhododendrons and lilacs, blue spiraeas and white or yellow hollyhocks were acceptable, and Koehler thought he could interest her in blue-flowering *Vitex agnus-castus* and blue *Hibiscus syriacus*. But the plantings all needed to be in bloom by mid-summer, including the water plants. James required a planting cost estimate for this garden as well as for other areas on the estate still incompletely planted.[16]

Implementing the Idea: Early Construction

Although not mentioned in the record, the blasting to flatten this space must have already been accomplished, because by March 1912, the garden plan had been dimensioned, the arcs calculated;

the outline had been surveyed and staked on site, reviewed and adjusted, inspected and approved; and construction had started on the boundary walls. The construction was under the supervision of Greatorex, and by May he had most of the walls and piers built, although these still had to be covered in stucco. Simultaneously, the utilities and drainage pipes were being installed, as well as the central square pool-water supply system, the only one contemplated at this time. Adjustments had to be made to deal with the stiff blue clay found about eighteen inches below the surface.[17]

Charles Wait proceeded with designs for the pergolas, beginning with the one on the southwest. Harriet James had definite ideas about the development of this garden concept. The early plan for this pergola was based on her ideas and on her insistence that it be pushed further back against the ledge, necessitating more blasting.[18] She wanted to find a place in this structure for six marble columns she had acquired. In addition,

(facing page) Pergola at West End of Formal Garden, Plan No. 353, May 7, 1912. This dimensioned drawing includes the re-use, as requested by Mrs. James, of six roughly-textured granite columns, originally from the loggia at the former Glover house.

(above) View of southern pergola, looking west, July 1915. The pergola was constructed of concrete, granite and stucco, with inlaid tile patterns in the concrete paving at each end. The water course on the hillside can be viewed through the columns.

(below left) Sketch showing elevation and sections of the ledge area behind the pergola, Plan No. 390, undated. The waterfall was a variation on the water theme in the garden. (below right) Waterfall at south end of garden, July 1915, photograph by Harold H. Blossom.

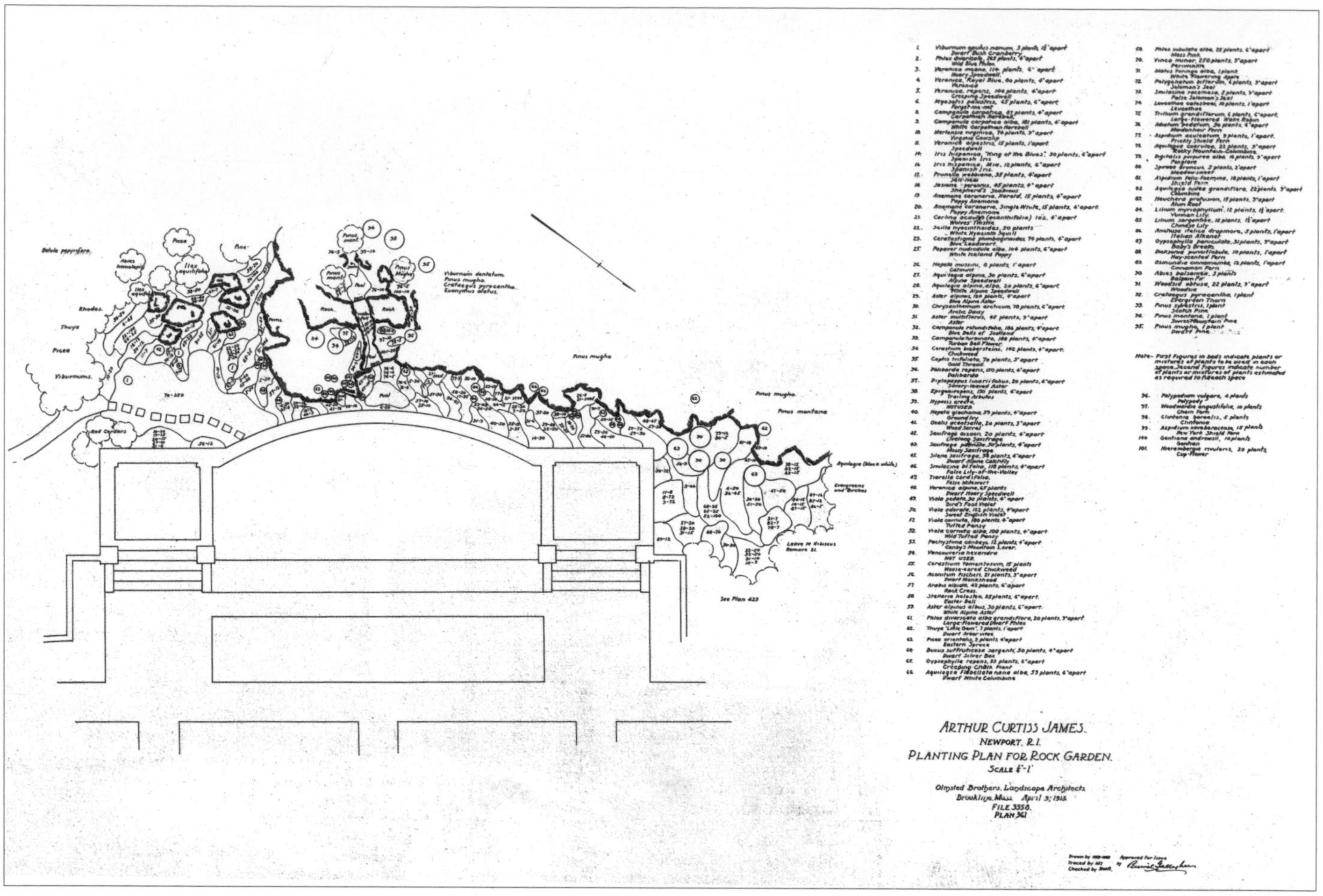
ARTHUR CURTISS JAMES.
NEWPORT. R.I.
PLANTING PLAN FOR ROCK GARDEN.
Olmsted Brothers. Landscape Architects
FILE 3558.
PLAN 361

(above) Planting Plan for Rock Garden, Plan No. 361, April 9, 1913. A plant list of ninety-five items, including herbaceous material, some small trees and shrubs, accompanied the plan. The effect was that of a lush and textured tapestry behind the south pergola. (below right) View of the rock garden and water course behind the southern pergola, July 1915.

(facing page, above) Sketch showing Lotus Pools at North East Pergola, Plan No. 408, November 9, 1912. This pergola terminates the view from the south pergola. Broad lawn steps unite the upper terrace with the *plaisance*, the expanse of lawn that connects the walled garden to the north pergola. Plans for this pergola, drafted in June and July 1912, are no longer extant.

(facing page, below) The wellhead, surrounded by marble columns Mrs. James had acquired, provided a vertical accent to the *plaisance*, July 1915.

there were six roughly textured granite columns rescued from the loggia of the former Glover house, which she also wanted to use. Wait rejected the use of the thin marble columns for the southern pergola structure as too spindly, but agreed to insert the more robust granite columns as a screen in front of the ledge.[19] The pergola piers were to be constructed of stucco, painted to contrast, yet harmonize, with the native stone. Months after this pergola was constructed, in September 1912, Wait devised a scheme to provide interest on the steep slope visible behind this columned screen and extend the sense of space. On a slope to be planted with low shrubs, ferns

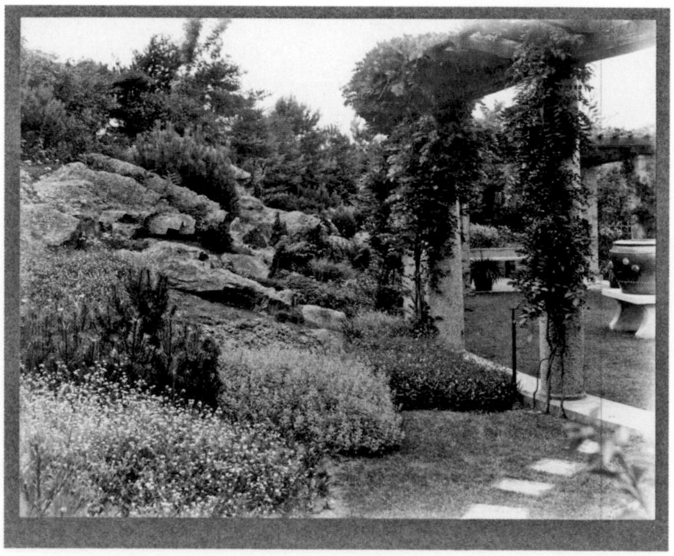

A.C. JAMES, ESQ
NEWPORT, RHODE ISLAND.
SKETCH SHOWING LOTUS POOLS
AT NORTH EAST PERGOLA.

File Nº 3558
Plan Nº 408

Olmsted Brothers
Landscape Architects

and wildflowers, he suggested a meandering waterfall among the boulders, a variation of the water theme in the rest of the garden.[20]

The northern pergola, located beyond the *plaisance*, was to be a curving structure, similar to the southern pergola, set on an elevated platform with square gazebos at either end to terminate the broad expanse of lawn. Not confined by a rocky slope, this pergola was more open, offering protected seating with vistas across the moors east of Beacon Hill Road. Its broad flat steps on the garden side were intended "to unite it with the lawn and make the two play together in a very pleasing way." Plans for this structure (most no longer extant) were made by July 1912, so that Greatorex could begin its construction. The wellhead, to be surrounded by four of the red marble columns which had been rejected for other places, was located on the central axis in front of this pergola to provide a vertical accent in this lawn space.[21]

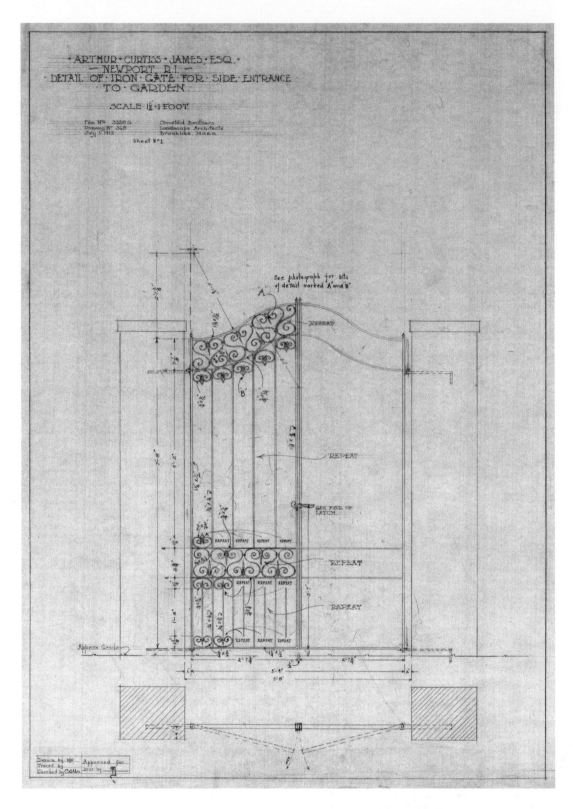

Mrs. James was also determined to use another prior purchase, antique gates, somewhere in the Blue Garden space, suggesting that these could close off the end of the walled garden. Reminding her that gates imply "seclusion," Wait again had to defend the principles of the Olmsted plan, saying,

It is distinctly our feeling that to introduce a gate at the northeast end of the garden, separating it from the plaisance and the pergola beyond would be a great mistake. Such a division would destroy the unity of a large composition and tend to make it two distinctly marked compartments. This would

mar the interesting play of one feature into the other which jointly forms the single unit of design ... Your wish to mark this point by introducing some interesting but widely separated side masses appeals to us as being highly appropriate and far preferable to any scheme by which this throat would be nar-rowed ... We hope that you may concur with us as we feel very strongly upon this point.[22]

Instead, he sketched a place for gates at the side entrances of the apses, making them harmo-nize with the surroundings, the slopes and the proposed piers to form a single composition "in sympathy with the rising movement of the hedge and lattice at the two entrances." F. Krasser, a Boston metal fabricator, was selected to duplicate the gates, making necessary adjustments to the decorative wrought iron so that they would fit between the piers.[23]

Tile was planned as a decorative element on the floor of the southern pergola. Wait inquired at the Enfield Pottery & Tile Works in Enfield, Pennsylvania about tiles of "Della Robbia" blue.

They forwarded examples of what they had of royal, Persian blue and turquoise, none exactly the sought-after hue. Although they could create the correct color, this firm was concerned about abrasion from use as a floor and from weather exposure.[24] Instead, Mrs. Jeannie Rice of the newly formed Durant Kilns in Bedford, New York was contacted. Socially prominent, with a great interest in arts and crafts, she had become a potter, establishing these kilns in 1910 with Leon Volkmar, a member of a notable family of ceramic artists. With their pooled artistry and practical scientific knowledge, they aimed "to give fresh impetus to ceramic art in America by ... reproducing classical forms and glazes of the old masters." In particu-lar, they were interested in reviving the richly hued glazes, which had once flourished in the Middle East, especially "the elusive Persian blue." Their endeavors to recapture this art were called at the time, "the best work being done in any country."[25] Indeed, the Durant Kiln work, char-acterized by its unique depth of color and iridesc-ence, appealed to both client and designers for this project. However, the production techniques were still experimental and problematic, and the Jameses' installation was plagued by numerous delays. Instead, for the northeastern pergola, Mrs. James intended to use Grueby tiles, known for their matte green glazes, to coordinate with the rosier tones of the marble columns surround-ing the wellhead, now in front of this structure.[26] However, in a November progress report, Wait not-ed the decision to lay the floor of the gazebo ends of the northern pergola in local stone instead.[27]

Regarding other decorative objects which Harriet James desired to place within the garden, Wait promised to review this task with Rick Olmsted and to provide her with a colored per-spective sketch to show where the statuary, etc.,

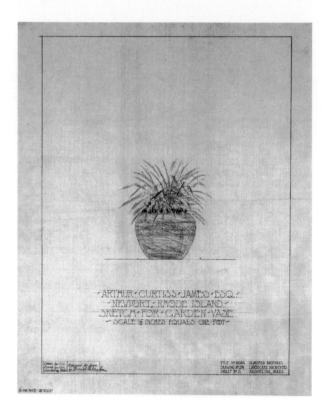

Sketch for Garden Vase, Plan No. 374, July 24, 1912. Multiple copies of this vase were used along the main axis of the garden and were originally planted with agapanthus, and later with conical evergreen trees, possibly holly.

locations throughout the grounds, in particular under the pergolas, may have been purchased through A. Olivotti & Co., an Italian company specializing in antiquities, with offices in New York and Florence.[30]

Prior to work concerning the reproduction of garden vases, Emerson & Norris had been contacted in April 1912 concerning "pink granite composite for the garden." The record is unclear as to where this material was to be used. At that time, the Olmsted firm was engaged with the installation of the southern pergola and the square pool, in addition to developing special stepping stones, since the natural site rock was too friable to be easily worked into steps or stepping stones. This company's unique craft of cast stone would become an essential component in the fabrication of many specialized decorative features that were to characterize the garden.[31]

Refining the Idea—the Persian Water Garden

In late summer of 1912, Rick Olmsted presented a refinement of his previous ideas for the Blue Garden, which totally transformed what would have been an elegant space into an inventive and brilliantly cohesive conception.[32] At an August 20 meeting with Arthur and Harriet James, Rick proposed suffusing the core of the design with the ambiance of a Persian garden within the classical Italianate framework already constructed. He thus brought water, with all its reflective vibrancy and symbolic characteristics, into this landscape on a site surrounded by, but not within direct view, of its seaside environment.

Until this time, the square pool in the center of the apse cross axis was the only water feature.[33] Instead, his new proposal changed the central grass panel along the long axis into a shallow rectangular pool, only two and a half inches deep, covered with patterned blue tiles, with fine spray jets along the sides. He suggested "… running a thread of water, Persian fashion, from the head of the garden through the turf and practically flush

could be located. Unfortunately, no such sketch remains to reveal the Olmsted intentions, although the Seasons statuary does show up in the historic photographs, tucked into the long flowering borders. Of the ten plans which the Olmsted firm originally produced for various vases and sundials for the garden, only three remain. It is difficult to know whether these were original designs or whether the antique vases which she owned became prototypes for copy.[28] However, the correspondence indicates that Emerson & Norris, a company in Brighton, Massachusetts, specializing in composite stone fabrication, successfully reproduced numerous large and small vases for the garden according to Olmsted plans. Many of these were produced in blue-colored cast stone, others in so-called "imitation Istrian marble." Wait took particular care to simplify the design, making them "more English in character," particularly for the large vase, which was to be a central accent at the southern pergola.[29] Benches, needed at various with it to the long basin." Like the long pool, this rill would be set with the varied blue tiles, produced by Durant Kilns, which would be arranged in a pattern and set in a gray marble dust mortar. To border this pool, he proposed an edge treatment with perforations into which "myosotis or verbena or something small, blue and delicate growing" would be planted. His report included sketches to illustrate the long pool and rill treatment. Although not revealed in the record of this meeting, this sophisticated idea must have greatly appealed to the Jameses, who agreed to implement these changes, even at this late date. Since they wanted the garden ready for the 1913 summer season, the Olmsted firm had to exert maximum effort to develop these concepts and make the necessary site changes.[34]

To develop details of his Persian idea, in early September 1912 Rick sent William White, a young drafting assistant working on the garden plans, to the Boston Public Library to research Persian patterns. In an 1883 volume, entitled *Ornements de la Perse*, by E. Collinot and Adalbert de Beaumont, a volume still held by

the library, White found design ideas, several of which he photographed and sketched. Over the next month, he worked on various decorative patterns for the pools and pergolas, based on Rick's original sketches, which were ultimately to give this garden its distinctive character. The long pool was to be tiled with specially produced azure blue-green tiles in several sizes. The central area consisted of two-and-a-half-inch squares with three outer rows of five-inch squares; separating these were two rows of rectangular tiles of differing sizes. Moreover, at either end and in the middle of the central panel were to be intricate medallion-like designs. These drew directly from White's research and sketches.[35] Plans for an unusual coping were developed to surround this pool by January 1913.

Plan for Layout of Water Features in the Formal Garden, Plan No. 400, October 1912. Until the summer of 1912, the square pool in the center of the apse was the only water feature planned for the garden. Rick Olmsted's August 1912 proposal significantly changed

this when he recommended that the central rectangular planting bed become a shallow pool. He proposed connecting it to the lily pond with a small rill, a detail based on Persian decorative elements.

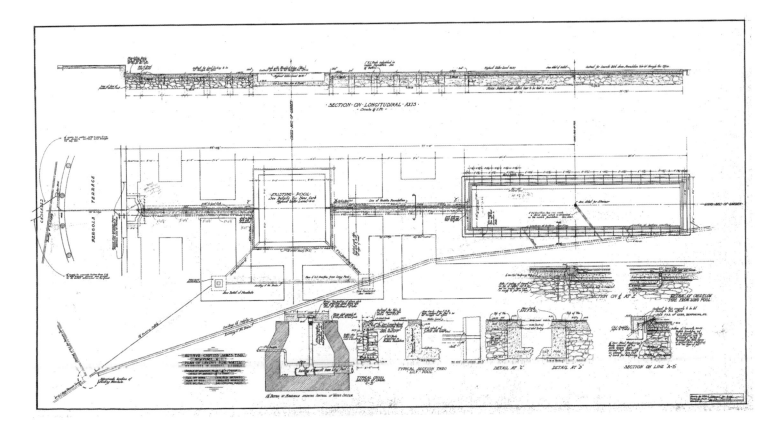

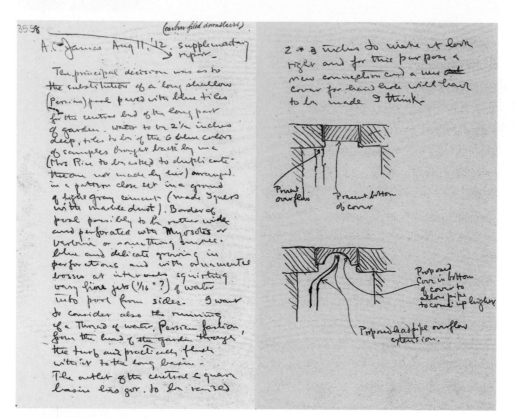

(left) Pages with sketches from a supplementary report by Frederick Law Olmsted, Jr., dated August 11, 1912 for the meeting with Arthur and Harriet James, where Olmsted proposed design changes for the water features in the garden. A head pool was designed at the base of the south pergola from which the rill emerged, connecting the lily pond and long pool, providing an axial spine for the garden.

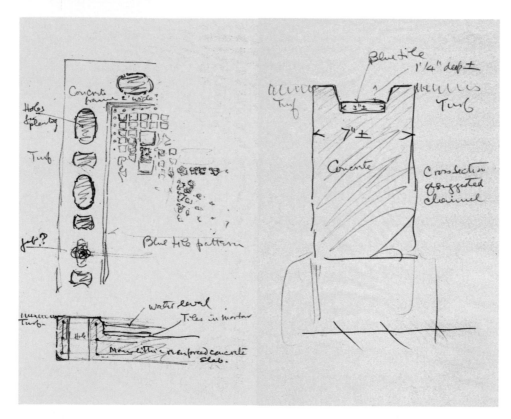

The coping consisted of an elaborate pattern of cast stone blocks forming an intricate series of cutouts as planting holes.[36] This design stemmed directly from Rick's sketch and from an image of a Persian rug that White had photographed at the Library. Finally, for the square pool, a coping was added with a blue Greek key-like pattern inlaid into the concrete. This design was a variation upon a screen, attributed to "S. Appollinare [sic] in Nuovo," probably from the Byzantine Basilica in Ravenna, Italy, which was found in an article on early Roman patterns from *The American*

Photographs of decorative elements found in *Ornements de la Perse* by E. Collinot and Adalbert de Beaumont, 1883, a volume found in the Boston Public Library. These were photographed by William White, a draftsman at the Olmsted firm, to aid in the tile design for the Blue Garden. The photograph of the Persian rug (right) was the inspiration for the cutouts in the long pool coping that were used for planting.

Architect. These undated periodical pages still exist in the Olmsted collection.[37] White was also responsible for tile patterns intended for the pergola floors, but these drawings are no longer extant.

The changes required to implement this Persian water concept reverberated along the entire long axis of the Blue Garden. More than design and construction drawings for the added elements of the rill and the long tiled pool with its elaborate edge treatment, these changes involved consideration of a complex system of waterworks. New outlets, controllers, drainage overflows and other elements were needed to service the expanded system, as well as grading changes along this axis to enable the water to flow naturally from the south toward the north. A head pool or seeming "source" was designed at the base of the southern pergola from which the rill emerged, to be made of cast stone with embedded tile.[38] The square pool, already

constructed by late 1912, had to be adapted to accept the rill in coordination with its newly designed decorative coping. Finally, to bring a water element to the northern pergola, two lotus pools were added on either side of the broad central steps.[39]

Between September 1912 and April 1913, over forty plans were produced for the various aspects of this remarkable system, of which only about twelve working drawings or sketches still exist in the Olmsted firm archives. No longer extant are working drawings which would have revealed aspects of tile layout and construction elements for the pools, rill and pergolas. However, the plans that do remain demonstrate the imaginative design skills and careful attention to decorative detail and proportions that characterized the Olmsted aesthetic.[40] The correspondence reveals that rough construction of this design on the site was to take place from October 1912 through spring 1913. Over the winter, in their

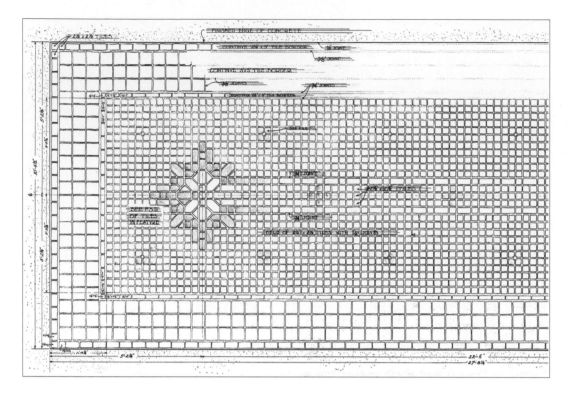

(left) Layout for Tile-work in Long Pool, Plan No. 430, January 14, 1913. Once the special color was approved by Mrs. James, the tiles were fabricated by Durant Kilns. (below) Detail of Border Stones Around Long Pool, Plan No. 432, Sheet No. 1, January 20, 1913. The tinted concrete blocks were fabricated by Emerson & Norris and formed an intricate series of cutouts for planting.

(facing page) Details of the Square Pool, Plan No. 415, January 14, 1913. A blue Greek key-like pattern was inlaid into concrete blocks of the coping.

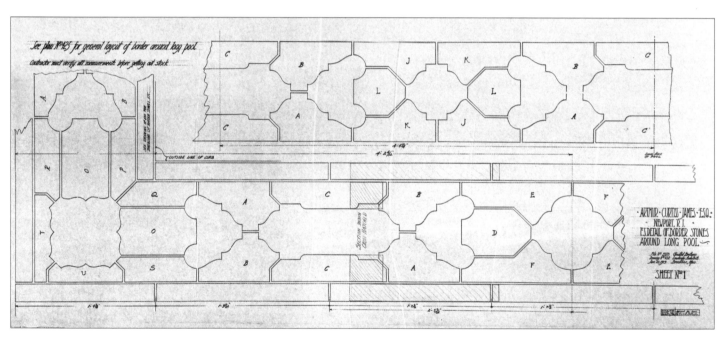

Brighton, Massachusetts shop, Emerson & Norris were to fabricate in tinted concrete various components of the garden water system, such as the rill, to be done in units. These would then be assembled on the site in the spring, at which time the tiles would be inserted. In November 1912, Harriet James, pleased with Durant Kilns color samples, directed that 300 three-inch tiles of a mottled blue-green be ordered for the water channel, needed within six weeks in order to be set in the concrete sections. Wait tried to caution her that these tiles were unproven for their weather resistance and were expensive—tiles for the long pool alone were estimated at $3,000— but Mrs. James was not interested in alternatives. Thus the tile orders were placed for the small pool and pergola ends, to be followed by that for the long pool.[41]

By January 1913, foundation slabs were laid and the stone basin castings begun. The first

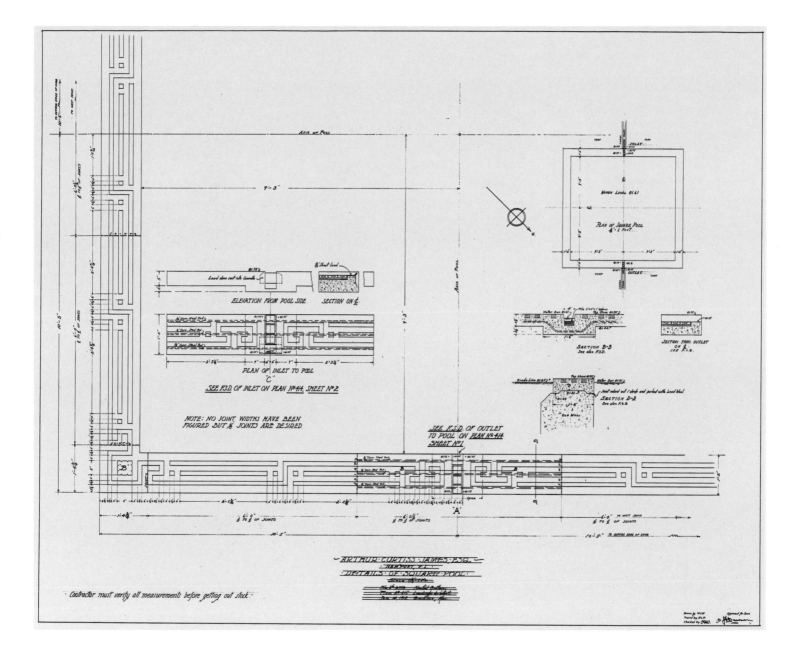

batch of tiles, delayed until February by glaze problems, was finally installed by the end of March, while the April batch was delayed until May, with corner pieces for the pool still missing in June. Production problems with matte gray tiles intended for the floor of the pergola ends resulted in the decision to simply install the blue border, letting the concrete substitute for the gray.[42] With the opening scheduled for August, an exasperated Harriet James expressed regret at ever having placed these orders.[43]

Other last-minute problems emerged which had to be resolved. Once the tile arrived and construction on the long pool could be completed, a member of the Olmsted firm's engineering staff set to work on various details regarding the fountains and water system throughout the Blue Garden. The long pool was intended to be supplied with multiple uniform jets of water along its length, all in the same direction, to sparkle when seen in strong light. Problems with piping and nozzles interfered with an effective water stream and had to be solved, although never totally satisfactorily. The waterfall, which Wait had designed to cascade down the slope behind the southern pergola, had been constructed in a manner typical for that era, by puddling clay into pools set among the rocky outcroppings.

Unfortunately, these would not hold water, so small basins of cast stone were substituted, to be hidden among the plantings. Since the slope was so richly planted with multi-textured materials, these pools were scarcely visible.

Finally, the issue of mosquito larvae, particularly in the square pool, had to be handled. A surface device was inserted to draw off water with larvae without emptying the whole pool, and fish were added.[44]

Planting the Garden — the Perimeter

From the earliest planting considerations made by Hans Koehler in March 1910,[45] even before formal garden discussions had melded into the Blue Garden concept, the area on the slope northeast of the house was given special attention. A natural hollow below the ridge, strewn with granitic extrusions, some of great size, provided a protective environment for plants. The original sharp curve of Beacon Hill Road intruded through this hollow around a large rocky outcropping. With the realignment of the road, space became available for new landscape considerations, such as a tennis court and specialized plantings. The March 1911 plan[46] treated this interior space with undulating drifts of perennial material set amid turf walks around the boulders, with attention paid to planning the vistas from various points along the road and paths. An outer layer of trees, deciduous and evergreen, underplanted with herbaceous material, was planned to enclose this "informal garden." Once the Blue Garden's classic form was fitted to this area, plantings planned for the perimeter of the hollow were adjusted to provide a suitable surround to enhance passage to this garden, while screening it from the drive and nearby tennis court.[47]

As construction permitted, plantings were installed around the developing Blue Garden to establish the desired vegetative enclosure. The hedge on the outside of the garden walls, intended to reinforce the shape by forming a green delineation between formal garden and enclosing plantings, was installed by mid-1912. Instead of using *Ilex crenata,* Japanese holly, for the hedge, as both Koehler and Charles Wait recommended for its good winter texture, *Crataegus pyracantha*, now called simply pyracantha, was the choice. A much more problematic plant, often subject to winter burn, it was also prone to scale, for which it had to be treated within a year of planting.[48] By 1915, this hedge planting had been removed. Shaded by shrubs and evergreens growing on its outer side and smothered by the rampant morning glory on the trellis, it had languished. Blossom's observation at this time was that it was "a distinct loss to the garden not to have this hedge."[49]

In the area between the mansion and the garden, low junipers blanketed the upper slope around the arrival circle at the house, gradually transitioning into a thick pine planting to edge the northern drive which entered the property at the junction of Beacon Hill Road and Hammersmith Road. A gently curving path from the circle down the slope into the hollow was realigned to accommodate the newly articulated garden. Paths were lawn where conditions would allow; otherwise, of gravel augmented by stepping stones or steps where needed, made of cast stone. One branch of this path entered the Blue Garden at the center of the apse, while another curved further east around boulders. According to the 1912 plans, east of this fern-lined path, rhododendron varieties, backed by pines, were to define the area; while on the western uphill side, herbaceous

(facing page) Planting Plan for the Vicinity of Flower Garden, Plan No. 423, April 15, 1913. A list of trees, with some shrubs and herbaceous material, is included in this plan. The plan delineates the surrounding paths and outlines the tennis court to the north of the garden, screened by climbing vines on the fence. The plan accentuates the ledge outcroppings with mixed plantings. A substantial border of juniper, spruce, and pine extends to include the north pergola, defining the enclosure of the space and making a transition from the formal garden to the rocky landscape beyond.

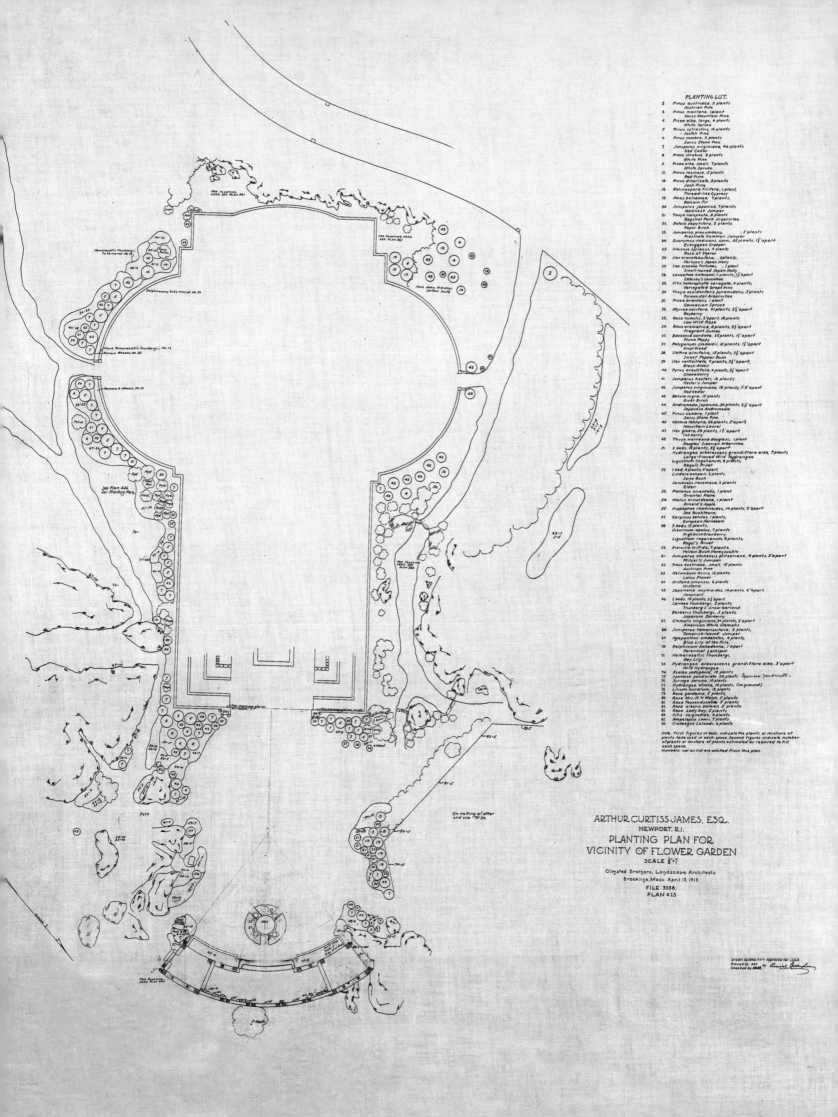

ARTHUR CURTISS JAMES, ESQ.
NEWPORT, R.I.
PLANTING PLAN FOR
VICINITY OF FLOWER GARDEN
SCALE ⅛"=1'

Olmsted Brothers, Landscape Architects.
Brookline, Mass. April 15, 1913.

FILE 3558.
PLAN 423

ARTHUR CURTISS JAMES, ESQ.
NEWPORT, R.I.
REVISED PLANTING PLAN FOR OUTSIDE OF SOUTH ENTRANCE TO FLOWER GARDEN.
SCALE 1/16"·1'

Olmsted Brothers, Landscape Architects.
Brookline, Mass. April 30. 1913.
FILE 3558
PLAN 446.

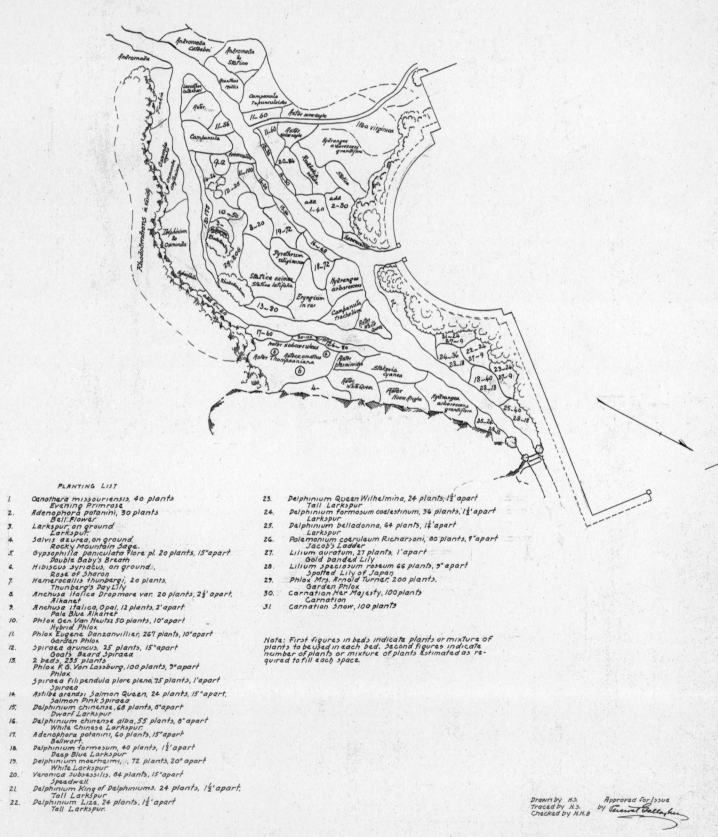

PLANTING LIST

1. Oenothera missouriensis, 40 plants
   Evening Primrose
2. Adenophora potanini, 30 plants
   Bell Flower
3. Larkspur, on ground
   Larkspur.
4. Salvia azurea, on ground
   Rocky Mountain Sage.
5. Gypsophila paniculata flore pl. 20 plants, 15" apart
   Double Baby's Breath
6. Hibiscus syriacus, on ground,
   Rose of Sharon
7. Hemerocallis thunbergi, 20 plants,
   Thunberg's Day Lily
8. Anchusa italica Dropmore var. 20 plants, 2½' apart,
   Alkanet
9. Anchusa italica, Opal, 12 plants, 2' apart
   Pale Blue Alkanet
10. Phlox Gen. Van Heutsz 50 plants, 10" apart
    Hybrid Phlox
11. Phlox Eugene Danzanvillier, 267 plants, 10" apart
    Garden Phlox
12. Spiraea aruncus, 25 plants, 15" apart
    Goat's Beard Spiraea
13. 2 beds, 235 plants
    Phlox F. G. Von Lassburg, 100 plants, 9" apart
    Phlox
    Spiraea filipendula flore pleno, 75 plants, 1' apart
    Spiraea
14. Astilbe arendsi Salmon Queen, 24 plants, 15" apart,
    Salmon Pink Spiraea
15. Delphinium chinense, 68 plants, 6" apart
    Dwarf Larkspur
16. Delphinium chinense alba, 55 plants, 6" apart
    White Chinese Larkspur.
17. Adenophora potanini, 60 plants, 15" apart
    Bellwort
18. Delphinium formosum, 40 plants, 1½' apart
    Deep Blue Larkspur
19. Delphinium moerheimi, 72 plants, 20" apart
    White Larkspur
20. Veronica subsessilis, 84 plants, 15" apart
    Speedwall
21. Delphinium King of Delphiniums, 24 plants, 1½' apart,
    Tall Larkspur
22. Delphinium Lize, 24 plants, 1½' apart
    Tall Larkspur.

23. Delphinium Queen Wilhelmina, 24 plants, 1½' apart
    Tall Larkspur
24. Delphinium formosum coelestinum, 36 plants, 1½' apart
    Larkspur
25. Delphinium belladonna, 64 plants, 1¼' apart
    Larkspur
26. Polemonium coeruleum Richarsoni, 80 plants, 9" apart
    Jacob's Ladder
27. Lilium auratum, 27 plants, 1' apart
    Gold banded Lily
28. Lilium speciosum roseum 66 plants, 9" apart
    Spotted Lily of Japan
29. Phlox Mrs. Arnold Turner, 200 plants,
    Garden Phlox
30. Carnation Her Majesty, 100 plants
    Carnation
31. Carnation Snow, 100 plants

Note: First figures in beds indicate plants or mixture of
plants to be used in each bed. Second figures indicate
number of plants or mixture of plants estimated as required to fill each space.

Drawn by H.S.   Approved for Issue
Traced by H.S.   by Percival Gallagher
Checked by H.H.B

(facing page) Revised Planting Plan for Outside of South Entrance to Flower Garden. Plan No. 446, April 30, 1913. The list consists of thirty-one shrubs and perennials that define the paths that lead from the house to and around the garden.

(above) These photographs from 1915-16 indicate how the established plantings were developed to heighten the experience of walking from the house along the paths. Material was planted for a tapestry effect of color and texture that carpeted the slopes. Shrubs such as *Vitex agnus-castus* and blue hibiscus served to hint at the color in the garden.

material was planted for a tapestry effect of color. Irregularly shaped swaths of single species were interwoven to carpet the slope, in a manner very reminiscent of William Robinson and Gertrude Jekyll. Large beds of yellow—rudbeckia, evening primrose, daylilies—intermingled with various blues—statice, salvia, sea holly, harebells, delphinium, aconite and shrubs such as *Vitex agnus-castus* and hydrangea—and whites with attractive gray foliage—asters, mallow—added to the overall effect. These planted verges served as a foretaste for the colorful horticultural splendors to come in the Blue Garden.[50]

On the west side of the Blue Garden, where space was more limited, shrubs such as mock orange and rose of Sharon, rather than perennials, were intended to furnish color, backed by a thick evergreen planting, including pines and fir. In April 1913, as the Garden's debut grew closer, a layer of shrubs and small trees, both deciduous and evergreen, was added around the entire perimeter of the garden, just beyond the hedge which followed the line of the wall. This planting, which included tall junipers, dwarf spruce and stone pines; birch and Arnold's crabapples; and shrubs such as clethra, kalmia and leucothoe, reinforced the garden's outline. This more sub-stantial planted border was extended to include the northern pergola and the *plaisance*, thus giving a more defined and graceful enclosure to this area than the various boulders could provide.

Plantings for other areas surrounding the Blue Garden were addressed. A Japanese Garden[51] had been discussed for this property from early in 1912, without being clearly located on the site. The estate's irregular terrain, with its eccentric boulders, some of great character, and slopes of creeping groundcovers and mosses, provided opportunities to develop this aesthetic. To reach the tennis court, various paths were needed which had to be threaded among the large rocks at the edge of the hollow, northwest of the Blue Garden. Since the courts were to be heavily screened with taller evergreens, such as firs, junipers and pines, Blossom developed a meandering path of lawn in sunny areas and gravel in the shade. He planted the edges with dwarf shrub material, particularly thread-leaf Japanese evergreens and azaleas, while at the ground plane, various sedum, thymes and creeping wildflowers were planted to populate the crevices between the boulders. Into this space, more a "Japanese path" than a garden, he placed various stone lanterns at scenic vista points. Evaluating this

(facing page) Planting Plan for Japanese Garden, Plan No. 360, April 3, 1913. The boulders and mossy slopes provided an opportunity to develop a Japanese aesthetic.

(left) The narrow path to the west of the garden was planted with dwarf Japanese evergreens and azaleas. Stone lanterns completed the effect.

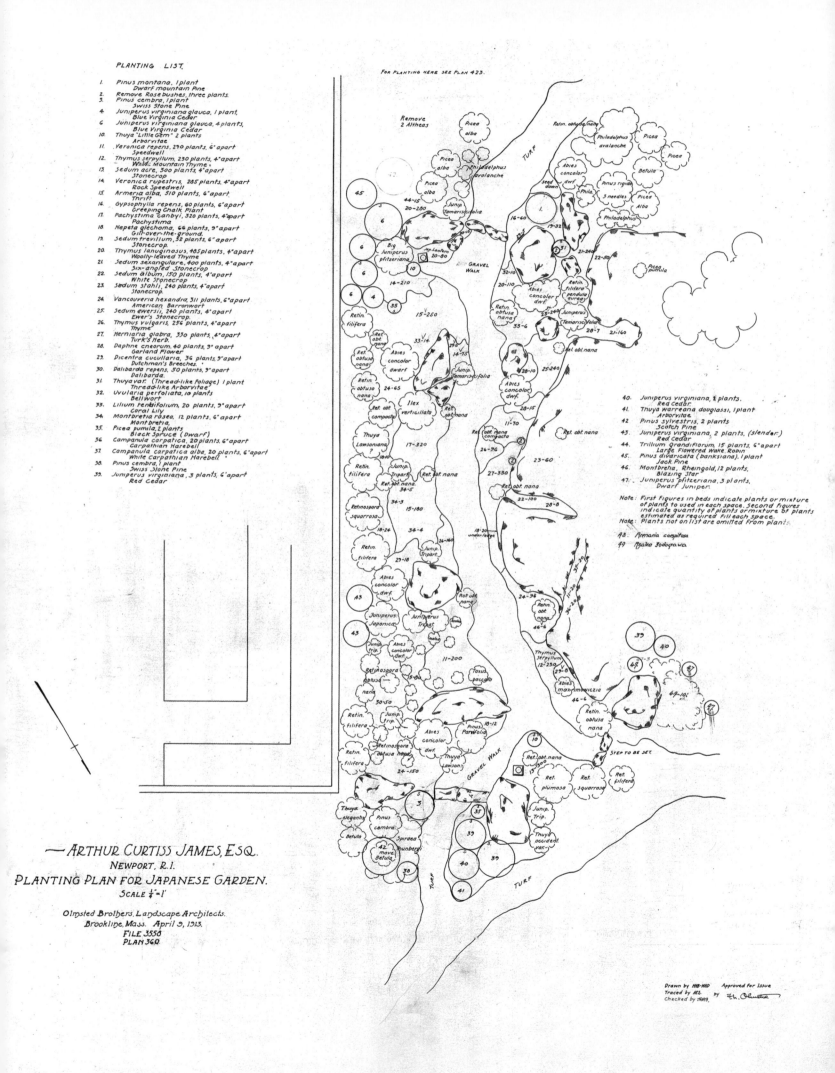

PLANTING LIST.

1. Pinus montana, 1 plant
   Dwarf mountain Pine
2. Remove Rose bushes, three plants.
3. Pinus cembra, 1 plant
   Swiss Stone Pine
4. Juniperus virginiana glauca, 1 plant,
   Blue Virginia Cedar
6. Juniperus virginiana glauca, 4 plants,
   Blue Virginia Cedar
10. Thuya "Little Gem", 2 plants
    Arborvitae
11. Veronica repens, 290 plants, 6" apart
    Speedwell
12. Thymus serpyllum, 230 plants, 4" apart
    Wild. Mountain Thyme
13. Sedum acre, 300 plants, 4" apart
    Stonecrop
14. Veronica rupestris, 285 plants, 4" apart
    Rock Speedwell
15. Armeria alba, 510 plants, 6" apart
    Thrift
16. Gypsophila repens, 60 plants, 6" apart
    Creeping Chalk Plant
17. Pachystima canbyi, 320 plants, 4" apart
    Pachystima
18. Nepeta glechoma, 66 plants, 9" apart
    Gill-over-the-ground.
19. Sedum trevillium, 32 plants, 6" apart
    Stonecrop
20. Thymus lanuginosus, 485 plants, 4" apart
    Woolly-leaved Thyme
21. Sedum sexangulare, 400 plants, 4" apart
    Six-angled Stonecrop
22. Sedum album, 150 plants, 4" apart
    White Stonecrop
23. Sedum stahli, 240 plants, 4" apart
    Stonecrop
24. Vancouveria hexandra, 311 plants, 6" apart
    American Barrenwort
25. Sedum ewersii, 240 plants, 4" apart
    Ewer's Stonecrop
26. Thymus vulgaris, 256 plants, 4" apart
    Thyme
27. Herniaria glabra, 330 plants, 4" apart
    Turk's Herb.
28. Daphne cneorum, 40 plants, 9" apart
    Garland Flower
29. Dicentra cucullaria, 36 plants, 9" apart
    Dutchman's Breeches
30. Dalibarda repens, 50 plants, 9" apart
    Dalibarda.
31. Thuya var. (Thread-like foliage) 1 plant
    Thread-like Arborvitae
32. Uvularia perfoliata, 10 plants
    Bellwort
33. Lilium tenuifolium, 20 plants, 9" apart
    Coral Lily
34. Montbretia rosea, 12 plants, 6" apart
    Montbretia.
35. Picea pumila, 2 plants
    Black Spruce (Dwarf)
36. Campanula carpatica, 20 plants, 6" apart
    Carpathian Harebell
37. Campanula carpatica alba, 20 plants, 6" apart
    White Carpathian Harebell.
38. Pinus cembra, 1 plant
    Swiss Stone Pine
39. Juniperus virginiana, 3 plants, 6" apart
    Red Cedar

40. Juniperus virginiana, 2 plants.
    Red Cedar.
41. Thuya warreana douglassi, 1 plant
    Arborvitae
42. Pinus sylvestris, 2 plants
    Scotch Pine
43. Juniperus virginiana, 2 plants, (slender.)
    Red Cedar
44. Trillium grandiflorum, 15 plants, 6" apart
    Large Flowered Wake Robin
45. Pinus divaricata (banksiana), 1 plant
    Jack Pine
46. Montbretia, Rheingold, 12 plants,
    Blazing Star
47. Juniperus pfitzeriana, 3 plants,
    Dwarf Juniper.

Note: First figures in beds indicate plants or mixture
      of plants to used in each space. Second figures
      indicate quantity of plants or mixture of plants
      estimated as required for each space.
Note: Plants not on list are omitted from plant.

48. Armaria carpitata
49. Azalea Yodogawa.

FOR PLANTING HERE SEE PLAN 423.

— ARTHUR CURTISS JAMES, ESQ.
NEWPORT, R.I.
PLANTING PLAN FOR JAPANESE GARDEN.
SCALE ¼" = 1'

Olmsted Brothers, Landscape Architects.
Brookline, Mass.   April 9, 1913.
FILE 3550
PLAN 360

Drawn by HMB-MHD   Approved for Issue
Traced by ACS.
Checked by   by Fh. Olmsted

space in January 1915, nearly two years after its installation, Blossom was pleased with the effects of mat-like groundcovers and dwarf shrubs, but the taller material, now too dense, needed pruning in the Japanese style.[52]

Finally, plans for planting around both pergolas were also prepared in April 1913. On the steep slope behind the southern pergola, where blasting had left an assemblage of rough outcroppings, work was underway to construct the meandering waterfall that Charles Wait had sketched in September 1912. This area, now called the rock garden, was accessed by stepping stones leading to the pergola. Along the path and tucked among the rocks was to be an embellishment of diverse wildflowers, which included, among others, spring-blooming acquilegia, arabis, tiarella and violas, summer-flowering aconites, asters, bellflowers, gentians and veronicas, all interspersed with ferns. This delicate tracery in whites and various blues expanded the formal garden's aesthetic into a wilder, seemingly less structured area.

In contrast, the northern pergola, with its numerous surrounding boulders and rugged stone piers, was backed by a more robust shrub planting. Sizable groupings of mountain laurel, rhododendron, clethra and gray dogwood were planted beneath its northern wall, intermingled with taller needled evergreens at the edges to frame the views out across the boulder-strewn Aquidneck moors, still relatively uncluttered by mansions. Photographs taken in October 1920 by Rick Olmsted reveal that the perimeter planting behind the northeast pergola had filled in, giving a sense of enclosure to this end of the garden.[53] On the eastern side of the *plaisance*, some tall conical evergreens are staked, possibly indicating that they were newly planted. These may be the *Cryptomeria,* the Japanese cedar, which eventually ringed the garden. With its resistance to wind and salt spray damage, this graceful evergreen became popular in Newport gardens.[54]

Planting the Garden—An Interior of Blue with a "touch of white"

Once the classic axial design for the formal garden, as conceived by Rick Olmsted and Charles Wait, had been accepted by Harriet and Arthur James, a frenzy of construction began. The mansion, essentially completed, had opened for a housewarming in February 1912, and the Jameses planned to be in residence for the summer. The grounds, though unfinished in many areas, were expected to be available for the social season. As productive as the contractors could be, there were too many unanticipated site exigencies for this complex design, which slowed the formal garden's completion. By April, realizing that the time would be too short to get enough showy growth from the perennial palette as desired by Mrs. James, Blossom prepared a simplified scheme of mostly annuals and summer-blooming bulbs, interspersed with some perennial material. After reviewing with Blossom her choices of annuals, she approved the plan so that plants could be ordered and seeds dispersed as soon as the beds were ready.[55]

Since this was also prior to the Rick Olmsted epiphany to create the Persian water garden, the central area to become the long pool was to be filled with bachelor's buttons, edged by ageratum. The parallel long beds on either side of this long central bed were to be planted as mirror reflections of each other, a tapestry of blue and white. With blue morning glories along the trellises, the beds were filled with dahlias, phlox, poppies, snapdragons and stock, all in white, intermingled with blue-purple larkspur, Japanese iris, and edged by ageratum, candytuft and alyssum.

(facing page) Planting Plan for Formal Garden of Annual Plants, Plan No.348, June 1912. This plan was developed using annuals and some perennials so that the garden would be in bloom for the 1912 season. The central planting bed was to be planted with bachelor's buttons and edged by ageratum. This was prior to Rick Olmsted's change that transformed the long bed into a shallow pool.

A.C. JAMES ESQ.
NEWPORT R.I.
PLANTING PLAN FOR FORMAL GARDEN OF ANNUAL PLANTS

SCALE ⅛"·1'
FILE No.3558
PLAN No.348

Olmsted Brothers·Landscape Architects
Brookline, Mass., June 7, 1912

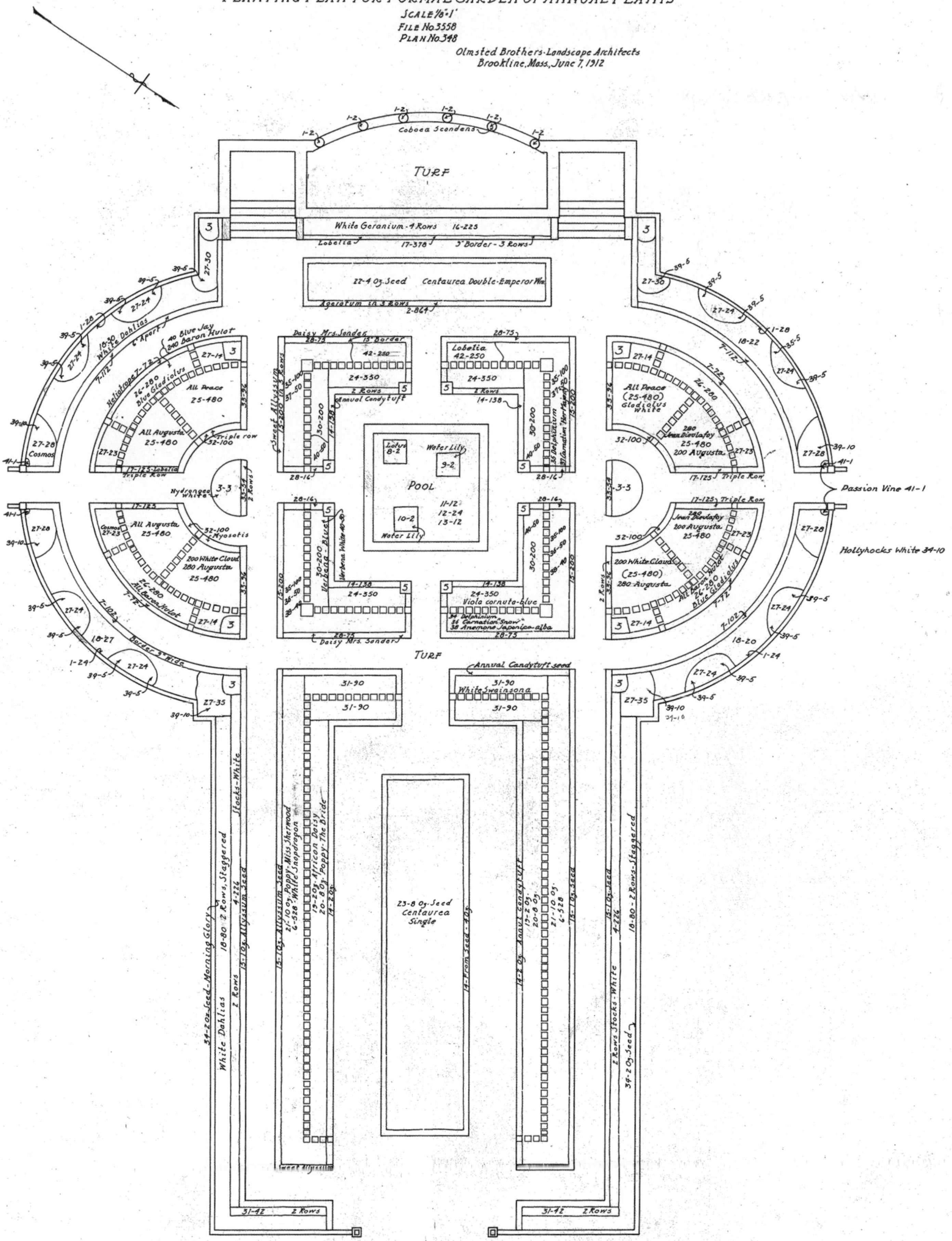

Cobaea Scandens

TURF

White Geranium - 4 Rows   16-225
Lobelia   17-378   5' Border - 3 Rows

27-4 Oz. Seed   Centaurea Double-Emperor Wm.
Ageratum in 3 Rows   2-864

White Dahlias
40 Blue Jay
200 Baron Hulot
Heliotrope
26-280
Blue Gladiolus
All Peace
25-480
All Augusta
25-480
Triple row
Lobelia
Triple Row
Cosmos
Hydrangea
white
Cosmos
Myosotis
All Augusta
25-480
200 White Cloud
280 Augusta
25-480
All Baron Hulot

Daisy Mrs. Sander
5' Border
42-250
2 Rows
Annual Candytuft
Verbena White
Daisy Mrs. Sander

Lobelia
42-250
2 Rows

Lotus
Water Lily
POOL
11-12
12-24
13-12
Water Lily

Viola cornuta-blue
24-350
Delphinium
Carnation Snow
Anemone Japonica-alba

All Peace
(25-480)
Gladiolus
White
Jean Nicolafay
25-480
200 Augusta
Triple Row
Jean Nicolafay
200 Augusta
25-480
200 White Cloud
(25-480)
280 Augusta
All Peace
26-280
Blue Gladiolus

Passion Vine 41-1
Hollyhocks White 34-10

TURF

31-90
31-90
Annual Candytuft seed
White Swainsona
31-90
31-90

Morning Glory
White Dahlias   18-80 - 2 Rows, Staggered
Stocks-White
Alyssum Seed
Poppy Miss Sherwood
White Snapdragon
African Daisy
Poppy-The Bride

23-8 Oz. Seed
Centaurea
Single

Annual Candytuft
Stocks White
18-80 - 2 Rows Staggered

Sweet Alyssum

31-42   2 Rows
31-42   2 Rows

Drawn By HHB. Approved for Issue
Traced by ELK   By
Checked by ELK

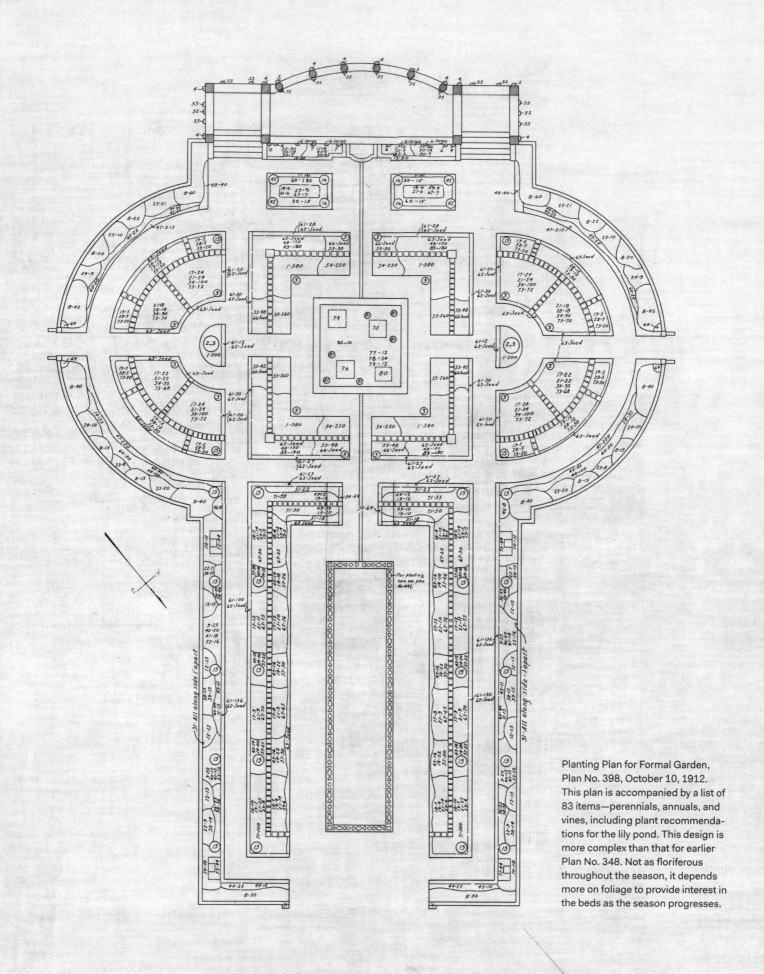

Planting Plan for Formal Garden, Plan No. 398, October 10, 1912. This plan is accompanied by a list of 83 items—perennials, annuals, and vines, including plant recommendations for the lily pond. This design is more complex than that for earlier Plan No. 348. Not as floriferous throughout the season, it depends more on foliage to provide interest in the beds as the season progresses.

A.C. JAMES ESQ.
NEWPORT-R.I.
PLANTING PLAN FOR FORMAL GARDEN
SCALE 1/8"=1'

Olmsted Brothers - Landscape Architects
Brookline - Mass., Oct. 10, 1912
FILE Nº 3558
PLAN Nº 398

PLANTING LIST.

1. Viola cornuta, blue, 3002 plants, 4"apart
   Tufted Pansy
2. Hydrangea Avalanche, - , 6 plants
   Hydrangea
3. Agapanthus umbellatus, 16 plants
   Blue Lily of the Nile
4. Wistaria chinensis blue, 11 plants
   Blue Chinese Wistaria
5. Wistaria chinensis, white, 3 plants
   White Chinese Wistaria
6. Evonymus radicans reticulatus, 3 plants, and 4 large.
   Narrow-leaved Evergreen Creeper
7. Hedera helix, 2 plants
   English Ivy
8. Delphinium hybridum, tall, 608 plants, 1"apart
   Hybrid Larkspur
9. Delphinium belladonna, 90 plants, 9"apart
   Larkspur
10. Baptisia australis, 58 plants, 15"apart
    False Indigo
11. Veronica longifolia subsessilis, 56 plants, 1"apart
    Speedwell
12. Aconitum autumnale, 120 plants, 1"apart
    Monk's Hood
13. Veronica incana, 60 plants, 6"apart
    Hoary Speedwell
14. Phlox, Miss Lingard, 298 plants, 1"apart
    Garden Phlox
15. Paeonia, Marie Lemoine, 24 plants, 2"apart
    Hybrid Peony
16. Paeonia festiva Maxima, 4 plants, 2"apart
    White Peony
17. Iris, pallida dalmatica, 222 plants, 1½"apart
    German Iris
18. Iris, pallida mandralacea, 68 plants, 18"apart
    German Iris
19. Iris, kaempferi, Gold Band, 170 plants, 1½"apart
    Japanese Iris
20. Phlox Czarina, 68 plants, 15"apart
    Garden Phlox
21. Iris, kaempferi, blue, 403 plants, 1½"apart
    Japanese Iris
22. Lilium myriophyllum, 90 plants, 1½"apart
    Lily
23. Lupinus polyphyllus, blue, 36 plants, 15"apart
    Lupine
24. Lupinus polyphyllus, white, 38 plants, 15"apart
    Lupine
25. Digitalis purpurea, alba, 78 plants, 1"apart
    Foxglove
26. Not used
27. Not used
28. Iris germanica, Mme. Chereau, 174 plants, 1½"apart
    German Iris
29. Iris, Mrs. H. Darwin, 46 plants, 15"apart
    German Iris
30. Lilium speciosum album, 26 plants, 1½"apart
    Showy Lily
31. Ipomea, Heavenly Blue, 428 plants, 1"apart (from seed)
    Morning Glory
32. Clematis jackmanni, 4 plants
    Blue Hybrid Clematis
33. Clematis paniculata, 6 plants
    Virgin's Bower
34. Gladiolus, Blue Joy, 770 plants, 6"apart
    Blue Gladiolus
35. Cobea scandens, 6 plants, 1"apart
    Cobea
36. Campanula persicifolia alba, 100 plants, 9"apart
    White Peach Bells
37. Not used
38. Campanula pyramidalis, 82 plants, 15"apart
    Chimney Flower
39. Campanula pyramidalis alba, 30 plants, 15"apart
    White Chimney Flower
40. Campanula medium calycanthemum, 74 plants, 9"apart
    Canterbury Bells
41. Campanula medium alba, 66 plants, 9"apart
    Canterbury Bells
42. Paeonia, Mt. Blanc, 4 plants, 2"apart
    Peony
43. Phlox, F.G. Von Lassburg, 216 plants, 15"apart
    Garden Phlox
44. Delphinium chinensis, blue, 380 plants, 9"apart
    Chinese Larkspur
45. Lilium candidum, 150 plants, 1½"apart
    Madonna Lily
46. Statice latifolia, 16 plants, 1"apart
    Sea Lavender
47. Veronica, Royal Blue, 870 plants, 6"apart
    Speedwell

48. Campanula carpatica, 680 plants, 6"apart
    Carpathian Harebell
49. Iris germanica, Pres. Carnot, 44 plants, 1½"apart
    German Iris
50. Not Used
51. Stokesia cyanea, 80 plants, 1"apart
    Stoke's Aster
52. Adenophora potanini, 60 plants, 1"apart
    Gland Bellflower
53. Ruellia ciliosa, 356 plants, 6"apart
    Ruellia
54. Viola cornuta purpurea, 1128 plants, 4"apart
    Tufted Pansy
55. Plumbago larpentae, 1040 plants, 4"apart
    Leadwort
56. Platycodon mariesii, - plants, 6"apart
    Japanese Bell Flower
57. Platycodon grandiflorum, 306 plants, 9"apart
    Balloon Flower
58. Campanula carpatica alba, 756 plants, 6"apart
    Carpathian Harebell
59. Myosotis palustris, 26 plants, 6"apart
    Forget-me-not
60. Arabis albida, 660 plants, 6"apart
    Rock Cress
61. Iberis sempervirens, 920 plants, 9"apart
    Hardy Candytuft
62. Sweet Allyssum, by seed, 582 sq. feet
    Sweet Allyssum
63. Viola cornuta, white, 486 sq. feet
    White Tufted Pansy
64. Passiflora coerulea, 4 plants
    Passion Flower
65. Papaver, The Bride - Seed
    Poppy
66. Papaver, Miss Sherwood - Seed - 128 sq. ft.
    Poppy
67. Delphinium ajacis, 702 plants, 9"apart
    Larkspur
68. Delphinium hybridum
    Hybrid Larkspur
69. Not used
70. Cactus, dahlia, white
    Dahlia
71. Antirrhinum, dwarf white, The Bride, 410 plants, 9"apart
    Snapdragon
72. Campanula lactiflora, 176 plants, 6"apart
    Bell Flower
73. Antirrhinum, Giant white, 924 plants, 1"apart
    Snapdragon
74. Nymphaea marliacea albida, 1 plant

75. Nymphaea zanzibariensis, 2 plants
    Water Lily
76. Nymphaea coerulea, 2 plants
    Water Lily
77. Eichornea crassipes major, 12 plants
    Water Hyacinth
78. Myrophyllum proserpinacoides, 24 plants
    Parrots feather
79. Pistia stratiotes, 12 plants
    Water Lettuce
80. Nymphaea Gladstoniana, 2 plants
81. Nymphaea pygmaea, 6 plants.
82. Lymnocharis Humbolti, 12 plants.
    Water Poppy.
83. Nepeta mussini, 72 plants
    Cat Mint.

Drawn by NHB
Traced by ELK
Checked by SWB

Approved for issue
By F.L. Olmsted

Looking to the west end of the south pergola across the iris beds, 1917. The boulders of the water cascade can be seen through the pergola columns.

The curving beds in the apse ends mixed plumbago and asters with white dahlias, edged by anchusa; while in the inner curved beds, various ground-hugging campanulas in blue and white were contrasted with vertical blue gladioli edged by lobelia, heliotrope and forget-me-nots. The angled beds which surrounded the square water-lily basin mixed white daisies, carnations, platycodon and anemone japonica with the blues of delphinium, violas, scabiosa and ladybells (adenophora), edged by alyssum. Touches of yellow were provided by other gladioli, evening primrose, and the daisy-like chrysocoma and heliopsis tucked into corners, with other blues, such as salvias, verbenas and aconites, added in various pockets.

Planning for the more permanent perennials for the 1913 Blue Garden began in October of 1912. After meetings with both Charles Wait and Harold Blossom, the Jameses agreed to the necessary adjustments to reconfigure this garden to include the new Persian water features. In addition to the various construction alterations to provide for the necessary water, the rill now provided a definite spine to the space, requiring subtle changes to the layout. What had once been two long rectangular beds fronting the southern pergola now became four smaller beds, bisected by the rill and its "source," a small basin with a shell feature, attached at the base of the pergola. A different aesthetic seemed to emerge in the Olmsted planning, perhaps expanding upon the Persian theme. Since many plans produced from

View to the west gate along the central lawn path
and across the lily pond in the apse, 1917.

August through October 1912 no longer exist, it is
difficult to get the full picture of their thinking.[56]

Correspondence indicates that Blossom
sent Mrs. James three color charts, which unfortunately no longer exist, to indicate the relationship "between blue and white masses and also
foliage masses that are without bloom" for May–
June, for July–August and for September. To
accomplish the full effect over the entire summer,
the firm suggested that Greatorex be instructed
to grow pots of blue annuals, which could be
inserted to fill out weak places. Blossom cautioned
that the perennial garden would not be as fulsome
throughout the summer as the annual garden had
been, but the foliage would be more substantial
and certain plants, such as German iris and lark-

spur, would provide more character with their
foliage. With this design, they hoped to achieve a
better preponderance of blue to white than they
had obtained in the annual garden. Also at this
time, responding to Mrs. James' complaint that
the hillside above the garden was very bare, they
suggested covering the ridge around the Telescope
House and flagpole with heathers and other such
low materials, using select shrubs to provide
protection so these plants could naturalize. This
planting addressed the garden's larger context,
the extended focal points of the Blue Garden's
main axis.[57]

The perennial plan was much more complex
than that for the annuals, which had used broad
sweeps of a few species to cover large areas. In

View along lawn path between the planting beds on the east side of the garden, 1917. Note the abundant iris plantings to the right and the mixed perennials to the left, along the wall surmounted by the trellis.

the later plan, each side of the rill along the long axis was a mirror image of the other; likewise, each side along the cross axis in the oval was mirrored by its other side. Within each bed were intricate arrangements of perennials, with some annuals, in groupings combined for color, texture of leaves and flowers, for height and period of bloom. Perennials provided an expansive array of the desired blue, blue-purple and lavender hues, with leaves of all shades of green through gray, some like the various iris, vertical and strappy; others such as larkspur a feathery filigree and still others—aconite—substantial and shiny. Intertwining through the trellises or across the pergola beams, to carry the color up to another

level, were blues and whites of wisteria, clematis, morning glories and the more exotic cup-and-saucer and passion vines. The resultant effect was that of a three-dimensional tapestry of interrelated and repeated motifs, which engaged both mind and the senses.

In the rectangular area centered on the long pool, four statues of the Seasons on pedestals were inserted at each end of the beds backed by the walls. Five white peonies—*Festiva maxima*—placed at intervals along this bed provided a rounded shrubby presence among the spiky verticals of baptisia, veronica, delphinium and tall campanulas. Iris and lilies of several varieties and blooming times, together with phlox and the

Looking along the lawn path on the west side of the garden, 1917. Note the lushly textured perennial borders and the vine-covered trellis enclosing one of the "Four Seasons" sculptures.

cup-shaped platycodon, added flowers of another shape to the irregular swaths of color. In the foreground, mounds of smaller campanulas, violas and rows of white snapdragons were edged by white candytuft and alyssum. In the adjoining long bed with turf paths on both sides, similar perennials in clusters of three or four different but complementary species were grouped to create a more horizontally striped effect, with repeated clusters at each end of the bed. To enhance the azure iridescence of the long pool, clusters of low veronica, ageratum, lobelia and alyssum were suggested for the planting spaces in the decorative stone border. In June 1913, this poolside planting was simplified to be mostly blue verbena.[58]

The curved beds on either side of the cross axis at the oval area of the Blue Garden were likewise treated with clusters of complementary plants, varied for texture, type and bloom time. Along the curving walls, the beds were to be filled with large groups of tall spring-blooming lupines, to be followed by delphinium mixed with various white lilies for the summer. Fronting these plants were medium height blue phlox and shorter delphinium with low campanulas as edging. The curved interior beds were separated into wedge-like groups of several iris cultivars, varied by height and bloom time, intermingled with blue gladioli and tall white snapdragons and edged by white iberis and alyssum. Around the central

Looking to the east gate in the apse from the lily pond, 1917.

square water-lily pool, the beds were filled with plants with an airy texture, annual white poppies, various violas and low catmint. At the four inner corners of these beds, pots of agapanthus were intended. The basin was planted with different cultivars of water lilies, flowering water lotus and other exotic aquatic plants.

Orders for the perennials were sent out in October 1912 to numerous nurseries from New England to Rochester, New York, so that they could be planted in the beds as soon as weather permitted. In addition, several of the intended plantings, the annuals in particular, were to be raised from seed in the greenhouses. In January 1913, Greatorex had begun to work the soil in the beds, as frost would allow; by April, they were

already thinning out the young phlox plantings, preparing to plant the lily bulbs and scurrying to clean up the site. By May, they were pruning wisteria and seeding in bare areas. In June, Mrs. James fretted that there were no buds on the water lilies and the garden was showing more white than blue. She reiterated that what she wanted, according to Blossom's report, was "a dazzling blue all summer with a touch of white." To achieve this, Blossom noted that Greatorex would have to use traditional bedding-out practices of growing plants in pots ready to be installed where color was needed.[59]

In addition, Harriet James felt that the turf area beyond the long pool looked "open and blank." This complaint does not seem to have

View along the lawn path on the east side of the apse, curving between beds of varied perennial plantings, 1917.

been addressed until 1916, by which time the four Corinthian columns no longer surrounded the wellhead. At that time, Harold Blossom suggested giving the wellhead more presence by surrounding it with a circular planting bed, edged with stone roping, with stepping stones to approach the well. Three small boxwood, underplanted by dwarf pale yellow snapdragons with large heliotrope, would give a flash of color and character to this expanse of turf when viewed from the other end of the blue and white garden. Blossom also suggested some novelty plants which might be inserted into the garden that would pique Mrs. James' horticultural fancies.[60] Inspecting the garden after the 1913 debut party, Hammond Sadler, an Olmsted assistant, observed that all looked "very well though with lots of white because the morning glory seed had failed." Given his horticultural training, it was to be expected that Greatorex would make some plant substitutions in the garden. But on a 1915 visit to see the condition of plantings throughout the estate, Blossom noted that Greatorex had kept closely to their plan, praising the display of the blue pansies, gladioli and the ageratum. However, due to the climatic, often foggy conditions, which caused rot on certain plants, Greatorex was having difficulty keeping a continuous floral display. Rather, he could provide a good presentation in early July and another in the fall, a disappointment to Harriet James, who was hoping also for June splendor.[61]

Following the taste for Italianate design, various decorative elements enhanced the carefully crafted plant arrangements to complete the garden, whether statuary, jardinières, benches or other such embellishments. Large pots, originally numbering five on each side, lined the inner edge of the planted borders from the long pool to the southern pergola.[62] These were probably the pots made in 1912 by Emerson & Norris, the cast stone fabricators, according to the Olmsted sketches. In June 1913 photographs by Blossom, these pots contained agapanthus; by 1915, they were shown planted with tall pyramidal shrubs which made a more dramatic statement, in keeping with the scale and style of this classic Italianate garden.[63] In September 1916, Rick Olmsted visited the garden with his sister Marion to meet with Harriet James. At this time he suggested "raising the concrete pots on little plinths with blue tiles on the tops … [and] blue tile inlay in the sides of plinths." Indeed, later photographs reveal the pots elevated on square pads.[64]

Carved baskets of fruit or flowers were often pictured on the edge of the square pool or the southern pergola.[65] Other jardinières of flowering plants adorned the pergolas, particularly at the northeastern end, which was surrounded by less floriferous plantings. In some photos, these pots contain hydrangeas; at others, they are shown with small spruce. Amphorae on wrought-iron stands had been added in front of this pergola by 1916.[66] Two other amphorae, shown as deep blue in the hand-colored images of the period, were placed on the back wall at both ends of the southern pergola. These matched in color a great blue pot, probably antique, which, in the summer of 1914, was given a signal placement in the front center of this pergola, elevated on a bench, where it terminated the long axis. By July 1917 this pot had been relocated to a plinth in the center of the long pool, where Frances Benjamin Johnston photographed it.[67] The 1923 report of the tour through the Blue Garden after the annual meeting of the Garden Club of America referred to this bowl as Ming, calling it "Lord Kitchener's Fish Bowl," its color "the essence of its surroundings."[68]

The wellhead, a focal feature on the main axis, was an important decorative device characteristic of a classic Italianate garden. It had been the subject of much early discussion before it was settled into its place in front of the northern pergola and surrounded by its four columns. However, the latter do not remain long in this locale, having disappeared as early as September 1916.[69] Improvements to the wrought-iron superstructure over the wellhead were considered by Rick Olmsted in late 1916, which Charles Wait designed by May 1917, suggesting the addition of a pineapple, the symbol of hospitality, to the top. Instead when the wellhead was relocated to the amphitheater in 1923, it was without its decorative wrought iron.[70]

Benches of diverse styles also decorated the garden. Originally, a simple stone bench was placed on both sides mid-garden by the enclosing wall, a good vantage point for the differing views in both directions. By 1917, photographs indicate a bench with elaborate ends had been located across the axial grass path on both sides by the square pool. Benches also populated the end bays of the northeastern pergola, while on the southwestern structure elaborately decorated benches provided shady resting spots for garden vistas under the pergola greenery.[71]

The tall piers bracketing the gates at each end of the cross axis in the oval were capped by classic urns rising high above the planted trellises. These entrances at the cross axis of the oval were frequently photographed as marking successful portals between the formal interior of the garden and the wilder exterior planting.[72] The carved figures of the four Seasons placed into the beds along the walls, had by July 1917 acquired arched trellised enclosures covered by clematis or other vines, which eventually enshrouded them, doing little to highlight the sculptures.[73]

"The Masque of the Blue Garden"

As finishing touches were being made to the Blue Garden's structures and planting, elaborate plans, veiled in secrecy, were underway to give this uniquely beautiful space a proper dedication. With her flair for the artistic and the dramatic, and with the help of her friend and artistic collaborator, Joseph Lindon Smith, theatrical impresario *extraordinaire*, Harriet James presented a pageant on a bravura scale and with a distinctiveness befitting her remarkable garden. In Newport, where ostentatiously grand events reigned supreme in this pre-war era, the "Masque of the Blue Garden" on August 15, 1913 would top them all for many years to come, with the ingenuity of its artistic conception, its skillful execution and, of course, the extraordinary setting it was to celebrate.

Joseph Lindon Smith was an artist and educator of many talents. Trained at the Boston Museum of Fine Arts (MFA) as a painter, he returned from European travel to become a decorative arts instructor at the MFA in 1898 and a member of Isabella Stewart Gardner's circle of protégés. He produced portraits, landscapes and murals, one of which can still be found at the Boston Public Library. A restless spirit, with a fondness for travel and an interest in archeology, he began painting what he saw at the monuments he visited. His fascination with Egypt and with recording in detail the art of temple and tomb, sometimes as full-scale paintings, became a new career, his work desired by galleries and museums in this era before color photography. An artist with a flair for the dramatic, he managed to imbue his works with a pictorial realism and an emotional quality which gave life to these historic artifacts. This quality also informed his parallel career, that of producer of theatrical spectacles. Beyond his coterie of wealthy clients desiring a grand event, Smith produced pageants

Joseph Lindon Smith was trained as an artist at the Boston Museum of Fine Arts and produced numerous paintings of antiquities. With his flair for the dramatic, he produced theatrical pageants for cities, institutions and private clients, such as the "Masque of the Blue Garden," which he developed with Mrs. James to inaugurate her unique monochromatic garden.

for municipalities celebrating anniversaries, for schools and museums, for charity benefits and for educational purposes. He coordinated text, music, costumes, artists and even historical feasts to follow the program, as he did for the Blue Garden's Renaissance pageant.[1]

In a letter to Mrs. James, found in the Scrapbook for the Masque of the Blue Garden,[2]

Harriet Parsons James, costumed as Lady Sapphira, in a Renaissance gown of blue brocade glittering with sapphires, was hostess for the festivities of the Masque and invited friends to "witness the dedication" of her Blue Garden.

Smith recorded his developing thoughts about the prologue for this pageant, adjusting ancient Greek and sixteenth-century poetry to his purpose to "make a beautiful and rather unusual effect." He ended his letter with a cartoon of himself "praying for a visible full moon."[3] His wish was granted. The evening of the event was moonlit and clement for the 350 guests, the fifty-four actors, dancers and musicians, including the crew of James' yacht *Aloha II* performing as Neptune's followers, and the numerous costumed staff who would later serve a Renaissance banquet

of boar and fruits in the mansion following the theatrics. The exclusive guest list incorporated the *crème* of the Social Register, family, friends and select members of the press who would circulate news of the evening's enchantment.

With great attention to detail and the guests' comfort that characterized the Jameses' events, the Masque was planned to entertain and entrance, maximizing the effects of the garden's magical scenery.[4] At the arrival circle to the mansion, guests were led along a path, canopied in blue, accompanied by soft music, to the garden periphery, where they were greeted by Arthur Curtiss James, elaborately costumed as Cosimo di Medici. They were seated at the south end in a stadium-like structure constructed within the pergola, covered with Oriental rugs and blue cushions. The long axis of the garden with its pools stretched out before them, "a-quiver in the soft blue [electric] light", all terminating at the wellhead with its four Corinthian columns. The festivities began with a welcome from Harriet James, resplendent in a Renaissance gown of blue brocade, glittering with sapphires, amethysts and diamonds, as she invited her "dear friends … to witness the dedication" of her Blue Garden.[5] A musical interlude of harp and baritone was followed by Joseph Smith's poetic synopsis of the pageant to follow. He set his theme in a short poem,

> *This lovely spot old ocean laves,*
> *And woody coverts fringe the waves.*
> *Happy the Art that could dispose*
> *What e'er in sea or garden grows.*
> *And summoned to the enchanted land*
> *The naiads and nereids band.*

He then proceeded to explicate his fanciful tale of a vintage time when Ceres and Flora with the earth sprites make offerings to Zephyrus, the gentle West Wind, to celebrate "the ecstasy of life." Sea gods join the celebration, led by Neptune on a "gold-hoofed steed" and Amphitrite, his queen, borne by tritons on an enormous shell. With the coming of dawn, brought by Apollo's chariot, all the deities flee, leaving only the "lovely garden … [and] the perfume of the flowers."[6]

For three-quarters of an hour, flitting amid the shrubs and flowers, splashing through the pools, all illuminated by twinkling blue bulbs, a troupe of actors and dancers, including Smith's two young daughters as wood-sprites, carried out this scenario to its dramatic culmination. Mermaids in blue emerged from shells to dance through the pool in preparation for the main feature, the interpretative dance of Florence Noyes as Amphitrite. Leaping from her throne, a giant conch shell placed at the far end of the long pool, this "high priestess of rhythmic expression" danced with "reckless grace" through the sprays of the long pool before disappearing into the

Arthur Curtiss James in costume as Cosimo di Medici greeted guests, guiding them from the arrival court at the house through paths to the Blue Garden.

"depths"—not much more than four feet—of the square lily pond. The appreciative applause triggered a display of colored lights sparkling like "a myriad of fireflies" throughout the gardens, spotlighting the actors assembled around the wellhead with its columns. A trumpeting herald appeared to lead the guests to the mansion, bedecked with peach trees, garlands of fruit and grand candelabras, to enjoy the Renaissance feast and the *dansant* to follow.[7]

(top and facing page) Florence Fleming Noyes, an interpretive dancer, costumed as Amphitrite, wife of Poseidon, leapt from her throne and danced with "reckless grace" through the sprays of the long pool, before disappearing into the "depths" of the lily pond.

(above and facing page) The cast, which included Joseph Smith's young daughters and a gold-hooved horse, assembled by the wellhead and columns. Mermaids in blue emerged from shells in the garden, which was illuminated with hundreds of twinkling blue lights. Joseph Smith wrote to Mrs. James that "We made a dream come true."

After the Pageant

The following day, the *New York Times* extolled the event as "striking and original … one of the most notable entertainments of the Newport season," sentiments echoed by the *New York Tribune*, the *New York Evening Telegram* and carried by smaller newspapers across the country, particularly in those locales with an economic connection to the James enterprises.[8] One astute column, entitled "Saunterings," from an unknown newspaper, while praising the event as "the most original and beautiful entertainment given at Newport this Summer," commented upon the numerous anachronisms in the production. Noting that Wagner was one of the chosen composers, the article suggested that the more appropriate Palestrina might have been "beyond the capabilities of Conrad's orchestra." Paul Swan, noted dancer of his day, lightly clad in leopard skin for the role of Zephyrus, danced in the Russian style, which "greatly pleased the Russian Ambassador." As for the setting, the anonymous author prophetically observed the following:

… [A] fairy demesnes of gleaming white arcades, fountains and luxuriant bloom which the taste and inventive genius of artists supply to millionaires nowadays over night … We are entirely too progressive to wait centuries for anything, so our gardens like our pedigrees are made up out of books and the Jameses have a perfectly good garden that entrances the casual eye and will last them their lifetime. After that, who cares?[9]

Another unidentified writer, but one who knew Harriet James, broached a different topic. Calling her a "genius" as "a woman so lately accepted by Newport" to have pulled off such a triumph, both in garden and in event, the writer wondered if Mrs. James would really want "the leadership of the Circus," referring to the social set of Newport's leading matrons, "Fish, Oelrichs, Belmont and Company."[10]

The numerous thank you notes, preserved in a Scrapbook of the Masque of the Blue Garden in the collection of the Redwood Library and Athenaeum in Newport, record the pleasure, enjoyment and genuine respect and affection for Harriet James that many guests felt at being present for this fete. Interestingly, these preserved notes are all addressed to "Mrs. James." From fete to feast, all who wrote were spellbound at the visual beauty, the artistry of the conception and its execution, the splendor of such a setting and the gracious and kind hospitality. They praised Harriet for managing such a complicated event with dignity; for the poetic "feast of beauty you laid before us," and for "lifting Newport Society to this high plane." In her note, Mrs. John Nicholas Brown wrote that she was grateful for "an opportunity to see and enjoy such a perfectly artistic and wonderfully carried out dream in reality. All Newport owes you a debt of gratitude."[11]

The wild dance in the water pool before the guests.

Cartoon illustration of costumed guests watching the dance of Amphitrite. The *New York Times* wrote that the event was "striking and original. . . one of the most notable entertainments of the Newport season." An unidentified writer called Mrs. James a "Genius. . . both in garden and in event."

In a letter from Joseph Lindon Smith, signed "your life long friends" by his wife Corinna and their daughters Rebecca and Frances who had participated in the masque, he wrote:

We made a dream come true. It couldn't have been done, if it had not been for your stead-fast faith in the dreamer, and the wealth of beautiful material, animate and inanimate which you gave into his hands. When you walked down the long path towards your guests you epitomized my purpose and struck the key note of our praise of beauty, our dedication of the garden of flowers—the "Blue Garden." May serene skies mirror their heavenly blue in your pools and fountains on the Beacon Hill and azure Summer seas surround your "Aloha."[12]

Using the Blue Garden

After such a notable debut, the Blue Garden was firmly established as the venue of choice for major entertainments. With war clouds rumbling in Europe after the June assassination of Archduke Ferdinand, the July 4th, 1914, social events in Newport were celebrated with particular intensity. The Russian and German ambassadors and the Duchess of Marlborough were among the guests present in Newport that summer. At Beacon Hill House, "all society seemed to be present" for a tea dance presentation by Miss Margaret Hawksworth and Basil Durant, who danced the latest "Lulu Fado" on a dance floor erected in the Blue Garden, followed by the release of hundreds of balloons. By August, however, celebrations had changed into fundraisers for International War Relief at the Breakers, where Harriet James was to have a Blue Garden table.[13]

The war altered social schedules and habits over the next several years. For the 1915 season, the *New York Times* noted that many more prominent people would occupy their Newport estates, rather than traveling, although fewer grand social events made the headlines. To ensure that their friends and colleagues had opportunities to join them in Newport, that summer and fall Arthur Curtiss purchased various nearby estates, amounting to seventy-five acres, developing the properties to lease or resell[14], including land near Fort Adams to build a new large pier. Additionally, he became the President of the Motor Craft Association, part of the Naval Training Association, to ensure civilian support for the active navy, with yachtsmen offering their boats and crews for coastal defense.[15] Harriet, meantime, became the vice president of the Newport Garden Club and worked diligently at numerous philanthropic efforts in Newport, New York and at their Coconut Grove estate to raise funds for war efforts.[16]

In 1917, to benefit the American Red Cross, Harriet again set a unique and financially successful example that "was the charity event of the Summer season" according to the New York papers, enticing visitors from throughout the coastal region. In collaboration again with Joseph Lindon Smith, she staged a social gathering of several parts, entitled "Gardens in Poetry and Color." On one part of the grounds, decorated with Allied flags, a little theater had been set up, where noted garden photographer Frances Benjamin Johnston showed her slides of famous American gardens with accompanying poetry recitations. In particular, there was a reading of the 1911 Rudyard Kipling poem, "The Glory of the Garden," a nostalgic celebration of simple landscape tasks, illustrated by Johnston photographs of men at work on the Beacon Hill grounds.[17] The band from Fort Adams provided musical entertainment, and there were various booths selling plants and objects. In the late afternoon, Smith presented a masque, called "The Standard Bearers." Using the Blue Garden as backdrop, he set up a series of tableaux in which the women of Newport, in appropriate costumes, represented aspects of the Allies' history and culture. Scenes such as "Greece No Longer Blind;" "Britannia, Her Sustaining Daughters;"

"Russia, The Peasant Awakened;" and "France: The Birth of Liberty Through Disorder, Revolution and Bloodshed" were accompanied by selected readings by notable actors. Patriotically, the final tableau was America, in which Harriet's niece, Harriet de Forest Manice, represented Liberty.[18]

With this event and others by the Beacon Hill Auxiliary, an organization that Harriet developed with her neighbors, funds were raised to buy ambulances and pay for other services critical to the war effort. She provided a theater for the sailors stationed at Fort Adams, paid for actors to perform and inveigled the women of the colony to volunteer at dances. In turn, the seamen of the 6th Regiment staged their own surprise event for the Jameses at Beacon Hill House in September 1917, to celebrate Harriet's birthday, showing up in formation with the Navy band, to thank the Jameses for their ongoing generosity by presenting them with a silver cup.[19]

Such efforts, social events tinged with philanthropy and patriotic service, continued well beyond the 1919 Paris Peace Conference, with fundraising to aid the devastated countries. Even in the postwar years, the Jameses generously opened their estate, especially the Blue Garden, for a myriad of causes. In 1921, members of the New England Federation of Harvard Clubs were entertained at several notable Newport venues, including the Blue Garden. They were followed the next year by the Toparian Club of Boston, which included several faculty members of Harvard University's Graduate Schools of Architecture and Landscape Architecture, who viewed the garden and delighted in the picturesque eccentricities of the Surprise Valley Farm.[20] The Blue Garden sparkled during the June tour by the Garden Club of America, held in conjunction with its 1923 annual meeting in Newport. The iridescent blue appealed to the romantic soul of the report's writer as she enthused over the delphinium, salvia patens, anchusa, veronica and lupines among other blue perennials. Among the annuals receiving praise were the torenia, the

(above and facing page) Photographs by Frances Benjamin Johnston of men at work in the James garden, 1917, to illustrate the Rudyard Kipling poem, "The Glory of the Garden" which was read at a garden pageant to benefit the war effort:

"...And there you'll see the gardeners, the men and 'prentice boys Told off to do as they are bid and do it without noise;"

"For, except when seeds are planted and we shout to scare the birds, The Glory of the Garden it abideth not in words."

blue and white gladioli, the lasiandra and the tree form heliotrope.[21]

The whirlwind visit to Newport by the Swedish Crown Prince Gustavus Adolphus and his wife Louise in June 1926 was covered by newspapers across the country, which reported on the sightseeing, the dinners and the musicales given in their honor at many notable estates. As guests at Beacon Hill House, the royal couple was feted at a reception for 300 in the Blue Garden. The *New York Times* reported that the "garden was a mass of blue" with wisteria vines covering the pergolas with clusters of the light and dark blossoms; forget-me-nots tucked around the boulders; iris, delphinium and other blue flowers arranged in beds and "huge blue vases … here and there about the garden."[22]

The *Times* continued its rhapsodic coverage of the Blue Garden in a lengthy July 1928 article

by Virginia Pope, illustrated with the photographs of Mattie Edwards Hewitt, entitled, "The Gay Sun-Kissed Flower Gardens of Newport." Reviewing the many traditions that characterized the historical development of Newport's gardens, from its eighteenth-century simplicity to its nineteenth-century French-inspired formality to its twentieth-century intimate flower gardens where "color runs riot," the author compared the planting effect of the Blue Garden to diving into the Blue Grotto. Noting the separating "barricade" of pines, spruce and other evergreens which enclosed the garden, admitting the privileged through Italianate gates, she praised the "sea of blue" created by the layering of blossoms. The "cerulean posies," augmented by pots of agapanthus and hydrangeas, look as if "a bit of the sky had come down to earth."[23]

*"...But they can roll and trim the lawns
and sift the sand and loam,
For the Glory of the Garden
occupieth all who come."*

*"...Oh, Adam was a gardener,
and God who made him sees
That half a proper gardener's work
is done upon his knees,
So when your work is finished,
you can wash your hands and pray
For the Glory of the Garden that
it may not pass away!"*

Assemblage of sailors from Fort Adams
and the Jameses on the south side terrace.
Harriet is in the center, possibly surrounded
by her sister, Amie Ferry, and her niece
Harriet Ferry, with Arthur Curtiss James
to their left, September 1917.

In 1922 Harvard University faculty from the Graduate Schools of Architecture and Landscape Architecture and members of the Toparian Club toured Newport sites, including the Blue Garden and Surprise Valley Farm, the latter designed c. 1915 by Grosvenor Atterbury.

Changes in the Blue Garden

While there were, no doubt, variations within the plant palette used in the garden, the general noteworthy effect of iridescent blue and white seems to have been maintained, even if Greatorex could only achieve his two peaks of bloom, July and fall, rather than the desired three. The most significant alteration to the garden was to the architecture of the northern pergola. In the 1921 correspondence of the Olmsted firm concerning the rhododendron planting and rose garden development, there is a cryptic note that they are preparing studies for the extension of the shelter which closes the east end of the Blue Garden and that Rick Olmsted was planning to meet with Harriet James on the site to discuss ideas. In October of 1920, Rick Olmsted had visited the garden and photographed the northern pergola in particular, at that time densely overgrown by large-leaved vines. There is nothing further in the Olmsted record.[24]

However, sometime after 1922 and probably before 1928, the northern pergola was substantially rebuilt to accommodate an Italianate exedra-like structure with side panels. While this gave a very classic terminus to the main axis of the garden, it was a significant alteration of the Olmsted concept. The original pergola at this end, with its fieldstone columns, though somewhat classic in its shape and proportions, was of a much more rustic nature. It was intended to play upon the forms used in other parts of the garden, while marking a transition from formality to the boulder-encrusted landscape beyond the James property to be viewed from this location. The wellhead surrounded by the four free-standing Corinthian columns, which once stood in front of this pergola at this end of the *plaisance*, had modulated this shift from classicism to rusticity.

Even at the zenith of the garden's fame, this pergola had been treated rather anachronistically by the Jameses. The decorative elements placed in and around it, the benches, pots and amphorae, were more formal and Italianate than the character of this structure, hewn from the rock of the surrounding area, seemed to require. For some reason Harriet James decided to dramatically change the effect created by the Olmsted plan. The rusticated stone and wood pergola was removed and a classically articulated structure with accompanying walls and columns was inserted in its place. With no documentation yet located and with scant photographic evidence, often undated, this architectural element is enshrouded in mystery.[25]

What is discernible from the record is that this transition, made after 1922 and probably before 1928, in the heyday of mid-1920s exuberance, brought about several significant changes to this end of the garden. The wellhead, without its wrought-iron superstructure, found a new home as the central feature of the amphitheater, which opened in July 1923.[26] The exedra was in place in the Aiglon aerial photographs for this garden, found in the collection at the Frederick Law Olmsted National Historic Site, which were purchased by the Olmsted firm before 1928.[27]

The exedra was composed of a central niche, with side wings consisting of low walls intersected by vertical piers to which overhead trellising was attached. Into this niche, probably painted blue, a large pot was centrally placed on a pedestal. This all rested on a platform, elevated above the lawn level as the rustic pergola had been, with several large pots decorating the edge. At the outer edges on each side of this central unit the square trellis-covered "rooms" remained.

From Harriet Jackson Phelps' description of her "garden archeology" trek through the detritus of the Blue Garden, it seems that the exedra had survived in some form until the 1970s. She wrote "… I found myself standing on the terrace of the north gallery among a clutter of formal columns … [with] a blue alcove circled over my head." In the early 1980s, a house was built on the site of this pergola, at which point the exedra was either removed or destroyed and its trail disappeared.[28]

Looking east, in an undated photograph, across the exedra that was installed sometime after 1922. The condition of the walls, columns and steps would seem to indicate that this is not a new structure, supporting the supposition that this exedra was possibly a purchased antique. Although this form had been alluded to in Plan No. 284, the classical structure altered the effect in the Blue Garden originally created by the Olmsted-designed pergola of fieldstone and wood.

Other Garden Rooms: The Rose Garden

Ever restless about her garden, Harriet James had sought the Olmsted firm's advice in late 1920 regarding maintenance issues and the development of new garden areas. At this time they planned a large rhododendron area and a new rose garden for her in the southwestern corner of the property, at the junction of Hammersmith and Brenton roads. In the first phase of estate planting, rhododendrons, intermingled with alders, had already been inserted inside the boundary walls to the west of the Gate Lodge. The aim now was to expand this planting, mixing azaleas and rhododendrons, to enclose an irregularly shaped lawn area with a continuous mass of June blooms, visible from the road. From this space, paths were to lead to an expansive new rose garden that Hans Koehler designed.[29] The former rose collection on the James estate had been associated with the formal vegetable and cutting garden, where rose garlands punctuated the path borders and a hillside "room" of shrub roses was established on the periphery. As the panoply of new cultivars became available, rose gardens were very much in vogue at this time.

Soon after the original Olmsted work on the estate, a rose garden with trial beds had been set up around the glacial erratics on the west lawn south of the garage complex, defined by stone walls and paths in some places, by rustic trellis in others and by naturalized shrub plantings.[30]

The Olmsted firm's aim was to improve the existing scheme, to produce a rose garden "of a much more distinctive character, something that would be notable both from a rose-lover's standpoint and from that of garden design." Organized to give cohesion and some formality to the current space, Koehler made use of the topography by planning for a central grass "valley" punctuated at one end by a sunken circular feature, with the curvilinear beds of the trial garden branching out on either side. A low wall, defining the eastern boundary, was to separate the gardenesque portion from the wilder area, where native rose species would be mingled with tree peonies and groundcovers. Within the rose garden, in curvilinear beds, over 2,000 species of tea roses, hybrid perpetuals and climbers on arches, arbors or poles would be bordered by turf paths. To retain privacy from the road, a border planting of dogwoods, hollies, inkberries and yews, under-planted with sheep laurel, rhodora, juniper, ferns and native orchids was planned. Praising the scheme as "very attractive," Harriet James considered the cost estimates too expensive, saying they would pay for the plans and work on these ideas with their own crews under Greatorex.[31]

Retaining the circular core, Mrs. James and her team, which might have included advice from Joseph Lindon Smith, enlarged the Olmsted

The rose standards along the paths in the vegetable and cutting garden, c. 1917, with a rose-embowered shelter terminating the central east-west axis of this garden. Rose gardens were very much in vogue at this time, as new cultivars were developed. On the James estate, design of new rose gardens competed with the Blue Garden for attention.

Looking south across the amphitheater with its trellis shelters and statuary, c. 1930s. This garden room, with its rose plantings, debuted on June 27, 1923, for a Garden Club of America meeting. The central wellhead was relocated here from the northern end of the Blue Garden. This garden became another venue for social and philanthropic events.

idea into a two-tiered sunken amphitheater, defined by low stone walls with plantings. An upper circle to the north provided automobile access and parking, a broad turf path linking it to the garden circles. There is scant documentation about the shaping of this space, although a 1925 newspaper account attributed the design to Mr. Smith. The core of what was built clearly reflects the 1921 Olmsted ideas. Aerial photographs from sometime in the 1920s reveal its shape and surrounding plantings. Densely enclosed on the lower side by what appear to be evergreen plantings, which would have created privacy from the road, the upper slope appears to have a sloped planting bed incorporating the boulders, separated from the drive by vertical conifers.[32] The wellhead which had once graced the *plaisance* in front of the northern pergola in the Blue Garden was relocated as the central feature of the circular lawn, surrounded by a low clipped hedge. On the first tier of the amphitheater, on either side of the main entrance, four sculptural figures were located to bracket two arbors of climbing roses.[33]

Development of this rose garden was expedited so that it could have its debut on June 27, 1923, during a dinner for the Garden Club of America meeting. Smith devised a pageant with dancers from Boston representing roses of England, France, Persia, China and America, all enhanced by his theatrical mastery and dramatic illumination.[34] Two years later, in July 1925, Smith staged yet another rose garden pageant, this one, "A Summer Night in the Rose Garden," as a farewell party before the Jameses sailed for Europe aboard the *Aloha II*. With the roses in full bloom, perfuming the air, the garden was again

artfully illuminated to enhance individual plants and the architecture of the space. Four hundred guests from the colony and "away" were seated on the tier while dancers and actors enacted another complicated musical fairytale of yore of separated lovers, nymphs and shepherds, nobility and peasants, with mummers and Japanese acrobats to enliven the mix. The cast of forty, made up of some members of the summer colony, also included some notable professionals. The female lead was played by Estelle Winwood, an English actress then appearing in Broadway plays; the principal dancer was a young Martha Graham, lately of the Greenwich Village Follies and about to launch her own company.[35] This garden theater became yet another venue for Newport social and philanthropic events, in particular for yearly fundraising dances to benefit the Berkeley Memorial Chapel in Middletown.[36]

The Rose Garden was to have yet one more incarnation. In those heady days before the 1929 Black Tuesday stock market crash, Harriet James embarked upon her last major Beacon Hill House construction, to build a linear rose garden, intended, according to early reports, to be more than a mile long, following the ridge below the southeastern entrance drive from Beacon Hill

Road. Newspapers from as far away as Canton and Cleveland, Ohio, reported that 200 men were at work dynamiting rock, building walls and trellises to create a world-class rose garden, estimated to cost $250,000.[37] The long-time and trusted estate superintendent, John Greatorex, had died in July, so Harriet James turned to landscape architect Herbert J. Kellaway for design advice.

Originally from Kent, England, Kellaway had trained at the Olmsted firm from 1892 until 1906, when he left to establish his own practice. He was a skilled designer and a knowledgeable horticulturalist whose design commissions involved residential landscapes as well as public open space, parkway and other town planning projects for communities around Boston.[38] He had formed a collaboration with Harriet Risley Foote, a noted rosarian and Smith alumna, specializing in the design of remarkable rose gardens, often in difficult terrain. Prior to the Jameses' commission, they had developed award-winning gardens for clients such as Henry and Clara Ford at Fairlane, Dearborn, Michigan. Their Massachusetts work included designs for Mrs. Edwin Webster in Falmouth, for Henry S. Hunnewell at the Cedars in Wellesley and for Richard Crane at his Castle Hill estate in Ipswich, among many others. Foote's working methods involved first the site selection, then an analysis of the soil, followed by selection of the roses, to be grouped in beds or on structures to make "a harmonious whole," blending colors like a painting. As she wrote to Smith alumnae, "I believe the great object of a rose garden is to touch the heart."[39]

The James Rose Garden was laid out on a series of terraces on a southeastern-facing hillside, with views of the water. Integrated around the natural rock outcroppings, this garden combined rusticity of material with formality in its axial arrangement. Rooms on various levels were defined by stone walls connected by stairs of differing lengths; some with rustic pools, others with sculptural elements; still others with pergolas, arches, and rustic umbrellas. These "rooms" gave architectural presence to the uneven terrain while providing microclimates to protect some roses from the windy conditions. Over 5,000 rose bushes were planted of many different classes: Hybrid teas, Bourbons, Noisettes, polyanthas, rugosas, multifloras, etc. As Harriet Foote noted, "climbers … to clothe pergolas and arches, pillars … for height; standards for landscape effect, creepers for boulders and rocks."[40] After 1933, the James garden no doubt contained the "Mrs. Arthur Curtiss James," a vigorous, cold-tolerant large-flowered yellow climber, hybridized by their friends, Walter and Josephine Brownell of Little Compton, Rhode Island. This rose, praised in the press at that time for its color and fragrance, was considered by noted rosarian Dr. J. Horace McFarland as "a rose of great richness and beauty … of high rank among the yellow climbers."[41]

A tea for "several hundred" guests was held in these newly established gardens to celebrate July 4th, 1931. Later that month Mrs. James entertained members of the Newport Garden Club in the garden to hear a lecture on roses by Dr. Hugh Findlay, assistant professor of agriculture at Columbia University. Called by *Horticulture Magazine*, "one of the outstanding rose gardens of America … especially attractive because of its seaside location," this garden room became as much a venue of choice for meetings and events on the James estate as was the Blue Garden.[42]

View along the main linear axis in the new Rose
Garden, c. mid-1930s. Reputed to be more
than a mile long and to contain over 5,000 rose
bushes of different classes, this garden, along
a ridge below Beacon Hill House, opened with
a tea to celebrate July 4th, 1931.

The Depression Decade

The decade of the 1930s brought change everywhere, even among people of extraordinary wealth such as Arthur Curtiss and Harriet James. The full impact and the depth of misery that the recession would bring nationwide was a slowly realized process. The usual whirlwind of social and philanthropic events at Beacon Hill House and at their other homes continued to be reported in the press in 1930 and 1931: a fete for Polish midshipmen or the British ambassador, benefits or meetings for various organizations and charities, Harriet James's activities for the World Service Council of the Y.W.C.A. But it was the intrigue over the rail negotiations in the West that kept Arthur Curtiss at the forefront of news coverage, with quotes concerning the nation's economic health and "the well-being of the nation's railroads."[1] While he was jubilantly pounding the golden spike in November 1931 to achieve his long-held dream to link the rail

systems, his wealth was decreasing by millions, and Harriet, his constant companion, was too ill to attend the ceremony.[2]

Whatever her health issues at this time, press coverage about Harriet James became minimal over the next several years. Even her attendance at Board of Directors' meetings for Christodora House in New York, a charity of great personal significance for her since 1904, lapsed, many of the duties taken on by her niece and her husband, William and Harriet de Forest Manice.[3] Lavish theatrical evenings in the Beacon Hill House gardens ceased, as did reports of similar events presented by other Newport social leaders. They were replaced instead by more modest coverage of musical benefits at the Casino, or flower show honors. The events planned for the gardens by the Newport Civic League during 1936 Music Week were one of the last references to such a happening.[4]

Without Harriet's personal attention, and with Arthur Curtiss distracted by business issues

THE ARCHITECTURAL RECORD.   509

VIEW OF GARDEN AND HOUSE, BEACON HILL HOUSE.

Into the mid-1930s, the Blue Garden continued to be featured in magazines, heralding its architectural and horticultural beauty, and in the press as a venue for social and philanthropic events. The impact of the Depression curtailed such coverage. Other garden rooms on the James property competed for resources, reducing the needed maintenance of the intricate Blue Garden grounds.

as well as his own deteriorating health, the gardens at Beacon Hill House must have suffered. With all the specialized garden rooms, these were extensive and intricate grounds to maintain even in the best of circumstances. Even the knowledgeable John Greatorex had struggled over a decade earlier to keep up with the weeding and pruning. At that time, Arthur Curtiss had commented, "it would be better to do the weeding badly than not to do it at all." But, as Rick Olmsted had warned earlier, the carefully planned character of the whole estate could be easily ruined by rash removals or reckless and unskilled work.[5]

The Passing of Arthur Curtiss and Harriet Parsons James

At the cusp of the next decade, in 1941, months before war had reached American shores, both Harriet and Arthur Curtiss James succumbed to their ailments. Mrs. James's passing was discreetly and quietly noted in the press, with articles acknowledging her "unceasing hospitality," her elegant social leadership and her extensive charitable endeavors. In her tribute to her friend and fellow leader of the Y.W.C.A., and fellow Smith alumna, Vera Scott Cushman articulated the deep respect shared by many who had benefitted from Harriet's leadership and generous public service. She praised her "passionate allegiance to whatever promised welfare and security for others," living a "Christian life of large vision … in an era that is closing."[6] In her will, Mrs. James continued her generous support of Christodora House, Smith College, the Y.W.C.A. and the Lincoln School of Nursing in the Bronx, among other charities, along with personal bequests to family and to various members of her household. The four mansions, in New York City, in Tarrytown, in Coconut Grove, and in Newport, which had been in her name, were bequeathed to her husband.[7]

In contrast, the death of Arthur Curtiss James was given expansive coverage in newspapers small and large, from coast to coast. Called the "Last Railroad Mogul," James' extraordinary accomplishments in the railroad and financial worlds, the sources of his great wealth and the extent of his quietly effective, ecumenical and socially conscious generosity were heralded in a manner which would not have pleased him in his lifetime, when he preferred his philanthropy to be anonymous. As a tribute at his death, the trains of the Western Pacific Line stopped for one minute simultaneously with the start of his New York funeral service.[8] Among the 600 mourners at his funeral at the First Presbyterian Church were J. P. Morgan, John D. Rockefeller, Jr., President Stanley King of Amherst College and other leaders of the financial, cultural and educational worlds. The Rev. Henry Sloane Coffin's eulogy was poignant in his praise for Arthur Curtiss in his devotion to his wife and friends; for his modesty and fidelity in discharging "a weighty trust … [and] for his single-mindedness who wished only to be wisely useful … and his stalwart devotion to things true, just and honorable."[9]

Reflective of the deeply held conviction he shared with his father, Daniel Willis James, that he was only the temporary steward of their great wealth, Arthur Curtiss set up a self-terminating foundation to administer his bequests, rather than the perpetual organizations which Rockefeller, Carnegie and Ford had created. At his death in the waning days of the Depression, the estate of Arthur Curtiss James, reputed to be the twelfth richest man in America, was worth approximately $35 million. After taxes and specific bequests to family, friends, staff and retainers, with no direct heirs, eight-tenths of the estate's residue, approximately $25 million, was directed to the James Foundation, with its seven person Board, to be managed and distributed to diverse cultural, educational and charitable organizations, some pre-specified, some at the discretion of the Foundation, over a twenty-five-year period.[10] The Foundation invested wisely over that period, considerably increasing its net worth, so that when it chose to terminate, in June 1965, it had

given away $144,000,000 to educational institutions from Ivy League colleges to Tuskegee Institute to the American Union of Beirut to nursing schools, to religious organizations of all denominations, to social service entities such as Christodora House, to hospitals serving poorer populations and to diverse museums and cultural establishments.[11]

The Post-James Tenure

The Foundation retained the James New York mansion in Lenox Hill as its headquarters. During the war years, the third floor became a service club for the Women's Military Services, providing beds for 100 enlisted women and a dining hall. After the war, this space became a dormitory for women students of the Union Theological Seminary. In 1958 this splendid marble mansion, which had cost over $1 million in 1916, was sold to Tishman Realty to be demolished for construction of a twenty-story luxury apartment building. The Foundation then leased offices in the Seagram's Building. An illustrated *New York*

Times article of May 1959 described a swarm of men in "Ivy League suits ... armed with screwdrivers ... [women] in high heels and flowered hats," with their workmen, stripping the mansion of its interior decorations, its fixtures and wall paneling—a sad demise for a such an elegant domicile.[12]

The demise of Beacon Hill House with its magnificent gardens was even sadder. Initially, the Foundation tried to maintain the grounds around the still-furnished but unoccupied mansion, possibly hoping that an educational institution could acquire the property. These were difficult times in Newport in the post-Depression and post-war decade, and most schools were not affluent enough to manage such a property. By June 1944, the Foundation authorized a sale at the mansion of furniture, glass, china, drapery, the Kimball organ and iron garden furniture. It was rumored that some plant material was also dug up and sold.[13] In 1951, as the assessed value of Beacon Hill House with all its acreage had declined to $186,000, the James Foundation gave the 100-acre estate to

(facing page) View along the main entrance drive to the now vandalized Beacon Hill House, c. late 1966, showing that windows and much of the roof are missing.

(right) Damaged door, window and debris at the entrance to Beacon Hill House, c. mid-1960s. A fire in 1967 resulted in complete demolition of this once great mansion.

the Roman Catholic Diocese of Rhode Island, which stated at that time that it planned to use it for a children's home. The Sisters of Cluny set up a residence and novitiate at Zee Rust, the James guesthouse, which had been occupied earlier by their friends, artist Hubert Vos and his family. Many of the ancillary buildings in what had been the former vegetable garden were modernized to become a school, with the flat planting beds reutilized for recreation grounds.[14]

Two years later, a newspaper clipping illustrated the unoccupied mansion, describing its once tastefully opulent interiors as crumbling.

High up on the hill, the great house lies empty, shuttered and spectral. The formal gardens are neglected and the greenhouses empty save for some tomatoes which the caretaker, Peter Gillan, planted. The lawns are well cared for and green. It takes Peter and his staff three or four days to keep them trimmed.[15]

Even though Newport began to emerge from its doldrums in the late 1950s, with preservation efforts and reinvestments rescuing some of the architectural "grandes dames," there was to be no such aid for Beacon Hill House, whose grounds were used at that time for a Knights of Columbus summer day camp. This property was clearly well beyond the means of the Diocese to manage. They were unable to stem the unabated vandalism of the mansion—the removals of quantities of decorative elements, the wild parties and the squatters. A destructive fire in May 1967 and the mansion's subsequent demolition were an undeserved fate for this once elegant great house.[16]

Retaining twenty-two acres for the school and the Gate Lodge, where the chaplain of Mary Immaculate Novitiate resided, the Diocese sold the remaining seventy acres to Interliving Corporation for $400,000. Other than a condominium development in the former garage complex, the developers' intended 200-unit clustered townhouse proposal fortunately was not realized on this rugged landscape that had been so thoughtfully crafted by the Olmsted Brothers planning efforts and protected by the original James stewardship.[17] Thus, many of the unique features and garden rooms of the Jameses' celebrated landscape could succumb to benign neglect and nature's weedy *couverture*, rather than to the irrevocably destructive blade of the bulldozer. Over the years, the memories of earlier grandeur and garden splendors receded as the garden structures disappeared under the mantle of briars and seedlings, which grew so well in Newport's beneficial climate.

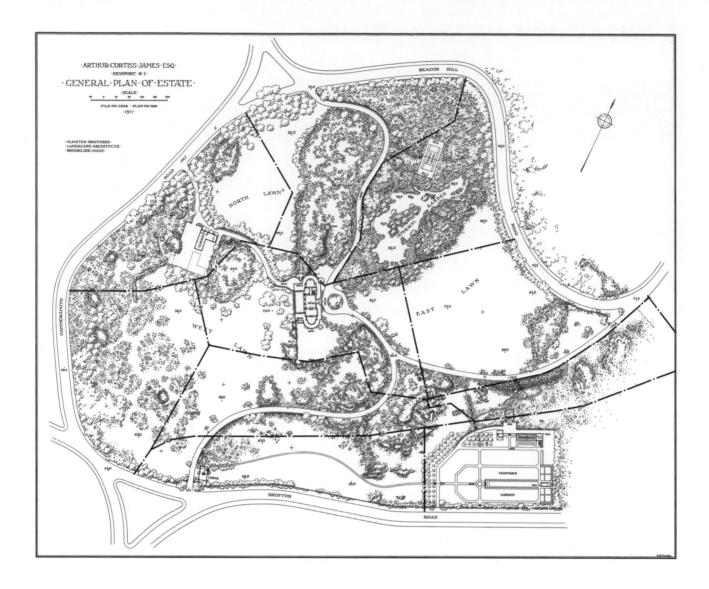

Early Reclamation

The land remaining from the Beacon Hill House estate which had escaped from its intended cluster development was eventually subdivided into multi-acre lots on which commodious homes were built in the 1970s and 1980s, taking advantage of the spacious scenery and many of the infrastructure improvements that remained from the James era, particularly the roads and boundary walls. One new owner retained the Telescope House atop its promontory, building a new house approximately where the James mansion once stood. Another chose a spot at the end of what had been the linear Rose Garden. Yet another unknowingly chose to locate on the ruin of the northern pergola, at the end of the once-heralded Blue Garden.

The late 1970s was the infancy of historic preservation for landscapes. Even as the movement to preserve and protect the nation's architectural heritage progressed, recognition that the landscape architecture was likewise an art form and a critical component of the same cultural continuum as architecture was not yet readily acknowledged. As this understanding slowly emerged, it was the restoration of iconic public spaces, such as recapturing Central Park from decades of decay and meddling, that led the foray. Recognition that the interrelationship between a carefully crafted structure, whether mansion or smaller, and its integrally planned surrounding landscape (garden or vast estate), involved the artistry of both disciplines, lagged a decade or more behind the rehabilitation of public parks. A unique and cogent separate discipline of land-

(facing page) The land from the Beacon Hill House estate was subdivided into multi-acre lots, but retained the original roads, drives, and many amenities that the Olmsted Brothers firm had planned in the early 1900s. The Gate Lodge and Carriage House remain as reminders of a past age of fine design and extraordinary craftsmanship. New homes were built where the original mansion and the north pergola of the Blue Garden once stood.

Frances Benjamin Johnston (left) and Mattie Edwards Hewitt (right) were photographers whose work documented the houses and gardens of the socially prominent, who wanted to record their accomplishments in creating taste-setting architectural and landscape beauty. Their photographs were featured in notable popular and professional publications.

scape preservation, with justifiable standards, guidelines and protection tools, was, and is, still evolving. Adequate funding to rehabilitate notable historic landscapes, both public and private, and effective protection mechanisms for gardens have been slow to develop, the latter particularly thorny when involving privately held heritage properties. To recognize original design intentions while accommodating changes over time; to recapture these landscapes from neglect or misguided interventions; to reconstruct what can be rescued and provide for a sustainable future; these are tasks requiring a long vision, enduring commitment and significant resources.

The first step in this evolving process was recognition and understanding of what had once been there, of what the various artifacts and landforms were revealing about a prior existence. This process was immeasurably advanced by the wisdom and generosity, tinged with self-interest, of earlier generations who saw to the production of memorable photographs and glass slides in the teens and 1920s. To record their accomplishments in creating taste-setting architectural and landscape beauty, these earlier owners, designers and craftsmen either hired or were amenable to having their properties photographed and reviewed in an array of print and visual media—newspapers and tabloids; periodicals, whether professional journals of all disciplines or popular magazines; and books. In the pre-Depression

heyday of these luxurious mansions and country places, the media coverage of the great and grand, both American and European, was also translated to the more modest level of the average home-owner, interested in domestic improvement, in gardens and in horticulture. This literary and photographic output had a vital civilizing and educational purpose, to entertain while elevating public taste, a noble goal that had, likewise, spurred on the nineteenth-century landscape practitioners and writers such as Andrew Jackson Downing and Frederick Law Olmsted, Sr., in their visionary endeavors.

Beyond these increased printed and visual media opportunities to explore the world of landscape and architecture of great estates, there had been, from the late nineteenth century on, an increase of civic and beautification societies, garden clubs and similar organizations, which were active sponsors of public lectures. The technological advancement of photography and the improvement of glass lantern slides, with its corollary expansion into hand-painted color renderings, coincided to mutual advantage with this educational effort to elevate taste. With their emphasis on visual topics, lectures illustrated by these richly evocative glass slides provided a vibrant immediacy which could only be exceeded by an actual tour to the sites. These slides were also a testament to a coterie of very talented photographers, many of whom were women, whose skilled eyes captured the architectural and spatial character, the opulence of ornament or horticulture, the grace, beauty and changing moods of this often ephemeral artistry of landscape architecture. Frances Benjamin Johnston and her early partner, Mattie Edwards Hewitt, whose images, both black-and-white and hand-painted, captured the ethereal beauty of the early Blue Garden, were both active leaders in this field. Johnston, in particular, used her photographic artistry, her business acumen and social connections to advance her progressive principles that included a passion for education and preservation. With her frequent lectures, exhibits or published articles, illustrated by her photographs, whether of gardens, of early southern architecture or of students in schools, north and south, she popularized landscape beauty, architectural history and cultural values, using her art as a "force for social change."[18]

That this very fragile medium of glass and emulsion was cared for, collected and eventually processed into an archive, making these recorded images available for future study, is a demonstration of the wisdom, generosity and perseverance of several notable women—the members of the Garden Club of America (G.C.A.) who originally collected these images; Harriet Jackson Phelps, the photographic editor of the G.C.A. *Bulletin* who realized their worth in the 1960s, after they had been forgotten and surpassed by other media; and several others, who pursued identification, cataloguing and copying of these slides.[19] They were among those responsible for finding a permanent home for this collection, at the Smithsonian Institution's Archives of American Gardens in Washington, D.C., where they now provide an invaluable resource. With its substantial collections of related documentary materials, nursery catalogues and ephemera, etc., and with the additions over the years of other photographs, slides and records of gardens, this Archive has become a vital resource for all those interested in uncovering and recapturing the American garden heritage.

Somewhat simultaneously, the rescue of other documentary and visual collections critical to an understanding of the history and importance of landscape architecture, urban planning and garden design also coalesced during the late 1960s and 1970s. And again, just as with the G.C.A. glass slide collection, serendipitous connections and individual commitments made these rescues possible. Of particular significance for the story of the Beacon Hill House estate with its Blue Garden is the creation of the Frederick Law Olmsted National Historic Site with its vast and protected archive of plans, photographs, documentary files and other ephemera. Establishing his home and office, Fairsted, in Brookline, Massachusetts in 1882, the senior Olmsted, followed by his sons and subsequent partners, developed a growing landscape architectural practice, which reached a zenith of productivity and influence in the 1920s, with far-flung national and international projects of all types. The Depression and the radical changes in national outlook and taste following World War II irrevocably altered the landscape profession. Olmsted, Jr., retired in 1949 and died in 1957; his succeeding partners aged, and by the mid-1960s this formerly thriving practice was on the verge of collapse. Although designated a national historic landmark in 1963, Fairsted, the nineteenth-century farmhouse to which several office wings and a plan vault had been attached, was in desperate need of repair. Within the buildings, 100 years of plans, photographs and documents from this once-busy office, recording the shaping of so much of the American urban, suburban and institutional landscapes, were rapidly disintegrating.

In 1971, the last remaining Olmsted firm partner, Artemas Richardson, citing the importance of Olmsted to the nation and to the landscape profession, sought assistance from the National Park Service, the American Society of Landscape Architects and other institutions, worrying that structural demolition and dispersal of the collection were his possible alternatives

(above left) Frederick Law Olmsted, Sr. established his home and office, Fairsted, in Brookline, Massachusetts in 1882. The Olmsted Brothers continued the practice, thriving through the 1920s and lasting until the mid-1960s. The National Park Service acquired this property in 1979.

(right) View in the vault at Fairsted, c. 1972. Since 1982, when Fairsted was designated as the Frederick Law Olmsted National Historic Site, a hundred years of plans, photographs and documents from the Olmsted office have been conserved and protected in the archives.

without some economic aid. Following Olmsted, Jr.'s lead beginning in the 1940s, Richardson had already given away many of the files, fortunately most to the Manuscript Division of the Library of Congress.[20] The Park Service initially was extremely reluctant, as were other entities, to take on a challenge of such unknown proportions—neither structural assessments nor an inventory of the documents housed in the Fairsted buildings had been prepared. Moreover, the Park Service was not at all convinced that

this Brookline farmhouse and its collections met any of the appropriate criteria to be included under its management.

Fortunately, a renaissance of interest and research in the senior Olmsted was developing at this time, as his significant contributions to American culture, to social philosophy, to environment preservation, among other endeavors, were being rediscovered. To celebrate the sesquicentennial of his birth, in 1972 simultaneous exhibits were developed, one at the Whitney Museum in New York, and one at the National Gallery in Washington, D.C., each highlighting a different aspect of Olmsted work and landscape artistry. Even with a resurgence of knowledge about Olmsted's significance, it took a group of dedicated historians, landscape professionals and preservationists more than seven years of byzantine negotiations to aggressively change the National Park Service considerations to include such cultural resources within its mandate.

This required intensive persuasion of Congress for the necessary legislation and funding to undertake such a project in order to buy out the Richardson holdings at Fairsted and to establish this unique National Park Service site.[21]

The legislation was signed in October 1979 and the site dedicated in April 1981. Given the impaired conditions of these buildings and the need to accommodate changed use from a working office to a research facility and visitor destination; given the vast size and deteriorated condition of a complex series of collections; and given the vagaries of federal funding for such an unusual undertaking, it has taken nearly three decades to preserve and stabilize the structures and to understand, inventory and conserve all the documentary holdings.[22] Among these now-conserved plans, photographs and miscellaneous documents is the collection relating to the Newport property of Arthur Curtiss James, which consists of 159 plans, over 230 photographs, three folders of planting lists and other miscellany, augmented by five folders of correspondence in the Library of Congress holdings.

In the 1960s, however, Harriet Jackson Phelps did not have the benefit of these resources. She was armed only with her familiarity with Newport, her savvy and curiosity about designed land and her knowledge of the variety of historic images, when she went exploring through the weeds and boulders on the former site of Beacon Hill House and other locales. What she discovered was a pitiable relic. In 35mm. slides in the Garden Club of America collection ascribed to her, dated "1960–70s," she documented a mansion with no windows, surrounded by dead and overgrown vegetation, yet with a mown lawn; shelters in the former rose garden with upright piers no longer supporting overhead trellising. In what was once the estate's gem, the Blue Garden, the columns of the northeast pergola lay on the ground like fallen warriors, while at the southwest end, the columns, still upright, were strangled by vines. The pools, filled with decomposing vegetation, were crowded by invasive maples and ivy. In one image, however, the specialized tile pattern at one end of the long pool was still visible.[23]

Although Mrs. Phelps' *Newport in Flower* was published in 1979, well-illustrated with glass lantern slides which documented the elegant garden architecture and horticultural opulence once gracing these Newport estates, it was too early in the evolution of landscape preservation for this to be more than an interesting reminder rather than a preservation stimulus.[24] Thus, when the property which once contained the Blue Garden was sold in 1979, the new owners,

In the early 1970s, Harriet Jackson Phelps discovered remnants of the Blue Garden covered with weeds. She recorded the ruins in slides that are preserved in the Garden Club of America collection at the Smithsonian Institution. These include the fallen columns from the former exedra at the north pergola (above) and invasive trees and shrubs around the columns still standing at the south pergola (below).

Mrs. Phelps' discoveries included the weeds encroaching upon the square lily pond (left), and the original blue tile patterns in the long pool (right). Her book, *Newport in Flower*, was illustrated with hand-colored glass lantern slides from the GCA collection which she had helped to save, which heralded the glories of the Blue Garden in its prime.

not realizing what they had, placed their contemporary house where the northeast pergola had been located.[25] Spurred on by Harriet Phelps and her subsequent article, "Garden Archeology," these new residents set to clearing much of the debris, revealing the rill and pools with their copings, the outline of the old walls and the southwestern pergola, and uncovering various blue-tiled pot bases. Slides from 1984, after some of their efforts, revealed water in the pools surrounded by a green carpet of grass rather than the once-exuberant floral borders. Correspondence from 1984–85 between Harriet Phelps and Eleanor Weller documented everyone's excitement at the unfolding discoveries, particularly in the Blue Garden, where a fountain had been added to the long pool. Likewise, at a nearby property, recently purchased by Dorrance Hamilton, rediscovery and transformation were also in process. Once the site of Harriet James' 1929 expansive Rose Garden along the Beacon Hill ridge, Mrs. Hamilton was energetically overseeing the removal of briars and vines, uncovering and restoring walls, shelters, pergolas, trellising and ironwork which once had shaped Harriet James's noted garden of yore.[26] With interest piqued, these owners continued to make improvements to their properties as a subsequent article, "Enchanted Gardens In Newport" explained. While keeping what remained of the Blue Garden in its simplest form, the new owners had "planted banks of blue hydrangeas, blue hostas,

blue impatiens and blue ageratum in masses." They had also "restored" the "blue-tile lake and lily pond."[27]

What is clear from the Phelps-Weller correspondence is that the work to improve these gardens was being done with personal dedication and great interest. What was unusual about recapturing these rooms from the former James estate landscape was that, like the fairy tale, they had "gone to sleep" under their weedy covering, without having been seriously altered by human use over the intervening decades to complicate the rediscovery process. What is also evident is that in the late 1980s and early 1990s, tools to guide these homeowners in their improvements were not yet readily available. Information about how to evaluate what they were discovering; how to work within preservation parameters being developed at the time to recapture the form and substance without compromising the integrity of "original fabric" and spatial character—such standards were only just coming into practice for the disciplines involved: archeology, landscape architecture, horticulture and landscape history.

Recapturing the Story

For two decades after the glorious "Masque of the Blue Garden" presented this unique landscape to society, articles about the garden and images of its architectural elements appeared in periodicals and books dealing with design, horticulture or Olmsted Brothers work. Beyond the emphasis on the distinctive palette of blue and purple blooms, the garden's classical proportions, its terminating pergolas and enclosing lattice walls with their articulated gates became exemplars of good design. Likewise, photographs of the Amphitheater, the Rose Garden and of the architecturally unique Surprise Valley Farm were subjects of interest in popular and professional magazines.[1] After the Depression years, the deaths of Arthur and Harriet James and World War II and its aftermath, coverage essentially ceased and this literature, like the landscapes that were its subject, receded from the forefront of interest to the back shelves of academic libraries. For those in Newport who had grown up with some familiarity with the James properties before they had totally slipped from prominence, there were retrievable echoes of something special that had existed on the former estate site, perhaps only to be remembered in somewhat mythologized tales.[2]

The work in the 1980s by the new property owners of this land to clear and retrieve some semblance of the Blue Garden grounds, and, indeed, to uncover the Rose Garden, was done without benefit of documentary research to guide their tasks. Harriet Jackson Phelps' access to visual aids in the glass slides and other photographic collections certainly had elicited interest, but it remains unclear whether she tapped into any of the published resources in the architectural and landscape literature available at that time to direct her advice about landscape renewal.

Retrieval of components of the special places that had been the James patrimony was a slow process, full of serendipitous connections over the three decades following Phelps' article on "Garden Archaeology" in the Garden Club of America *Bulletin*. Most fortuitous was the interest of Dorrance Hamilton who, with her husband Samuel, had acquired several acres of former James land, some of it with a dwelling along the ridge with southeastern ocean views and remnants of the former James Rose Garden, which she was rehabilitating.

Dorrance Hamilton, known as "Dodo" to her friends and family and as "Mrs. H." to many others, had grown up in New York and Philadelphia and spent summers in Newport with her family. Although she was too young to have known the James estate in its grandeur, there were friends of her parents who shared memories of Beacon Hill House events, even of the Blue Garden's celebratory Masque. A woman of exceptional resources and business acumen, Mrs. Hamilton directs her philanthropic efforts with a very hands-on and visionary approach and with oft-repeated advice to her associates, to have fun in their endeavors. She welcomes challenges, especially those that involve the rescue and preservation of significant places. Her diverse interests include, among many others, horticulture and gardening, which she had learned from "quality time" spent with her grandmother at her Radnor, Pennsylvania, estate; preservation of important components of artistic and cultural history; conservation of land and natural resources with a strong instinct for future sustainability; and educational outreach, providing opportunities at many levels and for differing populations.[3]

Prominent in her early memories of Newport are gardens, whether attached to the various dwellings her family rented, or at Bois Doré, the Charles Platt-designed mansion and grounds,

(left and below) Surprise Valley Farm is a compound of architectural gems designed c. 1915 by Grosvenor Atterbury. By 1998, the land and buildings were in disrepair and were slated for development. The property was rehabilitated and repurposed as SVF Foundation, now in partnership with the Smithsonian Conservation Biology Institute.

which her parents had purchased by 1941. Also among her Newport childhood memories were Sunday afternoon drives to see the animals at Surprise Valley Farm, the complex of Arts and Crafts buildings set on the hillside overlooking acres of meadows, which once housed the prized Guernsey cattle belonging to Arthur Curtiss James. Decades later, this remarkable property

was to be rescued by Mrs. Hamilton and her husband from the threat of development, just as she would undertake the retrieval and renewal of the Blue Garden beginning in 2012.[4]

The Surprise Valley Farm (SVF) rescue tale exemplifies the Hamilton philanthropic wisdom. Mrs. Hamilton remembers a visit from her local councilwoman in Newport, at some point in the late 1990s, expressing concern over the impending sale of nearby Surprise Valley Farm with its abutting mansion, Edgehill, the former home of the Ferry and Manice families which had become a rehabilitation facility.[5] More than the destruction of attractive and valuable agricultural land by the development of multiple residential lots, the Farm's unique and quaint rustic architecture, designed c. 1915 by Arts and Crafts architect Grosvenor Atterbury, was all badly in need of repair and would probably be destroyed. To forestall such destruction, the Hamiltons joined with others to submit a bid, ultimately winning the auction and the property.

By 1998, Mrs. Hamilton had set about a two-year process to resuscitate its textured architecture, as well as to find a creative repurposing of its original agricultural mission. She was concerned at this time about the loss of heritage domestic farm animals and wondered if the Farm could serve a role in this cause. A chance discussion with a veterinarian from Tufts University's Cummings School of Veterinary Medicine redirected her efforts toward an innovative solution. Since the Farm's acreage was insufficient for a conventional breeding ground, she embarked instead, at their recommendation, upon cryopreservation of genetic material from rare and endangered heritage breeds of food and fiber livestock. Therefore, while the buildings were restored to retain their unique external character of rubble masonry with tile or wood shingle roofs, the interiors were reconceived as state-of-the-art laboratories to maintain the tanks and specialized equipment needed to retain the frozen germ plasm. The site's infrastructure was upgraded to maintain this work, while its landscape was engineered for well-drained meadows, restored wetlands and diverse habitats, all sustainable ecosystems to add pastoral beauty to the Aquidneck area. With the 2002 completion of the reconstruction project, the cryopreservation mission of the non-profit SVF Foundation began in collaboration with the

Cummings School, and as of 2014 with the Smithsonian Conservation Biology Institute. Thus, Dorrance Hamilton's visionary philanthropy has enabled a multi-dimensioned preservation project with far-reaching implications, not only in the scientific world but also for Newport's cultural heritage.[6]

At the same time as the SVF project, Mrs. Hamilton was engaged in another heritage rescue—that of Wildacre, the property that would be her residence for over a decade. A distinctive Arts and Crafts house on a spectacular waterfront site, this was the first major residence to be designed on the East Coast by California architect Irving Gill. After advice in 1899 from his nephew, John Charles Olmsted, regarding purchase of the land, Hartford banker Albert H. Olmsted—"Uncle Harry"—half-brother of Frederick Law Olmsted, Sr., had commissioned the angled house and its ancillary structures to fit the chosen site overlooking Price's Neck Cove. John Charles then patterned the landscape to screen out Ocean Avenue and nestle the multi-leveled house into a textured green setting, appropriate to this site.[7] After decades of use and neglect, the property was a bit "tattered" at the time of the Hamilton purchase. With thoughtful rehabilitation, the well-proportioned house readily returned to its intended charm and the landscape to its lushly varied enclosure, to provide a commodious and elegant, yet understated, dwelling in a spectacular setting.

The story of the Blue Garden involves similar serendipity. As the varied floor levels in Wildacre became burdensome, Mrs. Hamilton began construction of a new home, the "Bird House," on a high swath of the former James estate known as the East Lawn. Along the western boundary, the abutting property containing the former Blue Garden came to market in 2012, and was purchased by Mrs. Hamilton. She then began consideration of its rehabilitation with the advice of Doug Reed of Reed Hilderbrand, a notable landscape architectural firm from Cambridge,

(left) The Olmsted Brothers sited a multi-leveled house, designed in the early 1900s by California architect Irving Gill, and laid out the grounds. This property, called Wildacre, was designed to take advantage of the scenic views of Price's Neck Cove. Their plan developed many separate garden rooms in the surrounding landscape which, along with the house, have since been rehabilitated, including the unique garden shelter.

Massachusetts, engaged to oversee the inter-connected projects, together with Mary Ellen Flanagan, a landscape designer who had worked on many previous Hamilton properties.

Before any clearing or reconstruction could take place on the site of this once-heralded garden, it was imperative to interpret the visible elements, to understand which were artifacts or "original fabric" remaining from two generations of Olmsted work, and which represented later additions or alterations. To make these distinctions required exploring the history of ownership of this land and understanding the intent and efforts of previous owners at shaping it to their needs.

Although the acreage which once constituted the Beacon Hill House estate had been subdivided

Aerial view over the Blue Garden property, 2012. A large house and swimming pool were built where the north pergola and tennis court once stood. Lawn now surrounds the remnants of the pools and rill, where once there were lushly planted beds. Invasive trees, shrubs, and vines encroach upon the space. At the top right, the roof of the Telescope House is visible, now on the abutting property.

into several separately owned parcels, the land-forms resulting from the senior Olmsted's 1884 subdivision planning and from the Olmsted Brothers twentieth-century estate design were still visible for interpretation. And, fortunately, because these were Olmsted firm projects, ample illuminating documentation was available in several repositories: at the Frederick Law Olmsted National Historic Site (FLONHS); in Washington, D.C. at the Library of Congress, both in the Manuscript Room and in the Prints

and Photographs Division; and at the Archives of American Gardens of the Smithsonian Institution.[8] Additionally, in various historical societies, university archives and other repositories in Newport, in various locales in Massachusetts, in New York, in Florida and elsewhere, there are collections of documents relating to the James properties. This wealth of material clarified the story of an extraordinary couple with vast resources and sophisticated aesthetic sensibilities who could pursue their architectural and landscape desires, in collaboration with the very best design professionals and crafts people in the country. What was created by this nexus of talent, taste and resources was a unique twentieth-century interpretation of classical landscape forms, skillfully inserted into a ruggedly natural setting, which, by its scale and decorative elements, epitomized the values of a special time in Newport's and the nation's cultural history.

Recapturing the Place:
Preparation for Reconstruction

To renew and reconstruct the Blue Garden for the twenty-first century, it was necessary to fully document its historical intent and form; to analyze the remnants on the ground for integrity to original purpose and for material stability; and to plan for a rehabilitation that could capture the essential character of the garden while being responsible in an environmentally changing future.

The renewal process began in 2012 with the acquisition of digital copies of plans and photographs, produced for the Jameses' project, retrieved from the archives at FLONHS. Additionally, the professional correspondence from the Olmsted collection at the Library of Congress was acquired and studied in conjunction with the plans. With such documentation in hand, the team at Reed Hilderbrand evaluated the site and its remaining built features in collaboration with the designated contractor and construction manager, Glenn Parker of Parker Construction Company of Providence, Rhode Island, and his team, all under the guiding hand of Peter Borden, the Client Agent for Dorrance Hamilton.

Degraded portions of the original stucco walls, no longer topped by lattice, still enclosed the garden. The long blue-tiled pool, the square pool and the rill were now surrounded by lawn instead of the planted garden beds, but the two pergolas had not fared so well. At one end of the garden, the fieldstone northern pergola had been removed and the surrounding ledge blasted to build a contemporary house, swimming pool and

driveways. At the other end, the southern pergola with its stucco walls and columns existed in severely compromised condition. The 1970s subdivision of the James estate had disregarded the garden structures in setting new boundaries, with the result that the line for the new property abutting to the south cut very close to the corner of the southern pergola. When a new house was built on land above the garden, boulders and debris had been pushed over the edge of the hill, severely damaging anything remaining at the western end of the structure. While the eastern corner of this pergola was still standing and contained remnants of the poured concrete steps and the original embedded tile borders, most of its stucco surface had disintegrated.

While the numerous site challenges were evaluated, there was an administrative hurdle to be overcome. Since this area is in a designated historic district, permission to remove the existing house had to be granted by the Newport Historic District Commission before any major renovations could commence. As the result of a hearing held in July 2012, where several consultants testified to the importance of the Blue Garden and to the inappropriateness of the house, the Commission agreed to its demolition, citing that this removal was necessary in order to recapture the garden, which would return an iconic and defining landscape component to the city's cultural palette.[9] By early fall, the house had been removed and anything of value either donated to Habitat for Humanity or recycled. Once the excavation was backfilled, the rest of the initial site work for the garden's rehabilitation could commence.

The Japanese cedar—*Cryptomeria japonica*—once an essential component of the evergreen enclosure outside the garden walls, had grown to out-of-scale proportions, while weedy vines and invasive Norway maples with their greedy root systems smothered the rest of the space. To reveal the garden's original "bones," these invasive plants, roots and all, had to be removed with great care to not compromise the extant wall

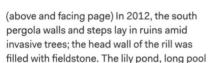

(above and facing page) In 2012, the south pergola walls and steps lay in ruins amid invasive trees; the head wall of the rill was filled with fieldstone. The lily pond, long pool and the rill remained, still enclosed by portions of the original stucco walls. A dense planting of hosta obscured the cutouts in the coping of the long pool.

footings. As the vegetative debris was removed, the massive rock outcroppings surrounding this garden space were exposed, emphasizing the distinct spatial enclave that the Olmsted Brothers firm had created. In keeping with Dorrance Hamilton's request to make this project sustainable, the wood from these tall straight cedars was milled to provide material for the overhead structure of the restored pergolas.

After the tree removals, extensive excavations revealed the conditions below grade—the depth and composition of the soil, the foundations of the walls, the southern pergola steps, the pools and rill, and the underground water systems. Critical components of the original fabric of the structures—the intricately patterned blocks around the long pool, the pool copings, the redeemable features of the south pergola such as the glazed tiles and the step slabs—were carefully removed, numbered and set on pallets to be stored away from the construction zone. They would be mended before being returned to their proper places and would provide material samples, dimensions and shapes to guide the manufacture of missing elements, such as steps, copings and tiles. To retain the steep slope along the south boundary that had once been defined by ledge, a dark gray concrete wall was built along the property line in cooperation with the neighbors,

leaving them with a stabilized driveway and providing room for an evergreen planting to screen their property.

The next challenge for this area of the garden was rebuilding the southern pergola, which could not be rebuilt in its original location due to the new property lines created in the 1970s subdivision. After studying several alternatives for its location, the solution was found in a preliminary plan that the Olmsted firm had produced in February 1912.[10] In this early garden iteration, the southern pergola was located directly along the south line of the oval at the end of the garden. It had been at Harriet James' insistence in April 1912 that the space had been enlarged by additional blasting to enable the pergola to be pushed several feet toward the southern ledge.[11]

Although returning to the originally contemplated location meant shortening the rill by several feet, it allowed the rest of the garden proportions to remain intact. But even in the recommended new location, the pergola would still be within the zoning set-back and would require a variance from the Newport Zoning Board of Review. The first hearing regarding this zoning variance was held on January 27, 2014 and continued to March 10 at which time the variance to rebuild the pergola was granted. As stated in the decision:

The requested variance would permit the restoration, preservation and rehabilitation of the Blue Garden to maintain its classic proportional relations, shape, orientation and setting with its connecting and existing pools, garden gates, pillars and walls as laid out by the Olmsted Brothers. Without the south pergola, which is a character defining architectural feature of the Blue Garden, the Blue Garden could not be historically and architecturally restored to obtain the appropriate preservation, restoration and rehabilitation.[12]

While the northern pergola had no such boundary issues, it had scant extant plans. It was rebuilt in its original location by garnering information from whatever Olmsted plans and sketches were available and from many photographs. The main challenge for this structure was to develop a suitable pattern from local stone that would reflect the original rustic character.

Several greenhouses existed on the original James estate to service the garden areas, in particular, the labor-intensive Blue Garden. These glass houses enabled seeds to be started and plants to be grown to optimal size before being planted in the garden beds, and provided storage space for the numerous potted plants. In con-templating the future of the renewed Blue Garden, it became clear that a greenhouse would likewise be necessary for storage and to house utilities. Careful design resulted in a structure that would be within the set-back requirements and be of a scale to provide for the garden's planting needs without visually intruding upon it.

Construction

Since the Olmsted firm archives contained extensive construction drawings for most of the garden's structures, the architectural team was able to develop plans necessary to recreate the historic structures and to update these into construction documents to meet current building codes. They paid special attention to maintaining the integrity of the historic details and proportions, while also accommodating contemporary structural requirements. With the advice of a masonry conservation consultant,[13] the walls and tiles of the pools were cleaned, revealing the true color of the original concrete, so that repairs could be accurately matched.

With August 2014 contemplated for the opening of the renewed Blue Garden, the construction schedule was very tight. The decision was made to enclose sections of the site under two tents. One enclosed the northern pergola

(above and facing page) The south pergola trellis was rebuilt using wood from cryptomeria trees that were on the site. A new sea creature for the head wall was fabricated based on historical drawings. Portions of steps that remained were used as molds for replacement treads. The lily pond and long pool were cleaned and repaired. Spray heads were designed for the long pool using modern technology.

area while the second covered the garden walls and pools, leaving an area between the tents for staging and circulation. These tents provided the necessary protection to enable the crews to construct the stucco walls and lattice tops and to build the northern fieldstone pergola and wooden overhead trellising. The small fountain basin attached to the garden side of the southern pergola wall—the source for the rill water—was recreated in a material to match the color and texture of the original ceramic sculpture.[14] Many of the extant glazed tiles in the rill and southern pergola floor had to be replaced with new material to match the hue and glaze variations of the original Durant Kiln tiles.

Working under these tented conditions presented its own set of challenges. In the distorted lighting, trying to extract and match the intended colors from the aged stucco of the garden walls and piers, and from the various pool surfaces, once cleaned, was difficult. The numerous photographs contemporaneous with the garden at its beginning were black-and-white or hand-colored, so while they could offer some direction as to texture, color choices had to rely on documentary descriptions, with the exception of the Frances Benjamin Johnston images.[15] Her historic photographs proved useful in deciding on stucco

tone and in revealing the texture of the granite columns, originally at the back of the southern pergola, which were to be recreated in textured precast concrete. The various construction teams were surprised to uncover the pink tonalities of the newly cleaned long pool; while the edge of the square lily pool revealed the intricate design of inlaid blue stones.

Earthwork and Soils, Irrigation and the Water System

For many months, heavy equipment traversed the bedrock-laden site, compacting the already depleted soil and destroying its physical structure. For a garden with such specialized planting beds and lawn paths, it was paramount to have good drainage, and friable, fertile soil conditions. Prior to planting the interior garden and lawn, all depleted material was removed to a depth of three feet and the bottom of the excavation pitched to subsurface drains. Specially designed horticultural soils, with a calibrated balance of the necessary organic material, minerals and structural profiles for adequate moisture retention and drainage, were installed in areas aligned to the eventual planting beds.[16] Sections of the garden were graded to transfer surface water

away from the walls and pools to area drains and to a subsurface system for collection and infiltration.

A traditional irrigation system was installed to water the lawns and turf paths. Together with soils designed to limit the need for supplemental water, and a planting design that incorporated a number of drought-tolerant plants, hose spigots were dispersed throughout the garden for hand watering. However, as a precaution against periods of long-term drought, an irrigation system was also extended throughout the perennial beds.

Although there were 1912 plans from the Olmsted office that detailed the water feature utilities to service the pools, little remained of an underground system when the site was excavated, except for a small manifold and a chamber east of the lily pond. Using contemporary technology, a new system was designed and constructed. Its main components are located under the new greenhouse and include three pumps to recirculate water to each of the water features. A new head pool feeds the rill, the lily pond and the long pool; while a manifold controls the spray jets for the long pool and the lotus ponds in front of the northern pergola. Care was taken in setting the rill tiles to precise elevations to ensure adequate water flow. To reestablish the effect originally intended, of a series of graceful sprays arcing

toward the middle of the long pool, a new system of pipes with brass nozzles was installed so that this water flow could be precisely adjusted. Finally, charcoal filters and ultraviolet sanitization were included to keep the water free from particles, cleansed of chemicals and safe for plant life.[17]

Planting

Planning for the specialized planting in the renewed Blue Garden and its surrounds engendered a great deal of thoughtful discussion by the team and detailed analysis of the Olmsted planting plans and lists. The original intent had been to create an elaborately textured garden room where the visitor would be sensually enfolded by the blended colors, the fragrance and lush beauty of a space of classical geometry in counterpoint to the rugged landscape of evergreens and rocky outcroppings beyond the walls. To achieve this carefully orchestrated effect, the Olmsted plans incorporated a complex palette of diverse species of blue, purple, and white-hued flowers with varied foliage to extend the period of bloom from late spring through early fall. In the original garden, it took a bevy of full-time gardeners to maintain the intended effect, in an era when there were fewer concerns about environmental responsibility.

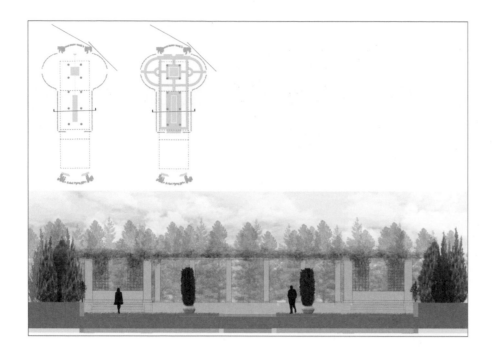

Alternative planting strategies were developed for a contemporary Blue Garden to require less maintenance and be more sustainable than the original garden. The basic question was, "How little blue was necessary to justify a Blue Garden?" In all the options explored, retaining blue flowering vines on the trellis and pergolas, with the blue tiles of the pools and blue pots, provided the essential requirements for a Blue Garden.

The plan in the upper left proposes lawn to replace garden beds. The plan on the right replaces lawn paths with peastone.

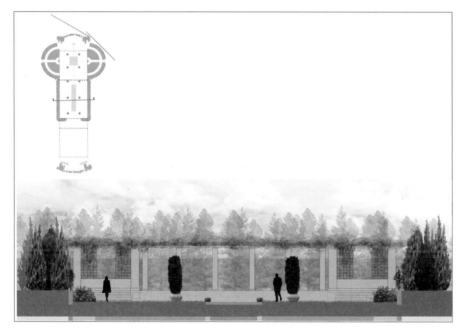

This option incorporates planting beds that reinforce the perimeter of the garden and could also be used as phase one of a fully planted scheme.

The final study evokes the intent of the original Blue Garden planting in terms of lushness and color, but uses fewer plant species and groups them together in fields of one type of plant, thus requiring less maintenance.

In 2014, however, concerns about an economically realistic maintenance schedule and several related environmental issues were given high priority in the planning process that also entailed discussions about retaining integrity of the original design intent. Mrs. Hamilton urged the team to consider alternative planting strategies. The team first considered the question of how much "blue" was necessary to justify a "Blue Garden." The "blue" was then defined as vines on the pergolas and trellis, the water and the pots. This provided the base for diagraming planting options. The first was to install lawn throughout the entire garden, floating the pools in a carpet of green. The second retained the lawn, but shaped the space by outlining the former planting beds in stone. A third alternative proposed planting flowerbeds only along the outer walls, leaving a large swath of open lawn surrounding the pools to give them a special focus. This opton could also be thought of as Phase 1 of a full planting plan. All of these alternatives, studied in plan and in section, retained only a scant echo of the garden's original character, raising questions as to whether these offered enough for a defensible preservation strategy.

These explorations enabled Mrs. Hamilton and her team to choose yet another option—a reconstruction of the garden beds, planted with a simplified palette to recapture the intended ambiance, while using techniques to make the garden environmentally sustainable and economically maintainable. This process was to be one of renewal and reinterpretation rather than a classic restoration. Choices of perennials and annuals for the interior beds adhere to several principles developed by Reed Hilderbrand. Rather than the Olmsted firm's complex planting palette, which relied heavily upon bedding-out practices to retain the garden in prime condition, a new model was developed whereby horticultural dependability, drought tolerance, ease of maintenance and longevity of bloom are factors of importance equal to the blue, purple, white and gray-green hues and the interplay of textures, height and seasonal diversity.

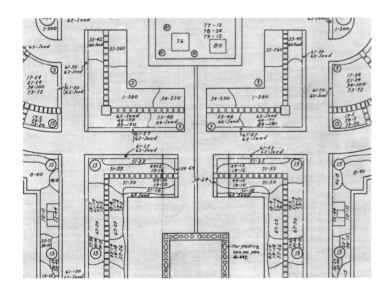

The inspiration for layout of the renewed planting beds was Olmsted Plan No. 398, dated October 1912, a detail of which is seen on the left. The Olmsted numbering system is augmented by a planting list with fuller instructions as to plant spacing, etc. The first number indicates the plant, the second number the quantity to be used.

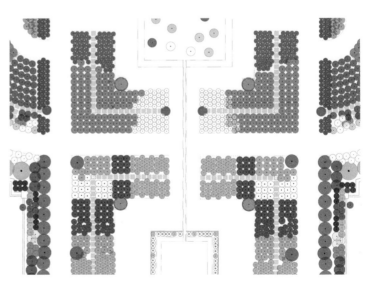

In the new plan, the complex plant groupings of the Olmsted drawing were reinterpreted and used as patterns for the new planting. The original planting plan was also simplified by removing the edging of alyssum, violets, and other seeded plants.

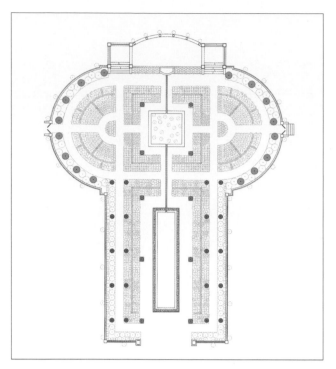

Evergreen Shrubs

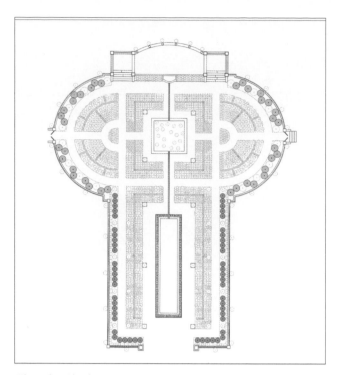

Flowering Shrubs

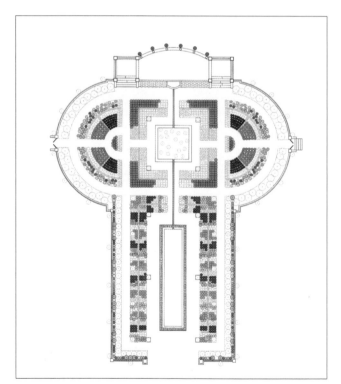

Perennials

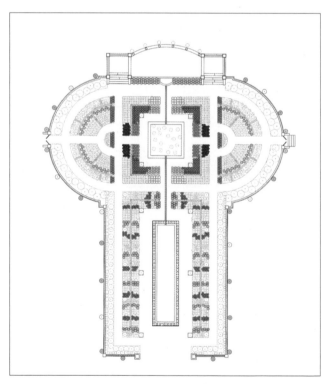

Annuals

The new plan incorporates select shrubs, not used in the Olmsted plans, to provide large masses, requiring little maintenance.

Evergreen Shrubs. Boxwood gives an evergreen definition for the lawn paths, with holly, planted in concrete containers, set along the long axis, where they had originally been located.

Flowering Shrubs. Bluebeard and Lace Cap Hydrangeas provide floral reinforcement for the perimeter of the garden.

Perennials. The new planting plan utilizes several flowering perennials from the original plans — Japanese and German iris, phlox, delphinium, balloon flower, nepeta and clematis, among others. Artemisia and lavender are included to provide gray green texture in the central beds.

Annuals. The annuals add an overlay of continuous color as the perennials come into bloom and fade. *Salvia patens* is the truest blue and complements the newly acquired blue pots and seats. Plumbago and morning glory, part of the original planting scheme, reinforce the blue ambiance.

(facing page) Enclosing the garden is a surrounding planting of moderately scaled evergreen trees with some deciduous material, to screen out the adjacent carriage house and greenhouse. Additionally, this planting reinforces the secluded status of the space as a secret garden or *hortus conclusus*, moderating the transition between the formal architecture and the rocky landscape beyond.

Greenhouse

Carriage house

The Olmsted planting plan of October 1912 indicated a compelling compositional strategy in its layout of plants in both the oval and linear beds of the original garden. The Reed Hilderbrand team analyzed the graphic components of the Olmsted planting patterns in intricate detail, extracting the individualized color sequences, heights and blooming times in order to understand how the spatial character and experience of the enclosed garden were defined by the plantings. In the original, the perennial groupings in the straight beds paralleling the walls changed species selection when the beds curved to follow the walls at the apse end, evoking a different character.[18] The straight central beds, on either side of the long pool and flanked by turf walks, were planted with numerous varieties of iris intermingled with phlox and balloon flowers, providing this passage with yet another textural experience.[19] In the oval area of the garden, the central square lily

pond was surrounded by generously sized beds, which the Olmsted plan planted like a parterre, to read as a distinct form, interweaving a complex pattern of several low-growing perennial and annual groupings. The adjacent half-circle beds, echoing the apse shape, were reinforced by one-foot square stepping stones to access the plantings. Wedge-shaped plant groupings held a concentration of vertical material—iris, gladioli and snapdragons.[20]

Inspired by this organizational pattern, the Reed Hilderbrand team, working with consultants specializing in herbaceous material, developed a plan utilizing fewer plant species grouped into blocks in the beds. Typical Olmsted planting methods were labor-intensive, setting individual plants often inches apart, with the intention of culling the bed as the plants matured.[21] Modernizations made to the 1912 plan included deleting the low flowering border plants around the bed perimeters. Additionally, masses of blue flowering shrubs such as *Caryopteris* and *Hydrangea* were incorporated to provide large swaths of height, structure and color. Because of the short and early blooming season, the peonies, originally planted along the main path as rhythmic punctuation points, were replaced with *Ilex glabra* to give year-round structure. Likewise, for the water plants, the original list guided the new choices for *Nymphaea,* now including King of Siam, Blue Capensis and *Marliac albida* for the blue and white water lilies, interplanted with blue and white *Pontederia cordata* in the square pool and with *Lotus grandiflorus* in the northern pergola pools.[22]

Originally, the concept of this garden as a *hortus conclusus*, separate and hidden from the rest of the estate, was reinforced by a dense enclosing planting of evergreen trees and deciduous shrubs. This planting, conforming to the wild character of the natural terrain with its irregular ledge outcrops, was intended to contrast with the defined symmetry of the ordered classical garden. Circumstances had changed since the garden had been surrounded by protected acres of the James estate. Now the roof of an abutting carriage house visually intruded to the east; on the hill above the western slope loomed the façade of a tall shingled house; and directly to the west was the newly constructed greenhouse. The goal for the new planting was to create a tree-shrub enclosure which would respond to the constraints of the current property boundaries, relate to the indigenous boulders and screen out the new visual intrusions, but which would be manageable in terms of growth patterns and heights.

Evaluating the Olmsted plans and historic photographs of the original planted frame enclosing the garden revealed to the Reed Hilderbrand team that many of the evergreen trees—the various pines, spruce, firs and Japanese cedars—would grow to heights of sixty to seventy feet with widths of thirty to forty feet, well beyond the limits of the space. Indeed, at the beginning of the project, the *Cryptomeria* that had outlived most of the other material had attained a height that overwhelmed the garden's scale, resulting in the decision to remove them. The team worked with a palette of native species, with a mature height of twenty to fifty feet and a tolerance for wind and salt air. This planting consisted of red cedar—*Juniperus virginiana*—a native tree which had been on the original lists, and would thrive in this windswept rocky terrain. In addition to the straight species, they used four smaller cultivars of this plant, "Burkii," "Idyllwild," "Hillspire," and "Emerald Sentinel," as well as arborvitae—*Thuja occidentalis*. Finally, American holly—*Ilex opaca*—with its dark glossy leaves and red berries, was chosen as a counterpoint to the palette of green, gray and olive of the other evergreens.[23]

This new frame planting is intended to be a more tailored, sustainable palette of native evergreen materials than was originally used, although still interspersed with drifts of *clethra* and groundcovers along the paths. To heighten the experience of the approach, hinting at the explosion of blue to come in the garden, rose of Sharon "Blue Satin," *Hibiscus syriacus*, and the Chaste tree, *Vitex agnus-castus*, which had been in the Olmsted plant list, were added. All the new plantings were designed to maintain the contrast between "outside and inside," the former being native, coarser and more rugged, while the latter provided for "[the] cultivated ... spectacular and, above all, Blue."[24]

The planting design of the garden and its

(facing page) The final plan for replanting the Blue Garden with its evergreen enclosure was based on original plans from the Olmsted office. These were analyzed to fully ascertain the original design intent—the context, views, topography, circulation, and planting. The trees in the newly planted frame are evergreens chosen to withstand the wind and salt air of the site—Holly, Arborvitae, and Red Cedar, the latter of which grows wild in the surrounding landscape. Five Red Cedar cultivars that grow to 15'-20' were also chosen for their variety of shapes and foliage texture. Blue-flowering shrubs, Vitex and Rose of Sharon, were planted as understory to provide a heightened sense of color awareness along the paths that lead to the garden. Drifts of groundcover define the lawn paths.

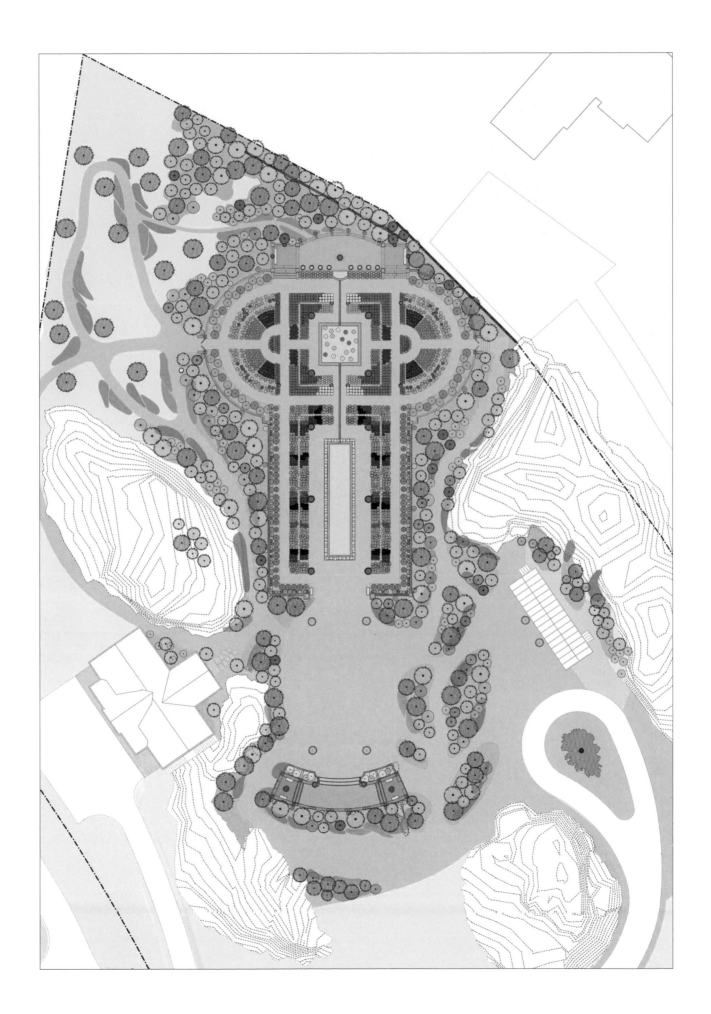

Dorrance Hamilton's vision, generosity and dedication to preservation and conservation of land and future sustainability, made the renewal of the Blue Garden possible.

She is pictured in the Blue Garden in September 2014, with her faithful companion, Louie, a Maltese.

enclosing landscape is evaluated each season to assess the effect created and to augment or change the flowering material selected in order to maintain prime conditions of bloom during the June to September period. Particular attention is paid to the trellis and arbor vines, both annual and perennial, to ensure that there is floriferous and textured coverage to intensify the sense of enclosure.[25]

Planning for a Sustainable Future

On August 20, 2014, the renewed Blue Garden was opened to a select group of guests who came together to celebrate the remarkable rescue of this iconic garden, with its classic architectural structure and unique monochromatic character, from the weed-filled and diminished condition in which it was found. Addressing an audience of preservation and horticultural leaders, of Newport dignitaries and of the many craftspeople who

had played a role in rehabilitating this site, Doug Reed paid tribute to Dorrance Hamilton for her vision and commitment to recapturing this notable component of Newport's and the nation's cultural history. He noted her strong sense of social responsibility to future generations so that they could learn about the people and the process which originally shaped this important cultural icon, in addition to her insistence that this renewal be relevant to contemporary times. Recapturing this work of landscape artistry is intended to teach others about the intellectual and pragmatic challenges of preserving a garden of such historic significance for today's circumstances. It is the hope that the Blue Garden serves as an inspiration to further this legacy of landscape artistry while reinforcing stewardship values concerning our collective culture.[26]

While every garden is a dynamic work in progress, for an historic garden to maintain the integrity of its artistic vision and be true to its intended spatial, visual and material character, even if it is not to be a classic restoration, it must be managed within clear parameters and shaped around its new purpose and educational mission. As a private place with limited visitation by invited groups, its nuanced balance of preservation, interpretation and sustainability is guided by strategic landscape management principles. These principles were developed to perpetuate the garden's spatial form and character for the two major components of its design, the interior garden and the surrounding plantings that form its enclosure. This strategy defines the tasks required to maintain the shape, color, texture and character of the plants within the garden's beds throughout the prime season. Likewise, the character of the surrounding planting is detailed with recommendations for pruning or successional planting. Daily, monthly and yearly maintenance requirements are directed toward keeping this garden at its prime to display its iconic horticultural character with interplay of color and texture within its classically structured setting.

Developing the mission for the Blue Garden is an ongoing educational process. Much can be learned from the panoply of stories associated with it—the history of the site, its owners and designers; its rich historical, geographical and multi-cultural contexts with their local, national and international implications; its original development and changes over time; and its resiliency, its rescue and its rebuilding with attention to its quest to be relevant to twenty-first century needs.

Conclusion

Retrieving the Blue Garden from the detritus of neglect has been an engrossing labor of dedication for a remarkable team of professionals from many disciplines. Over two years, architects, contractors, a historian, horticulturists and an army of craftsmen became increasingly engaged in the process, as lines of extraordinary beauty emerged from landscape remnants, revealing the artistry of Frederick Law Olmsted, Jr., and those who worked with him in the Olmsted office, and their ingenious response to Harriet James' request for a very special garden.

None of this retrieval would have occurred, however, without the discerning philanthropy of Dorrance Hamilton. Through her sound preservation instincts and love of gardens she recognized the potential for enjoyment and education that this unique landscape from Newport's past could bring anew to future generations. But, as with her support for Surprise Valley Farm, such preservation is not to have a static end result, solely of a rehabilitated property, but rather to be repurposed for a sustainable future that has socially productive implications far beyond its actual boundaries.

The artistry of landscape architecture, especially that developed by the Olmsted Brothers firm, is as governed by principles of pictorial art and spatial dimensions as are revered masterworks hanging in museums. They are intended to enjoyably engage the senses and perhaps challenge the intellect. Although seemingly works of natural beauty, the Olmsted landscape artifice was always planned with the fourth dimension—time—within its purview. Planning for sustainability, despite inherent change, growth and decay of natural elements, was always a major consideration of their projects, particularly those intended to remain in the public realm.

This then is the opportunity and challenge for Dorrance Hamilton and her team as they chart the mission for the renewed Blue Garden. To build upon the Olmsted credo of planned adaptability, not to be simply a demonstration of recaptured elegance from a bygone era, the Blue Garden seeks to define a progressive *raison d'être*. Advancing the enjoyment and understanding of garden art and horticulture on the cultural continuum is part of the mission of the Blue Garden, one that demonstrates that preservation and stewardship practices can be sustainable in a changing environment.

PHOTOGRAPHIC ESSAY

MILLICENT HARVEY *and* MARIANNE LEE

(previous) East gates at the entrance to the Blue Garden.

(left) Looking south along the east path with *Vitex agnus-castus* and *Clethra alnifolia* in bloom.

(next) First glimpse of the Blue Garden screened from view by a planting of evergreen trees.

145

View across the long pool to the south pergola. White fan flower (*Scaevola aemula*) is planted in the original decorative cutouts in the coping tiles.

The lily pond and south pergola are connected by a rill. Pots of agapanthus (*Agapanthus africanus*) enliven the pergola wall. Catnip (*Nepeta racemosa* 'Blue Wonder'), sweet alyssum (*Lobularia maritima*), wax begonia (*Begonia semperflorens*), and lobelia (*Lobelia laguna*) frame the pond.

(left) The south pergola is reflected in the lily pond. White hardy water lily (*Marliac albida*) and pickerel weed (*Pontederia cordata*) fill the pond. The blue stone pattern in the coping was restored to reveal the original design.

(next) Layers of gentian sage (*Salvia patens* 'Patio Deep Blue', Stokes aster (*Stokesia laevis* 'Peachie's Pick'), and meadow sage (*Salvia x sylvestris* 'Blue Hill') provide a foreground to the east gates and view of the meadow beyond.

(facing page)
Iris ensata 'Mt. Fujiyama'

(left)
Salvia patens 'Patio Deep Blue'
Gentian sage

Salvia x sylvestris 'Blue Hill'
Meadow sage

(above)
Gentiana 'True Blue'
Gentian

Stokesia laevis 'Peachie's Pick'
Stokes aster

(left)
Centaurea cyanus
Bachelor's buttons

Lavandula x intermedia
'Phenomenal'
Lavender

Platycodon grandiflorus
'Fuji White'
Balloon Flower

(facing page)
Central gardens are flanked
by lawn paths. Holly (*Ilex x*
'Nellie R. Stevens') are planted
in the stone pots.

(above)
Artemisia 'Powis Castle'
Wormwood

Salvia farinacea 'Victoria Blue'
Mealycup Sage

Salvia farinacea 'Victoria White'
Mealycup Sage

Passiflora caerulea
Passion Flower

Iris germanica
'Immortality'

(facing page)
West gate with evergreen
frame in the background.

(right)
Morning glory (*Ipomoea*) bloom
in profusion on the trellis.

(facing page)
A mix of delphinium (*Delphinium x belladonna* 'Blue Bird' and 'Blue Jay', and *Delphinium elatum* 'Summer Skies.'

(left)
View across the lily pond and
long pool to the north pergola.

(next)
The north pergola was reconstructed using local stone. The
wood trellis was fabricated from
Cryptomeria trees that remained
from the original garden.

(facing page)
View from the north pergola to the
plaisance, accented with bay trees that
belonged to the owner's grandmother.

Nelumbo 'Alba Grandiflora'
Lotus

(below)
Vitex agnus-castus
Chaste Tree

Hibiscus syriacus
'Blue Satin'
Rose of Sharon

(right)
The garden is screened by
evergreen trees along the lawn
path leading to the entrance.
The blue-flowering shrubs provide
a hint of the profusion of color in
the Blue Garden.

(left)
View through the east gate across the apse of the garden.

(next)
Lawn paths linked the garden to the mansion and were laid out based on the Olmsted Brothers plans. American arborvitae (*Thuja occidentalis*) dot the meadow with a drift of sweet fern (*Comptonia peregrine*) in the foreground.

(previous)
The north pergola blends within the evergreen frame and greater landscape.

(left)
The new greenhouse was built in the approximate location of the former tennis courts. A new drive was created to access the Blue Garden. Featured in the island is a weeping hemlock (*Thuja canadensis* 'Pendula').

(next)
The trial garden has been developed behind the north pergola to experiment with blue flowering plants before they are incorporated into the garden.

(pages 182–185)
Paths wind through old oak trees from the entrance to the Blue Garden to the lower clearing. The north pergola and greenhouse are barely visible from the road, nestled into a landscape of rocky outcroppings.

ENDNOTES

INTRODUCTION

1. Paul F. Miller, *Lost Newport: Vanished Cottages of the Resort Era*, (Carlisle, MA: Applewood Books, 2009), 114.
2. Olmsted Job #1380.
3. Olmsted Job #640.
4. Olmsted Job #2924. Stokes decided to subdivide his extensive property in the late 1920s, using the Olmsted firm to make these plans and giving them long-term design supervision over the architectural and landscape decisions of the individual plots. Many of the later homeowners for these lots also turned to the firm for their landscape planning.
5. Harriet Jackson Phelps, *Newport in Flower: A History of Newport's Horticultural Heritage* (Newport: The Preservation Society of Newport County, 1979); Harriet Jackson Phelps, "Garden Archaeology," *The Garden Club of America Bulletin*, Vol. 74, No. 4 (February 1986) 23–24. Correspondence between Harriet Jackson Phelps and Eleanor Weller Reade may be found in the Eleanor Weller Collection Garden Reference Files for RI Beacon Hill House, Archives of American Gardens, Smithsonian Institution.

CHAPTER 1

1. Frederick Law Olmsted, Jr., *Proposed Improvements for Newport* (Cambridge, MA: The University Press, 1913), 1.
2. Antoinette F. Downing and Vincent J. Scully, Jr., *The Architectural Heritage of Newport, Rhode Island: 1640–1915*, 2nd ed. (New York: Bramhall House, 1967), 129.
3. Ibid., 130.
4. Ibid., 129; David Schuyler, *Apostle of Taste: Andrew Jackson Downing, 1815–1852* (Baltimore: The Johns Hopkins University Press, 1996).
5. Schuyler, Introduction and Chap. 8 passim.
6. Cleveland, Amory, *The Last Resorts* (New York: Harper & Brothers, 1948), 23–24.
7. Downing and Scully, 139–156 passim.
8. Ibid., 172.
9. Ibid., 174.
10. This is the only joint project of the partners in Massachusetts. This park, for a city of spindles, with its predominant labor population, was being planned and built in time for the 1876 Centennial celebrations.
11. The Olmsted Job numbers are as follows: Theodore M. Davis #00684; John W. Ellis #01015; Anson Phelps Stokes #00640; King-Glover-Bradley #00681; Newport Land Trust #01070; Easton's Beach area #01211.
12. Olmsted's anxiety escalated into dementia, which caused him to be institutionalized in 1897 at McLean Hospital in Belmont, MA, the grounds of which he had planned two decades earlier. He died there in 1903.
13. The Olmsted Job numbers are as follows: William Dorsheimer #01073; Frederick W. Vanderbilt #01036; J. R. Busk #01299; Ogden Goelet #01203.
14. The work for Ellen Mason and her sister Ida is a case in point, Job #00257. Beginning in 1880, their grounds had been laid out in a formal manner according to a plan by Ernest Bowditch, a Massachusetts landscape engineer with a considerable following in Newport. Mason consulted the senior Olmsted in 1883 about planting. In 1902, for her new house, she returned to the Olmsted firm for advice to realign and redesign planting beds, but proceeded to work with Rose Nichols instead. In 1919 she again sought Olmsted advice, this time from Rick Olmsted, to mitigate the deleterious effects on her property from the widening of Bath Road, urban upgrades made in accordance with his recommendations to the city as part of his 1913 planning report *Proposed Improvements for Newport*.
15. Frederick Law Olmsted [Jr.], *Proposed Improvements for Newport: A Report prepared for the Newport Improvement Association* (Cambridge, MA: The University Press, 1913) 2–3, 5–6 and passim (Job #01824). The younger Olmsted cited the report prepared by the senior Olmsted in 1883 regarding Easton's Beach (Job #01211).
16. The Olmsted Job numbers are as follows: A.H. Olmsted #02221 and #02261; John Nicholas Brown #01220; Stuart Duncan #05432; H.D. Auchincloss #03794. Of these various Olmsted works, the Wildacre project is particularly noteworthy because of its eventual connection to the Blue Garden renewal. An innovative Arts and Crafts residence picturesquely set at the head of a cove on the rocky shore, Wildacre was the first large residence designed on the East Coast by California architect Irving Gill in 1900. John Charles Olmsted worked with his uncle and the architect to adapt this small lot to incorporate the unique architectural features into its waterfront setting. After nearly a century of varied ownership, by the 1990s this property was suffering from benign neglect when Dorrance Hamilton purchased it. With her respect for historic preservation, she returned the house and its grounds to its intended beauty while protecting the special character of its original design. She would also purchase several nearby parcels of land which had once been parts of the James estate, and would work to retrieve and reconstruct some of the original garden features. The notable Blue Garden is one of these projects.

CHAPTER 2

1. They were early and generous supporters of the Y.M.C.A., the Union Theological Seminary and numerous burgeoning cultural institutions in New York.
2. As his father, Daniel Willis James, had been before him, Arthur Curtiss James was a generous supporter of the college throughout his lifetime and later by bequests from the James Foundation. He was actively involved in many college programs and served as a trustee from 1904 to 1938. *Amherst College Biographical Record 1973* (Amherst: Trustees of Amherst College, 1973), 246.
3. Arthur D. Howden Smith, "The Men Who Run America: No. 20 Arthur Curtiss James: Unsung King of Western Railroads," *New York Post*, 5 December 1935; "Portrait of a Gentleman Funded Proprietor–this civilization's best example," *Fortune*, February 1930, 72–73; "Arthur C. James, 74, Rail Titan, Is Dead," *New York Times*, 5 June 1941; "James J. Hill," *Wikipedia*, URL: http://en.wikipedia.org/wiki/James_J.-Hill, 3–4.

4. Arthur Curtiss James, "Introduction," in [Dr.] Karl Vogel, *Aloha Around the World* (New York: G.P. Putnam's Sons, 1922), vii. The *Coronet*, built in Brooklyn in 1885, is listed today as one of the oldest schooner-yachts in the world. Originally owned by Rufus T. Bush, it became front-page news for the *New York Times* on 28 March 1887 when it beat the *Dauntless* (owned by Caldwell Colt of revolver fame) in a transatlantic challenge, winning a sizable purse. "Coronet is Over the Line," *New York Times,* 28 March 1887. By October 1893, Arthur Curtiss James had acquired the schooner as a gift from his father, and retained it until 1899. He later described it as "strictly a sailing vessel, without auxiliary power ... but an ideal type in which the young and inexperienced sailor could gain experience." Arthur Curtiss James, "Introduction," vii; Mabel Loomis Todd, *Corona and Coronet* (Boston: Houghton, Mifflin and Company, 1898), 1–3. The *Coronet* is presently undergoing restoration and rebuilding at the International Yacht Restoration School in Newport, RI.

5. Arthur Curtiss James, "Deep-Sea Yachting," in *Corona and Coronet*, xxiii–xxviii.

6. *Corona and Coronet*, 3–4. In addition to the hosts, Arthur Curtiss James (known as "the Captain,") and Harriet ("Mrs. Captain"), the guests included Professor David ("the Astronomer") and Mrs. Todd; John Pemberton ("Chief"), a retired U.S.N. chief engineer with Asiatic experience; Willard Gerrish ("the Musician") of the Harvard College Observatory; Dr. Vanderpoel Adriance ("the Doctor"), graduate of Williams College (Class of 1890) and the Columbia College of Physicians and Surgeons (1893) in practice in New York City; E. A. Thompson ("the Mechanician") of Amherst, in charge of the eclipse instruments; and Arthur W. Francis, an old friend and frequent sailing companion (Williams College, Class of 1890), known as the "General" for his financial management. *Corona and Coronet*, v–vi; 31; biographical material, Williams College Archives.

7. Arthur Curtiss James, "Advantages of Hawaiian Annexation," *North American Review* 165, No. 493 (December 1897): 758–760. *Corona and Coronet*, 24–124 passim.

8. The Todds had voyaged to Japan in 1887 for study of an earlier eclipse, at which time they had made many friends and acquaintances who now entertained the *Coronet* travelers with parties and tours. Likewise, the Jameses' social and business circles extended to Japan, including an Amherst classmate of Arthur Curtiss, Aisuke Kabayama, who introduced them to the Japanese social elite. Mabel's prior experience made her a valuable guide, especially her observations of the increased insertion of western elements into Japanese culture, food preparation and speech in the main cities. She traveled with the "unscientific contingent" as far as Kyoto; then she went north to the eclipse site, traveling with a young Japanese astronomer as interpreter, exploring Nara on the way. She also observed the devastation caused by a recent massive tidal wave, which had struck the northeastern areas of Honshu around Sendai on June 15, 1896. Text on the cover of a published edition of her *Coronet* journal (found in the Amherst Archives and Special Collections) advertised "A brilliant story of the longest yachting trip on record ... There are entertaining chapters on far away regions ... three hundred miles further north in the Japanese Empire than a foreign woman had ever before penetrated ..." *Corona and Coronet*, 172; 139–253 passim.

9. Arthur Curtiss James, "Deep-Sea Yachting," xxxiv–xxxvii; *Corona and Coronet*, 354; 343–356 passim. From San Francisco, the travelers' route took them by a special rail car, "The Buenaventura," from southern California across the desert of the Arizona territory to the Bisbee holdings of Phelps Dodge Corporation, where they explored the inner depths of the Copper Queen mine and its surrounding terrain. From there, they continued by rail through Texas to New Orleans, turning north through Georgia, Virginia, Washington, DC, finally arriving in New York. The *Coronet* repeated its voyage around Cape Horn with only its crew, arriving at its Brooklyn berth in February 1897, fourteen months and 45,000 miles after its departure. *Corona and Coronet*, 357–375.

10. The prestigious title of "Commodore" endured long after his tenure at the Seawanaka-Corinthian Yacht Club and later at the New York Yacht Club had expired.

11. Arthur Curtiss James, "Introduction," vii–viii; *Aloha Around the World*, 5; "Commodore James Orders Big Yacht," *New York Times*, 9 April 1909; "Flagship Aloha Launched at Quincy," *New York Times*, 24 March 1910; "Aloha Launched–New Yacht of Commodore James Afloat," *New York Tribune,* 24 March 1910; "Bark-Rigged Yacht, Flag Ship of New York Y.C., Put Over at Fore River Works," *Boston Herald*, 24 March 1910; "Carved Wood Panels in Aloha II," *The Lotus Magazine* 4 (May 1913), 319–24. The New York Yacht Club, established in 1844, was located in its new clubhouse on West 44th Street in New York when James was Commodore. In 1987, the connection to Newport was solidified with the acquisition of Harbour Court, the summer home of Commodore John Nicholas Brown, with its Olmsted Brothers and Harold Hill Blossom designed landscape.

12. Arthur Curtiss James, "Introduction," vii–viii; *Aloha Around the World*, 3–4, "Appendix" 263–264 and chapters I through XII passim.

13. "D. Willis James Dies in New Hampshire," *New York Times*, 14 September, 1907.

14. "News Items," *Torrea* (Journal of Torrey Botanical Society) 10 (January 1910), 25–28; "New Memorial Library for Mt. Hermon School," *Springfield (MA) Daily News,* 27 January 1913; "New Social Center for Italian Work ... ," *New York Times,* 19 May 1913; "March to New School," *New York Times,* 16 June 1913; "Mother of Arthur Curtis [sic] James Passes Away," *Watertown (NY) Daily Times,* 29 April 1916; "Arthur James, Financier, Dies," *New York Sun,* 5 June 1941.

15. "Real Estate in New York Is High but Worth Price," *Baton Rouge Times,* 8 November 1913; "Home to Cost $1,000,000–Arthur Curtiss James to Build at Park Ave. and 69th St." *New York*

Times, 8 February 1914; *Omaha World Herald*, 2 February 1928.

16. "Newport Looking Forward to Arrival of Atlantic Fleet," *New York Times*, 20 June 1915; "Will Build Newport Villas," *Washington Post*, 2 January 1916.

17. This property became the core of the estate of Marcellus Hartley and Geraldine Rockefeller Dodge, which she greatly enlarged and renamed Giralda Farms. Much of it is now a large corporate park.

18. "Arthur Curtiss James Developing Farm," *Miami Herald*, 8 September 1916; "Aristocratic Pigs Will Grunt on Newport's Lawns," *Duluth News Tribune*, 2 December 1917; Peter Pennoyer and Anne Walker, *The Architecture of Grosvenor Atterbury* (New York: W.W. Norton, 2009), 92–99.

19. The unique siting of Surprise Valley Farm, the shaping of the "bowl" in this rocky landscape, around which the farm build-ings are so picturesquely arrayed, reflects a skill and sensitivity to landforms. Without plans for this project, there is no record of whose hand might have been at work. There is nothing in the Olmsted Archives which indicate any work on this particular property, although Rick Olmsted and Atterbury were collabora-tors and advisors on several significant projects. At this time, Atterbury was designing the houses and apartments at Forest Hills Gardens in New York with Rick Olmsted as the landscape architect. This pioneering project, funded by the Russell Sage Foundation, was intended to prove that a well-planned community, with transportation connections, educa-tional and recreational amenities and attractive open space, could be designed with a distinctive architectural style and yet be affordable. Among Atterbury's contributions to this project were early innovations in low-cost modular build-ing units. Olmsted Job #3586; Pennoyer and Walker, 42–53 passim; 92–99; Susan L. Klaus, *A Modern Arcadia: Frederick Law Olmsted Jr. and the Plan for Forest Hills Gardens* (Amherst: University of Massachusetts Press, 2002), 12–13, 49–50.

20. Arthur Curtiss James was an accom-plished organist; thus organs were included in all their properties. "Home to Cost $1,000,000–Arthur Curtiss James to Build at Park Ave. and 69th Street," *New York Times*, 8 February 1914; "Artistic Park Avenue Residence for Arthur Curtiss James Nearing Completion ... ," *New York Times*, 26 December 1915; "The Real Estate Field–Arthur Curtiss James Rounds Out Park Ave. Corner at 69th St. ...," *New York Times*, 18 April 1916; "Arthur C. James Keeps on Buying ...," *New York Tribune*, 18 April 1916; "Real Estate Field ... ," *New York Times*, 21 July 1916; "Realty Event in Sale of ... Mansion on Upper Fifth Avenue," *New York Times*, 3 September 1916; "Park Avenue Block Restricted ... ," *New York Times*, 9 January 1931.

21. "Patriotism of Women Members of Navy League in Meeting and Work," *Miami Herald*, 4 March 1917; "Billy Sunday to Preach in Arthur Curtiss James Home," *Miami Herald*, 3 May 1917; "Mrs. James Talks on War Work of Red Cross and YMCA," *Miami Herald*, 12 February 1918; "St. Stephens Guild Benefit at Four Way Lodge," *Miami Herald*, 13 February 1918; "War Workers Guests at Delightful Luncheon," *Miami Herald*, 28 September 1918; "Japanese Pageant," *Miami Herald*, 21 January 1922.

22. "Prominent Citizens Aid Preparedness," *New York Times*, 5 November 1916; "Many Yachts and their Owners in Service of the Government," *Miami Herald*, 29 April 1917; "State Commissions on New York Ports Organize," *New York Tribune*, 23 August 1917.

23. "Newport Society Women Start War Relief Fund," *New York Times*, 16 August 1914; "Humane Side of War ...," *Miami Herald*, 20 March 1917; "$27,546 for Poet's War Aid," *New York Tribune*, 15 September 1917; "Sell Pearls and Furs, Mrs. James Tells Women," *Duluth News Tribune*, 8 November 1917.

24. "$115,000 to Armenia ... Arthur Curtiss James and Christian Herald Give $10,000 Each for Relief," *New York Times*, 29 May 1917; "Near East Drive to Go On," *New York Times*, 1 February 1919; "Story of Armenia's Woes Is Told ...," *Miami Herald*, 9 March 1921; "Aid for Near East Schools," *New York Times*, 29 April 1922.

25. *Biographical Record of Graduates and Former Students 1920*, Arthur Curtiss James files, Amherst College Archives, Amherst, MA; Baron de Cartier to Arthur Curtiss James, 30 December 1925, Arthur Curtiss James files, Amherst College Archives; "Association Is Formed to Lay Away Estate in France for an American Cemetery," *Fort Worth Star-Telegram*, 3 June 1919; "Hat for Paris ...," *Time*, 2 March 1925; "American Church Built in France," *Philadelphia-Trenton Evening Times*, 15 March 1929.

26. Earle Crowe, "New Move in Rail Contest," *Los Angeles Times*, 11 June 1926; "Arthur Curtiss James Leading Rail Stock Owner ...," *Washington Post*, 11 June 1926; "A. C. James Buys into Western Pacific ...," *Wall Street Journal*, 11 June 1926; Russell R. Clevenger, "New Railroad Factor Controls Vast Mileage ...," *New York Times*, 4 July 1926.

27. "King of the Rails," *Los Angeles Times*, 3 August 1926; "Get Bay City Terminal ...," *Los Angeles Times*, 11 November 1926; "James Explains Plan of Big Hill Railroad Merger," *Seattle Daily Times*, 11 November 1926; "James Roads," *Time*, 24 January 1927; "Rail Merger of North Detailed ...," *Los Angeles Times*, 15 February 1927; "Northern Railroad Merger Detailed ...," *New York Times*, 15 February 1927; "Powerful Rail Magnate Little Known to World ...," *Springfield (MA) Republican*, 29 September 1928.

28. "Battle in the West," *Time*, 25 November 1929.

29. Earle Crowe, "Rail Plans Scrambled Up," *Los Angeles Times*, 22 December 1929; "Portal to Nowhere," *Time*, 12 March 1934; "Rail Deal Has Parallel," *Los Angeles Times*, 22 May 1930; "End of an Era," *Time*, 16 November 1931; "Some New Rail Plans," *Los Angeles Times*, 16 November 1931; "The Men Who Run America," *New York Post*, 5 December 1935.

30. Arthur Curtiss James, "A Plea for Our Railroads," *The Saturday Evening Post*, 16 January 1932, 21, 102–103; "The Last Railroad Mogul," *New York Sun*, 5 June 1941.

31. [Arthur Curtiss James] "Jake" to Prof. William P. Bigelow, 24 July 1934, Arthur Curtiss James files, Amherst College

Archives; "Rails Hit Large Holders," *Los Angeles Times*, 28 November 1931; "West Moratorium," *Time*, 12 March 1934; "SEC Reveals Large Stock Holdings of James and Others," *New York Times*, 3 April 1935; "New Track," *Time*, 13 April 1936; "James to Retire as Western Pacific Chair, 'Empire Builder' helped Complete Line in 1931, Last Continental Route for Opening Country," *Wall Street Journal*, 4 November 1939; "Court Approves Plan for Western Pacific," *New York Times*, 17 August 1940.

32. "Ocean Travelers," *New York Times*, 8 August 1934; "Ocean Travelers," *New York Times*, 26 June 1937.

33. W. W. Carman to Margaret Hitchcock, 23 September 1935 and 4 November 1935; "Jake" [Arthur Curtiss James] to "Peggy" [Margaret Hitchcock], 20 March 1936, all found in Arthur Curtiss James files, Amherst College Archives; "Aloha to Be Broken Up," *New York Times*, 2 October 1937.

34. "James Furnishings Sold," *New York Times*, 5 December 1941; "James Left Fund for a Foundation," *New York Times*, 8 June 1941; "$35,525,652 Estate Left by A.C. James," *New York Times*, 29 July 1942.

35. Henry Parsons, *Parsons Family: Descendants of Cornet Joseph Parsons: Springfield, 1636–Northampton, 1655* (New York: Frank Allaben Genealogical Company, 1912), 180, 251; Charles F. Warner, *Representative Families of Northampton: A Demonstration of What High Character, Good Ancestry and Heredity have Accomplished in a New England Town*, Vol. 1 (Northampton: Picturesque Publishing Co., 1917), 7; "Northampton," *Springfield (MA) Republican*, 11 April 1876; "Northampton," *Springfield (MA) Republican*, 21 April 1876.

36. Amie Parsons, Smith class of 1885, was married in February 1889 to E. Hayward Ferry, a Harvard graduate, Class of 1886, who became a banker, first in Boston and after 1907 for the Hanover National Bank in New York. *Smith College Annual Circular*, October 1888, 31–34; *Harvard College Class of 1886 Secretary's Report*, June 1889, 26; *Harvard College Class of 1886 20th Reunion Report*, 55.

37. "The Coming Wedding," *Hampshire Gazette and Northampton Courier*, 15 April 1890; "Northampton," *Springfield (MA) Republican*, 20 April 1890; "A Brilliant Hampshire Event," *Springfield Republican*, 24 April 1890; "Mrs. Cleveland in Town," *New Haven Register*, 24 April 1890.

38. "Elizabeth Home for Girls," *New York Times*, 14 December 1892; "Incidents in Society," *New York Tribune*, 17 December 1895; "A Settlement Reunion–Fifteen Hundred Members of Christodora House Meet," *New York Tribune*, 9 May 1905.

39. "The Great Flower Show," *New York Tribune*, 13 November 1897; "Largest Chrysanthemum," *Idaho Statesman*, 21 November 1909.

40. A. W. F. and Wm. M. K. [Arthur W. Francis and William M. Kingsley], "First West Indian Trip," *Coronet Memories: Log of Schooner-Yacht Coronet on her Off-Shore Cruises from 1893 to 1899* (New York: F. Tennyson Neeley, 1899), 7–23; 316–364 passim.

41. H. P. J. [Harriet Parsons James], "Cruise to the Hawaiian Islands and Japan," *Coronet Memories*, 75.

42. Ibid., 80–81; 88–93; 136–145.

43. Ibid., 122; 134–137; 148–150; 129–145 passim; 173–76.

44. Ibid., 85–96 passim; 111–119 passim; 89; 114.

45. H. P. J. "Cruise …," 119–176 passim. For the trip to the Inland Sea, Mr. Halsey, a former tutor of Arthur's and now a missionary in Japan, accompanied them. At the Beppu baths, he showed them the real living conditions for this population, saying, "It is the Japan which the chrysanthemum and the cherry-blossom enthusiast does not see and the part which educated Japanese do not wish them to see if they can avoid it." Harriet's further observation noted the cost for Japan to support a large standing army to make it the "equal of Europe and America in power. They scorn to be compared with any Asiatic nation, and consider themselves more divinely descended than any," 155.

46. "The Amherst Party Back from Japan …," *San Francisco Chronicle*, 3 October 1896; "Took Several Pictures of the Eclipse,"

New York Times, 4 October 1896; "Star Gazers Are Back …," *Kansas City Star*, from *Chicago Time-Herald*, 25 October 1896; "The Craft and Those Who Sail Them," *New York Tribune*, 15 May 1899.

47. V. A. and A. P. A. [Dr. Vanderpoel Adriance and Andrew Peter Alvord], *The Maiden Cruise of the Aloha: Spring and Summer of 1900* (New York: William C. Martin Printing House, 1900) passim.

48. "Aloha Launched–New Yacht of Commodore James Afloat," *New York Tribune*, 24 March 1910; "Carved Wood Panels in Aloha II," *Lotus Magazine* 4 (May 1913), 319–24.

49. Arnold T. Schwab, "Conrad's American Speeches and his Reading from 'Victory'", *Modern Philology*, Vol. 62, No. 4 (May 1965).

50. "Newport Attends Unique Pageant for Red Cross…," *New York Tribune*, 11 July 1917; "Mrs. A.C. James Gives Rose Pageant at Newport," *New York Tribune*, 1 August 1925; "Arthur Curtiss James Gives Newport Pageant," *New York Times*, 1 August 1925; "Entertains at Tea for Garden Group," *New York Times*, 28 June 1929. In 1917, Frances Benjamin Johnston, and her former partner, Mattie Edwards Hewitt, were acknowledged leaders in the field of home and garden photography. From the beginning of the 20th century, their images captured the prominent properties of the time and were widely published as the era of architectural and horticultural magazines blossomed. There are 9 undated black and white images attributed to both of them in the photograph collection for Job #03558 at Fairsted. Two of these, plates #7 and 8, are dated summer 1914, and published as hand-colored images ascribed only to Johnston in *Gardens for a Beautiful America 1895–1935* by Sam Watters (New York: Acanthus Press, 2012). Other images for the Blue Garden, found in the Frances Benjamin Johnston Collection, Prints and Photographs Division, Library of Congress (hereinafter FBJ Collection), are dated 1917, some of which are also included in the Watters volume.

51. "Powerful Rail Magnate Little Known to World …," *Springfield (MA) Republican*, 29 September 1928.

52. "A. C. James Gives Newport Pageant," *New York Times,* 1 August 1925; "Mrs. Arthur Curtiss James Gives Dinner to Wives of Amherst '89," *Springfield (MA) Republican,* 21 June 1921.

53. Lida Rose McCabe, "Surprise Valley Farm: On the Estate of Arthur Curtiss James, Esq., at Newport, R.I.," *Country Life,* April 1924, 50–53.

54. "Rich Litany Book ... Presented to New York's Cathedral of St. John," *Los Angeles Times,* 31 March 1912.

55. ["Northampton,"] *Springfield (MA) Republican,* 15 March 1912. The President's Annual Report from 1912–1913 notes that a "New York donor, who insists upon withholding his name, generously contributed $75,000 for the establishment of a professorship in History to bear the name of Sydenham Clark Parsons. To this wise friend of education belongs the distinction of making the first large gift to the [Endowment] fund ...", *Annual Report of the President of Smith College 1912–1913,* Series 8, No. 2, (Northampton, MA: Smith College, 1913), 6. "Mrs. James Left Fund for Charity," *New York Times,* 22 May 1941.

56. "Calls Dwelling Bill Lax," *New York Times,* 28 November 1928; "YWCA Doing Big Work Abroad," *Ann Arbor News,* 4 November 1922; "No Flapper Styles Being Taught Girls in Foreign Lands by YWCA," *Muskegon Chronicle,* 6 November 1922; "Leading Woman Globe-Trotter to Lead Nation-wide Y.W.C.A. Drive," *Illinois State Register*, 11 November 1922.

57. "Luncheon by Y.W.C.A.," *New York Times,* 16 May 1926; "Four Leaders of Y.W.C.A. Coming," *Seattle Daily Times,* 5 November 1926. "YWCA Officers Feted," *Morning Oregonian* [Portland] 14 November 1926; "Wife of Visiting Financier Asks Support for YWCA," *Morning Oregonian* [Portland] 16 November 1926; "Praises Rich Women," *Cleveland Plain Dealer,* 6 and 7 November 1929.

58. "Just a Rail Magnate...," *Omaha World News,* 21 November 1931.

59. Cholly Knickerbocker, "Knickerbocker Brevities from Mayfair Scene," *Cleveland Plain Dealer,* 12 February 1939.

CHAPTER 3

1. Both Arthur Curtiss James and I. N. Phelps Stokes shared Anson Green Phelps as great grandfather, the family patriarch and source of the fortune.

2. Max Page, *The Creative Destruction of Manhattan, 1900–1940* (Chicago: University of Chicago Press, 1999), 222; Andrew S. Dalkart, *Morningside Heights: A History of its Architecture and Development* (New York: Columbia University Press, 1998), 413 fn 63.

3. Charles McKim, appointed to plan the new campus for Columbia University after its move to Morningside Heights, had chosen the senior Olmsted, his colleague from the Chicago World's Fair, to advise on the landscape layout for this long-range project. After FLO retired, Rick Olmsted took on the tasks of planning for path systems and planting around the new buildings for Barnard College and the Teacher's College. The new chapel designed by Howells and Stokes was among the buildings to be settled into its site by Olmsted design.

4. Max Page, 217–249 passim; Francis Morrone, "The Ghost of Monsieur Stokes", *City Journal,* Autumn 1997, www.city-journal.org/printable.php?id=251; Henry F. Withey and Elsie Rathburn Withey, "Stokes, I. N. Phelps," *Biographical Dictionary of American Architects (Deceased)* (Los Angeles: Hennessey & Ingalls, 1970), 575–76.

5. By 1909, interested individuals from many professions coalesced in Washington to hold the first National Conference in City Planning with Rick Olmsted as an acknowledged leader.

6. Arleyn A. Levee, "An Enduring Design Legacy: Frederick Law Olmsted Jr. in the Nation's Capital," in Thomas E. Luebke, ed., *Civic Art: A Centennial History of the U.S. Commission of Fine Arts* (Washington: U.S. Commission of Fine Arts, 2013), 38–55; Susan L. Klaus, "Olmsted, Frederick Law, Jr.," in Charles A. Birnbaum and Robin Karson, eds., *Pioneers of American Landscape Design* (New York: McGraw-Hill, 2000), 273–76.

7. Note that among the assistants who worked on this job was Frank Lloyd Wright, Jr., who apprenticed in the firm around 1910.

8. Unsigned, undated (ca. September 1909) memorandum describing John Greatorex's qualifications and proposed duties, found in B file #3558, Olmsted Associates Records, Manuscript Division, Library of Congress (hereinafter OAR). Unless another job number is indicated, the citation "OAR" will refer to documents in the correspondence file (B file) for Olmsted Job #3558, the Arthur Curtiss James estate in Newport. In an April 1924 article by Lida Rose McCabe, she notes that Greatorex had come originally from the Rothschild English estate. "Surprise Valley Farm," *Country Life,* April 1924, 53.

9. Lawyer and philanthropist Henry de Forest owned the abutting estate (Job #3175), where the Olmsted firm was engaged for nearly 30 years of advice, design and planting, beginning in 1906. His brother, Robert de Forest, also a lawyer and philanthropist who was engaged in tenement reform and the arts, eventually becoming president of the Metropolitan Museum of Art, lived nearby. Robert was Rick Olmsted's friend and colleague, with whom he worked on numerous projects, most notably the design of Forest Hills Gardens (Job #3586) and other projects for the Russell Sage Foundation, including the 1929 Regional Plan for New York and its Environs. Moreover, the firm was involved for more than 20 years with work on Burrwood, the nearby estate of oil tycoon Walter Jennings, who was also a friend and patron of Tiffany (Job #6287).

10. Alice Cooney Frelinghuysen, "Louis Comfort Tiffany's Country Residences," in Alice Cooney Frelinghuysen, *Louis Comfort Tiffany and Laurelton Hall: An Artist's Country Estate* (New York: The Metropolitan Museum of Art, 2006), 49–57. Greatorex's later work for the James estate as designed by the Olmsted firm was to greatly reflect William Robinson's principles of planting. See Chapter 5, notes 2 and 10.

11. Percy Reginald Jones (hereinafter PRJ), Report of Visit (hereinafter R/V), 1

January 1910, OAR.

12. Gradually, a crew of skilled men, such as William McGillivray, was hired. Hans J. Koehler (hereinafter HJK), R/V, 1 April 1912, OAR; Harold Hill Blossom (hereinafter HHB), R/V, 20 January 1915, OAR.

13. Frederick Law Olmsted, Jr. (hereinafter FLO) to Mrs. Arthur Curtiss James (hereinafter Mrs. ACJ), 8 October 1920, OAR; HJK, R/V, 22 December 1920, OAR.

14. Arthur Curtiss James (hereinafter ACJ) to FLO, 2 December 1929, OAR; *Newport City Directory for 1930*, 270; "Obituaries," *Newport News*, 10 July 1929.

15. Miscellaneous client job files (B files) from OAR. A file containing some personal correspondence between the firm and Jones was assigned Job #363, OAR.

16. This image exists as a slide in the archives at the Harvard Graduate School of Design. They have not yet located the original drawing.

17. Rebecca Spain Schwarz, "Pinewood House and Garden: Historical Documentation Research," (typewritten manuscript), March 1991, Bok Tower Gardens, Lake Wales, FL, passim. Appendix B contains a listing of Wait's architectural projects in the Mountain Lake community.

18. Olmsted Plan #03558–134 (February 1910), National Park Service, Frederick Law Olmsted National Historic Site (hereinafter FLONHS). FLONHS is located at Fairsted, in Brookline, MA, the former home and office of Frederick Law Olmsted, Sr. and his subsequent firms. In its archives it contains many of the historic records of the Olmsted firm, including plans, photographs, planting lists, business records, some correspondence and other material relating to the extensive work products of this firm over its more than 100-year history. [Hereinafter, unless another job number is noted, all plan numbers will refer to plans for Job #03558, the Arthur Curtiss James estate in Newport, RI.]

19. Charles Robert Wait (hereinafter CRW) to Mrs. ACJ, 16 July 1912, OAR; CRW, R/V, 15 June 1912, OAR; CRW, R/V, 21 June 1912, OAR.

20. Miscellaneous client job files (B files) from OAR. A file containing some personal correspondence between the firm and Wait was assigned Job #409, OAR.

21. Miscellaneous client job files (B files) from OAR. A file containing some personal correspondence between the firm and Koehler was assigned Job #394, OAR.

22. Olmsted Job #3175 for the de Forest estate; Job #3120 for the Pratt estate, both jobs spanning decades of Olmsted firm planning.

23. Olmsted Job #1220, Job #0726.

24. Arleyn A. Levee, "Blossom, Harold Hill," in Charles A. Birnbaum and Stephanie S. Foell, eds., *Shaping the American Landscape* (Charlottesville: University of Virginia Press, 2009), 22–25; miscellaneous client job files (B files) from OAR. A file containing some personal correspondence between the firm and Blossom was assigned Job #347, OAR.

CHAPTER 4

1. "What Society Folks are Doing," *New York Evening Telegraph*, 5 September 1908.

2. In her study of McKim, Mead & White, Mosette Broderick states that the plans for the Glover house were supplied by the firm in 1886 for $500.00. Michael Kathrens attributes the design to Stanford White, although the photographs of the structure show none of White's usual elegance. Mosette Broderick, *Triumvirate: McKim, Mead and White: Art, Architecture, Scandal and Class in America's Gilded Age* (New York: Alfred A. Knopf, 2010), 176; Michael C. Kathrens, *Newport Villas: The Revival Styles, 1885–1935* (New York: W.W. Norton, 2009), 253.

3. "Yachtsman Buys Newport Villa," *Kansas City Star*, from *New York Herald*, 24 September 1908. It is unclear whether the Jameses had stayed in Newport in earlier years before the 1908 rental.

4. Frederick Law Olmsted, Sr. to G. G. King, 7 January 1885, A file #681, OAR.

5. Text by F. L. and J. C. Olmsted, Landscape Architects, on the Lithograph of the General Plan, "Plan for the Subdivision of Properties in Newport, RI ..." dated 1 February 1885 (Olmsted Job #681), FLONHS.

6. *Newport Mercury*, 9 August 1902; *Newport Journal*, 25 August 1900; *Newport Mercury*, 19 September 1908; "Yachtsman Buys Newport Villa," *Kansas City Star*, from *New York Herald*, 24 September 1908; Frederick Law Olmsted, Jr. (hereinafter FLO), Report of Visit (hereinafter R/V), 22 September 1908, OAR; Olmsted Brothers (hereinafter OB) to W.H. Lawton (Newport City Engineer), 26 December 1908, OAR.

7. John Mead Howells to FLO, 27 March 1909, OAR; FLO, R/V, 11 June 1909, OAR; FLO, R/V, 9 July 1909, OAR; FLO and Percy Reginald Jones (hereinafter PRJ), R/V, 1 November 1909, OAR; PRJ, R/V, 24 November 1909, OAR; PRJ, R/V, 7 February 1910, OAR; Arthur Curtiss James (hereinafter ACJ) to OB, 11 February 1910, OAR; PRJ to ACJ, 21 February 1910, OAR; PRJ, R/V, 31 May 1910, OAR. The Olmsted archives originally held about a dozen plans for changes to Beacon Hill Road, of which only six are extant.

8. Plan #03558-35.

9. FLO, R/V, 2 September 1909, OAR. Greatorex was employed at $80.00 per month, plus his room.

10. FLO, R/V, 9 July 1909, OAR; FLO, R/V, 11 June 1909, OAR; R/V with Howells and ACJ at ACJ's office, 21 July 1909, OAR; FLO, R/V, 27 May 1909, OAR; FLO, R/V, 2 September 1909, OAR; Whitney–Steen Co. to OB, 20 October 1909, OAR; FLO and PRJ, R/V, 1 November 1909, OAR; PRJ, R/V, 1 January 1910, OAR; PRJ to Whitney & Steen Co., 25 March 1910, OAR.

11. Olmsted Job #01299. Olmsted office photographs from 1916 show that the James house could be glimpsed across the moors from the end of the Busk drive.

12. At this time, Mrs. James listed plants she expected to have included: large white German iris, delphinium, yellow and white lilies; *Rosa wichuraiana, Rosa rugosa alba* and other white roses; wisteria; white hollyhocks. In the greater landscape she wanted gorse, broom, bayberry, red cedars, prostrate juniper, *Pinus mughus* and kalmia. (FLO, R/V, 9 September 1909, OAR.) At a later September visit, James Frederick Dawson (hereinafter JFD), an Olmsted associate partner, noted that

tamarix, the *Rosa rugosa*, *Rhus glabra*, bayberry, hamamelis, *genista, cytisus* and *Amorpha fruiticosa* would all tolerate salt spray. (JFD, R/V, 17 September 1909, OAR.)

13. FLO, R/V, 30 August 1909, OAR; FLO and James F. Dawson (hereinafter JFD), R/V, 8 September 1909, OAR; OB to George Walter Dawson, 29 October 1909, OAR. To date, the Dawson watercolors have not been located.

14. On plans from May–June 1909 (Plans #03558-16 and #03558-28) a rectilinear enlargement around the Glover house outline is sketched in. By September 1909 (Plans #03558-41 and #03558-47) a rectangular extension had been added to the southwestern facade of the house. The former angular outline has been rounded at each end into graceful arcs echoed by terraces. This shape reflects the final form the mansion would have. This oval shape was later to be repeated in the Blue Garden.

15. "The New James House, All the Materials and Workmanship of the Very Best," *Newport Daily News*, 29 June 1910.

16. Olmsted Plan #03558-4. Apparently there were white rhododendrons with yellow markings among pine trees left from the Glover period of occupancy. FLO, R/V, 8 September 1909, OAR.

17. Hans J. Koehler (hereinafter HJK), R/V, 5–6 March 1910, OAR. They visited the estates of Alexander Agassiz, F.M. Davis, Marden Perry and Cornelius Vanderbilt, among others.

18. The visual record of Koehler's ideas, as shown on Planting Study #03558-146, FLONHS, also indicated the formal axial concepts for a large vegetable garden, for which he recommended a variety of fruit trees, some espaliered. HJK to ACJ, 24 March 1910, OAR. Also under development at this time were plans for various rusticated stone structures and greenhouses to service this garden. (Plan #03558-150)

19. ACJ to OB, 26 March 1910, OAR; ACJ to OB, 29 March 1910, OAR.

20. At this time, when General Plan #03558-188 was produced, the area later to become the Blue Garden was labeled "Informal Garden." See section below entitled "Considering a Formal Garden."

21. The planting study #03558-146 was elaborated into Revised Planting Plan #03558-248 of January 1911, which recorded what had been accomplished in 1910, as well as the planting agenda for 1911.

22. In April, Jones had noted that the grounds and associated buildings were costing nearly $100,000. He observed, "It all goes to prove that preliminary rough estimates are not worth a cuss ... in this case especially so as many difficulties have been struck all through the work which were impossible to see on the surface." PRJ, R/V, 23 April 1910, OAR; FLO to ACJ, 12 December 1910, OAR.

23. One of the office procedures for most projects undertaken by the Olmsted firm was to track each plan produced and received on a Plan Index card which was color coded to indicate the type of service it represented, i.e., architecture and engineering, planting, study, etc. While not all the original plans produced for a job still exist, in many cases the complete collection of Plan Index cards remains to provide a fuller sense of the complex course of a project.

24. Olmsted plan #03558-100; PRJ, R/V, 21 February 1910, OAR; PRJ, R/V, 12 March 1910, OAR.

25. Olmsted Plan #03558-134.

26. FLO to Howells & Stokes, 7 March 1910, OAR; PRJ to Whitney–Steen, 18 March 1910, OAR; HJK to ACJ, 24 March 1910, OAR; ACJ to OB, 26 March 1910, OAR; Charles R. Wait (hereinafter CRW) to Howells & Stokes, 28 March 1910, OAR; PRJ, R/V, 11 May 1910, OAR; FLO, R/V, 22 June 1910, OAR; PRJ, R/V, 5 July 1910, OAR.

27. PRJ, R/V, 30 July 1910, OAR.

28. CRW and HJK, R/V, 27 August, 1910, OAR; PRJ, R/V, 10 October 1910, OAR; PRJ, R/V, 7 December 1910, OAR.

29. Unfortunately, plans have not yet been uncovered for the Telescope House which was built. In the collection of plans from the Guastavino firm at Avery Architectural Library, Columbia University, there is an undated sketch for a classical structure labeled "Telescope Temple, Arthur Curtiss James residence, Newport, RI,

Howells and Stokes," which indeed resembles a *tempietto*, but is nothing like the Telescope House as finally developed. FLO to Isaac Newton Phelps Stokes, 24 June 1910, OAR; PRJ, R/V, 30 July 1910, OAR; CRW, R/V, 20 September 1910, OAR; PRJ, R/V, 21 October 1910, OAR; Olmsted Plans #03558-210, #03558-220.

30. Olmsted Plan #03558-248.

31. Frank Crisp, *Mediaeval Gardens*, (New York: Hacker Art Books, 1966), 23-31.

32. HJK, R/V, 10 March 1911, OAR, concerning Olmsted plan #03558-248; ACJ to OB, 11 March 1911, OAR.

33. "The Villa Colony at Newport Busy with Preparations for the Annual Dog Show," *New York Times*, 18 June 1911; "Notes from Newport," *New York Times*, 29 July 1911; "Evening in Newport Made Lively with Musicale and Surprise Party," *New York Herald*, 29 July 1911; "Diversions of Society at Fashionable Resorts," *Washington Post*, 12 September 1911.

34. The Olmsted firm worked on the grounds for Duncan's Bonniecrest over the next decade, Job #05432. They shaped the drives, richly textured plant groupings and a formal garden to surround a Tudorstyle house designed by John Russell Pope.

35. The Olmsted firm had provided plans in 1893 for the Harrison Avenue entrance, drives and planting for W.T. Burden (Olmsted Job #01387).

36. ACJ to OB, 19 September 1911, OAR; FLO to ACJ, 4 November 1911, OAR; ACJ to OB, 22 December 1911, OAR; PRJ to ACJ, 23 December 1911, OAR.

37. Whitney-Steen Co. to OB, 6 February 1912, OAR; Mrs. Clarke to OB, 28 September 1912, OAR; Harold Hill Blossom (hereinafter HHB), R/V, 27 April 1913, OAR; Olmsted Plans #03558-411 and #03558-442.

38. FLO to ACJ, 18 September 1911, OAR.

CHAPTER 5

1. Family members, the descendants of Harriet James' niece Harriet, Mrs. William de Forest Manice, were not aware of horticultural books which might have been in the collection of their mother or grandmother, Harriet's sister, Mrs. E. Hayward Ferry.

2. Gertrude Jekyll, *Colour Schemes for the Flower Garden,* reprinted, with a preface by T.H.D. Turner (Woodbridge, Suffolk: Antique Collectors' Club, 1983), 10–11, 221. Color, singly or in combinations, was addressed by many notable garden writers and planners of this period. William Robinson, the influential English garden theorist, who had revolutionized planting with his ideas about the wild garden, included discussions about color in his many books. (see note 13 below). Louise Beebe Wilder, an American garden writer of the early twentieth century, "translated" the English gardening ideas into what was appropriate for the American climate. She included a chapter entitled "Mid-Summer Blue" in her 1918 book. Louise Beebe Wilder, *Color in My Garden: An American Gardener's Palette,* reprint ed. (New York: Atlantic Monthly Press, 1990), 95–105.

3. "Told Under the Palms," *Miami Herald,* 26 February 1922.

4. Percy Reginald Jones (hereinafter PRJ), Report of Visit (hereinafter R/V), 9 December 1912, Olmsted Associates Records, Manuscript Division, Library of Congress (hereinafter OAR). Unless otherwise indicated, all citations to OAR will refer to the correspondence file for Job #03558, the Arthur Curtiss James estate in Newport.

5. "The Blue Garden–All Summer Long It Blooms only in Heaven's Color," *New York Tribune,* 2 July 1911. The Jameses and guests were aboard the *Aloha II* for a Mediterranean cruise from September to December 1911. "Society in Newport Entertained by Officers of German Cruiser," *New York Herald,* 8 September 1911.

6. Both the plan entitled "Study for Garden worked out by Greatorex under Mrs. James' direction," numbered #03558-254, and the plan called "Diagram on axis of Formal Garden as proposed by Mrs. James," #03558-272, are no longer extant.

7. The plan of December 30, 1911, Olmsted Plan #03558-278, was a conceptual sketch by Koehler of the area below the drive, indicating ledges and locating various plant groupings. On this planting sketch an outline of an axial cruciform space with a large oval at the southern end had been superimposed, possibly by Wait. This shape seemed to be an enhanced development of his earlier ideas from February 1910, Plan #03558-134, which simply sketched an axial form around a central bed, terminating in an apse, but not related to a ground plan.

8. PRJ, R/V, 9 December 1911, OAR: The oval shape of the cross axis was an echo of the form that Howells & Stokes had developed for the expanded new mansion.

9. Olmsted Plan #03558-284.

10. Suggesting alternative evergreens, Wait preferred the *Ilex crenata* also because "it would be something which few other people have," but he wanted to check on availability, price and hardiness. For reasons not clearly identified, the second choice of *Cratageus pyracantha* was selected instead. Charles R. Wait (hereinafter CRW) and Hans J. Koehler (hereinafter HJK) to Arthur Curtiss James (hereinafter ACJ), 14 February 1912, OAR.

11. In classical landscape parlance, a *plaisance* or "pleasance" is a pleasure garden, usually associated in the late Medieval and early Renaissance periods with orchard and kitchen gardens. Often secluded and usually enclosed by a wall or wood palings, it was characterized by trees, meadows and certain flowers. The idea extends from early Middle Eastern art, particularly as depicted in Persian art and on Persian rugs, to late Renaissance art in several media. Marie Louise Gothein, *A History of Garden Art*, Vol. 1 (London: J.M. Dent & Sons, 1928), 142–45. The senior Olmsted had used this concept in his 1871 Plan for Chicago's South parks as the "pleasure ground" or "kept ground," being managed in a more garden-like way "and enclosed by fencing." Frederick Law Olmsted, "Report to the Chicago South Park Commission," in Charles E. Beveridge and Carolyn F. Hoffman, eds., *The Papers of Frederick Law Olmsted, Supplementary Series Volume I: Writings on Public Parks, Parkways and Park Systems* (Baltimore: The Johns Hopkins University Press, 1997), 218. Rick was to design a garden with a *plaisance* for architect and colleague I.N.P. Stokes, who had imported a fifteenth-century English Tudor manor house and reconstructed it on his Greenwich, CT acreage.

12. CRW and HJK, R/V, 14 February 1912, OAR; Olmsted Plan #03558-284.

13. William Robinson, Irish born, established himself in London in his twenties (c. 1861) as a gardener, journalist and advocate for naturalized plant groupings of native herbaceous and shrub material. He was a vocal critic of the highly patterned plantings of exotic material which characterized the Victorian gardenesque practices of this time. Through his influential books, beginning with *The Wild Garden*, and his magazine *The Garden*, Robinson, together with his friend Gertrude Jekyll, revolutionized garden aesthetics and planting methods to emphasize freer designs of massed material.

14. CRW and HJK to ACJ, 14 February 1912, OAR; Olmsted Plan #03558-301A (February 1912). Unfortunately, of the 25 studies, perspective sketches and plans originally produced between February and May 1912 for the garden itself and its surrounding plantings, only nine remain. Thus, understanding the process whereby various permutations of design were attempted, discarded or refined is largely lost to the contemporary viewer.

15. In plan #03558-284, the "colums [sic] of old house" are noted along the back wall of the southeastern pergola; the "statues of seasons" are located in the beds around the square pool, and the "well-curb" is placed along the main axis in the center of the lawn area. As sketched on this plan, the northwestern pergola is depicted with a front colonnade, and an apse with a focal feature (depicted by an unspecified circle) centered along the back wall.

16. CRW and HJK, R/V, 14 February 1912, OAR; HJK, R/V, 15 February 1912, OAR.

17. Frederick Law Olmsted, Jr. (hereinafter FLO), R/V, 26 February 1912, OAR; PRJ, R/V, 16 March 1912, OAR; CRW, R/V, 12–14 April 1912, OAR; PRJ, R/V, 15 May 1912, OAR; Harold Hill Blossom (hereinafter HHB), R/V, 28–29 May 1912, OAR; Olmsted Plans #03558-320, #03558-326.

18. Probably Olmsted Plans #03558-349, #03558-353; CRW, R/V, 14 April 1912, OAR.

19. Olmsted Plan #03558-284 indicates the use of these materials.

20. PRJ, R/V, 30 July 1910, OAR; FLO, notes to PRJ, [30 July] 1910, OAR; CRW and HJK, R/V, 14 February 1912, OAR; CRW, R/V, 14 April 1912, OAR; Olmsted Plan #03558-390-tp1.

21. CRW and HJK, R/V, 14 February 1912, OAR; CRW to Mrs. Arthur Curtiss James (hereinafter Mrs. ACJ), 16 July 1912, OAR; CRW, R/V, 6 September 1912, OAR; FLO, R/V, 6 September 1912, OAR; Olmsted Brothers (hereinafter OB) to A. T. Stearns Lumber, 18 October 1912, OAR; Olmsted Plans #03558-406, #03558-408; #03558-419. The wood for the overhead structures of both pergolas was to be rough sawn red oak. There were several plans made for this pergola which are unfortunately no longer extant.

22. CRW to Mrs. ACJ, 15 June 1912, OAR.

23. CRW and HJK, R/V, 14 February 1912, OAR; CRW to Mrs. ACJ, 21 June 1912, OAR; CRW to Mrs. ACJ, 5 July 1912, OAR; Olmsted Plans #03558-365, #03558-368.

24. Enfield Pottery and Tile Works to OB, 22 June 1912, OAR; OB [CRW] to Enfield Pottery and Tile Works, 27 June 1912, OAR; Enfield Pottery and Tile Works to OB, 29 June 1912, OAR. Enfield Pottery and Tile Works was founded in 1905 by J.H. Dulles Allen in Enfield, PA. Their polychrome and terra cotta tiles, predominantly blues and greens, were installed in several notable venues: the Bok Singing Tower at Mountain Lake, FL; the Detroit Institute of Art; and the Pan American Union, Washington, DC. Specially molded tiles of African designs were installed at the Barnes Museum entrance, Merion, PA.

25. Hazel H. Adler, *The New Interior; Modern Decorations for the Modern Home* (New York: The Century Co., 1916), 298; Paul Evans, "Durant Kilns" and "Volkmar Kilns," *Art Pottery of the United States* (New York: Feingold & Lewis, 1988), 91–93, 307–309; Elizabeth Alexander, "Jeannie Durant-Rice," *New York Times,* 10 March 1919. FLO refers to Mrs. Rice in his R/V of 11 August 1912 (OAR) regarding the Persian water idea.

26. CRW to Mrs. ACJ, 14 and 25 October 1912, OAR. There is no further correspondence to confirm that this plan was carried out, and the October plans entitled "Study for tile work N.E. Pergola," (Olmsted Plans #03558-404 and #03558-405) are no longer extant. Inspired by Japanese matte glazes, as shown at the 1893 World's Columbian Exposition, the Grueby Faience Co. became a leader in the Arts and Crafts and Arts Nouveau movements, producing tiles, vases and other pottery, renowned, in particular, for its green tones. Grueby collaborated with Tiffany, Stickley and other leaders of this period, but went bankrupt, the factory closing in 1920. "Grueby Faience Company," *Wikipedia,* www.wikipedia.org/w/index.php?title=Grueby_Faience_Company&oldid=600717053

27. CRW, R/V, 10 November 1912, OAR.

28. CRW and HJK, R/V, 14 February 1912, OAR; CRW to ACJ, 14 February 1912, OAR; HHB, R/V, 28–29 May 1912, OAR. Household records would have helped to unravel this mystery.

29. CRW, R/V, 2 July 1912, OAR; Emerson & Norris to OB, 30 July 1912, OAR; CRW, R/V, 31 July 1912; CRW to Mrs. ACJ, 20 August 1912, OAR; CRW to Emerson & Norris, 12 September 1912, OAR; Mrs. ACJ to OB, 12 October 1912, OAR; CRW, R/V, 10 November 1912, OAR; CRW, R/V, 27 November 1912, OAR. Olmsted Plans #03558-373, #03558-374 sh. 2, #03558-380.

30. Mrs. ACJ to OB, 11 October 1912, OAR. A business card for A. Olivotti was found in an OAR file for correspondence from 1911–1912. Again, household records would have been invaluable here.

31. Emerson & Norris to OB, 23 April 1912, OAR; James W. Baston, R/V, 20 April 1912, OAR; HHB, R/V, 23 May 1912, OAR; Emerson & Norris to OB, 30 July 1912, OAR; Emerson & Norris invoice, 2 August 1912, OAR; CRW to Emerson & Norris, 27 November 1912, OAR; CRW, R/V, 6 December 1912, OAR; Olmsted Plans #03558-351, #03558-352, both no longer extant.

32. To date nothing has emerged from Rick's records which might indicate what stimulated this new idea for him.

33. Olmsted Plan #03558-348.

34. FLO, R/V, 11 August 1912, OAR.

35. White's sketches and photographs of the various ideas culled from his research in the Boston Public Library have been preserved in the FLONHS NAB-NAC collection. They also resulted in Olmsted Plans #03558-430; #03558-434 sh. 2 of January 1913 detailing the long pool tile patterns.

36. Olmsted Plans #03558-425 and 432 sh. 1.

37. Olmsted Plan #03558-415 shows the lily pool coping pattern. The sketches based on images found in the volume, *Ornements de la Perse,* and from *The American Architect* clippings are in the NAB/NAC Reference Collection of the Archives at FLONHS.

38. Olmsted Plans #03558-400 and #422.

39. CRW, R/V, 10 November 1912, OAR; Olmsted Plans #03558-408; #03558-419; and #03558-406.

40. This is not an uncommon situation for a project more than 100 years old, even in a collection as extensive as that of the Olmsted firm archives. Drawings and sketches were sent to the client or craftsmen in the course of construction. Over the firm's 100 years of active practice, the paper media of the plans disintegrated and files were weeded out. What does remain in many cases are the card files, the Plan Index cards, which tracked what was produced or received for a project.

41. HHB, R/V, 25 October 1912, OAR; CRW, R/V, 10 November 1912, OAR; CRW to Jeannie Rice, 20 November 1912, OAR; CRW to ACJ, 19 December 1912, OAR; CRW to Jeannie Rice, 24 December 1912, OAR.

42. CRW, R/V, 9 January 1913, OAR; Jeannie Rice to OB, 25 January and 3 February 1913, OAR; HHB, R/V, 27 April 1913, OAR; Jeannie Rice to OB, 29 May 1913, OAR; Mrs. ACJ to OB, 9 June 1913, OAR; Olmsted Plans #03558-432 sh. 1, #03558-425, #03558-426, #03558-430, #03558-432, and #03558-434 sh. 2.

43. Mrs. James continued to be a patron of the Durant Kilns. In April 1914, Jeannie Rice held an exhibit of her recent potteries at her New York City home. Among the works displayed to great praise was "a superb Egyptian blue and gold table decoration," made for Mrs. James to be a highlight in her yellow marble dining

room in Newport. Decorated with lotus blossoms and winged lions, this blue centerpiece bowl with candlesticks in "an especially beautiful lustre" was made with techniques not used since ancient Egypt. "Superb Pottery by Mrs. C. C. Rice Exhibited Here," *New York Herald,* 10 April 1914.

44. CRW, R/V, 6 March 1913, OAR; James W. Baston, R/V, 3–7 May 1913, OAR; Olmsted Plan #03558-390-tp1; CRW, R/V, 10 November 1912, OAR; FLO, R/V, 13 July 1913, OAR.

45. Olmsted Plan #03558-146.

46. Olmsted Plan #03558-248.

47. In December 1911 a sketch plan (Olmsted Plan #03558-278) inserted the formal shape into the chosen site. By February 1912, Wait had refined the shape and was exploring foliage massing on the garden's periphery. Olmsted Plan #03558-284.

48. This choice may have been based on size and availability. However, at Mrs. James' request, they were choosing red-berried material in the surrounding plantings to provide for winter interest. The pyracantha's fruit may have seemed an added bonus for this reason. CRW and HJK to ACJ, 14 February 1912, OAR; HHB, R/V, 10 April 1913, OAR.

49. HHB, R/V, 20 January 1915, OAR.

50. HHB, R/V, 22 May 1912, OAR; Olmsted Plans #03558-301A; #03558-340; #03558-446.

51. From the mid-nineteenth century on, *Japonisme* had been an important influence in art, architecture and landscape. The Jameses' interest in Japanese aesthetics could probably be dated from their 1897 research trip to Japan aboard the *Coronet,* to follow the eclipse. By the turn of the century, Japanese plant material was increasingly available to the Western market, with articles and books on Japanese landscape art and artifact, such as Josiah Conder's 1893 *Landscape Gardening in Japan*, providing suitable interpretations. Among the Newport *haute-monde,* several had added Japanese or Asian elements to their gardens, most notably the tea house installed by Alva Belmont in 1913 at Marble House. Additionally, *Cryptomeria japonica,* Japanese cedar, hardy enough to withstand the wind and salt spray, began to be added to Newport gardens.

52. HHB, R/V, 28–29 May 1912, OAR; HHB, R/V, 17 December 1912, OAR; HHB, R/V, 10 April 1913, OAR; HHB, R/V, 20 January 1915, OAR; Olmsted Plan #03558-360, with planting list.

53. Photographs #03558-ph 336–340, taken by FLO, Jr. found in Album #3 for Job #03558, Arthur Curtiss James. The remarkable collection of photographs, which were collected or generated by the Olmsted firm over its working history, has been preserved at FLONHS in Brookline, MA. These photographs, arranged by job number to coordinate with the projects, reveal the evolution of the firm's work in a specific locale from rough land to finished space. In many cases, retaining the name of the photographer and the date taken provides the modern scholar with a sense of these landscapes through the eyes of the designers. This collection also includes periodical clippings, postcards and other visual ephemera.

54. Arthur and Harriet James were introduced to *Cryptomeria* on their Japanese expedition of 1896, when they admired the ancient specimens which lined the drive in Nara and made up the woods which surrounded the temples at Nikko. See Chapter 2.

55. Plans #03558-347 (not extant) and 348 of 17 April 1912 with planting list for Plan #03558-347. Plan #348 is then redrawn in greater detail in October 1912, renumbered as Plan #03558-398 with its own accompanying plant list containing more perennial material. HHB, R/V, 28–29 May 1912, OAR; FLO and HHB, R/V, 3 June 1912, OAR; HHB, R/V, 15 June 1912, OAR.

56. FLO and CRW, R/V, 6 September 1912, OAR; HHB, R/V, 2 October 1912, OAR; CRW, R/V, 7 October 1912, OAR; Mrs. ACJ to OB, 11 October 1912, OAR. There were 22 plans produced between the beginning of August and early November no longer extant. Of these 6 are sketches of vases or sundials; 7 concern the northern pergola and one is about the south pergola; others concern water features and walls with one mysteriously entitled "Accents between Garden and Plaisance."

57. HHB to Mrs. ACJ, 25 October 1912, OAR; Mrs. ACJ to OB, 29 October 1912.

58. Olmsted Plan #03558-447; HHB, R/V, 24 May 1913, OAR; Mrs. ACJ to OB, 9 June 1913, OAR; HHB to John Greatorex, 9 July 1912, OAR.

59. HHB, R/V, 22 January 1913, OAR; HHB, R/V, 2 April 1913, OAR; HHB, R/V, 10 April 1913, OAR; HHB and Hammond Sadler, R/V, 24 May 1913, OAR; Mrs. ACJ to OB, 9 June 1913, OAR; HHB, R/V, 20 June 1913, OAR.

60. FLO, R/V, 13 July 1913, OAR; OB to Mrs. ACJ, 11 March 1916, OAR; Olmsted Plan #03558-454A. Unfortunately, Blossom's plant list has not been located.

61. Hammond Sadler, R/V, 25 August 1913, OAR; HHB, R/V, 20 January 1915, OAR.

62. Later photographs indicate that this central allée of planted pots was increased to seven or eight along the full length of the central axis, from northern to southern pergolas. Additionally, similar pots of tall conical shrubs are placed at other points in the garden. Aiglon aerial photograph #68-35, Aiglon Aerial Photograph Collection, FLONHS; Image #16542, July 1917, Frances Benjamin Johnston Collection, Prints and Photographs Division, Library of Congress (hereinafter FBJ Collection).

63. Photographs from Album #2 for Job #03558-ph 189–193.

64. FLO, R/V, 10 September 1916, OAR. Hand-colored photograph by Frances Benjamin Johnston, July 1917, Image #16541, FBJ Collection. A black-and-white version of this image was included in Louise Shelton, *Beautiful Gardens in America* (New York: Charles Scribner's Sons, 1924), Plate 75. Shelton also used a black-and-white image by Mattie Edwards Hewitt showing a corner of the Blue Garden, which included the pots on plinths (Plate 76).

65. Images #16541 and #16542, FBJ Collection.

66. The planted pots show up in Olmsted photograph #03558-268, Album #2 while the amphorae are seen in Olmsted photograph #03558-287, Album #3.

67. Images #16755 and #16774 (Summer 1914), FBJ Collection; Image #16757 (July 1917), FBJ Collection.

68. "Newport Gardens," *Bulletin of the Garden Club of America*, No. 12, new series (July 1923), 48–49. A later article in the July 29, 1928 issue of the *New York Times* (Virginia Pope, "The Gay Sea-Kissed Flower Gardens of Newport") also refers to "a large blue jar of the Ming period" as the "Kitchener Vase." Other available documents do not refer to such a bowl, and without the household records, the provenance of this object is difficult to verify.

69. Olmsted photograph #03558-280-81, Album #2.

70. FLO, R/V, 10 September 1916, OAR; CRW, R/V, 2 May 1917; Harriet Jackson Phelps, *Newport in Flower: A History of Newport's Horticultural Heritage* (Newport: The Preservation Society of Newport County, 1979), Plate 49, 103.

71. Images #125687 and #16774, FBJ Collection. The placement and style of some of these embellishments would doubtless have displeased the Olmsted firm, but this was after their active involvement. In fact, on the back of a loose copy of Olmsted Photograph #03558-ph 268 (FLONHS), which shows the elaborate urn and benches at the northeast pergola, someone wrote "Seat was not designed by Olmsted Brothers."

72. Olmsted Photographs #03558-ph 232 (July 1915) and #03558-ph 329, FLONHS; Image #3c25693 and #16750 (1917), FBJ collection.

73. Image #16539, FBJ Collection; Olmsted Photograph #03558-336, Album #3 (October 1920), FLONHS.

CHAPTER 6

1. Diana Wolfe Larkin, "Biography," *Monadnock Art* (2008), www.monadnockart.org/index.php/artists-past/joseph-lindon-smith. In an article in the 1948 *Providence Journal* [exact date unidentified] found in the Joseph Lindon Smith collection in the Archives of American Art at the Smithsonian, he noted that the subjects of his historical paintings "don't wiggle" and do not complain about the rendering of "the mouth or the nose" like the earlier subjects of his society portraits.

2. A compilation of photographs, "thank you" letters and newspaper clippings (some sadly unidentified), encased in an album, preserved in the collections of the Redwood Library and Athenaeum, Newport (hereinafter "the Scrapbook").

3. Letter fragment. Adding whimsical cartoons to illustrate his correspondence seems to have been a Smith characteristic. A collection of Smith's files at The Archives of American Art, Smithsonian Institution, contains several examples of these.

4. The Blue Garden, though still somewhat incomplete at the time of this article, had been noted in a June newspaper as a "wonderful scene" in the "magnificent grounds" where many landscape effects had been "designed by Mrs. James." ("All Newport Interested in Fruit and Flower Show," *New York Times*, 15 June 1913). In fact, in all the newspaper coverage of this event, there was no mention of Olmsted Brothers and their landscape design. Rather, if any mention was made about the garden's creation, it was ascribed to either Mrs. James or to Joseph Lindon Smith. (*The Club-Fellow and Washington Mirror*, a society weekly, undated, found in the Scrapbook.) The professional periodicals of this era—*Current Architecture*, *The Architectural Record*, *The Touchstone*, among others—were very clear to credit the Olmsted firm's ingenuity for this landscape design. *Current Architecture* (Boston: Boston Architectural Club, 1916), 3 plates; John Taylor Boyd, Jr., "The Work of Olmsted Brothers," *Architectural Record*, Vol. 44 (December 1918), 508–10; "The Great Gardens of America," *Touchstone*, (March 1918), 612, 616.

5. "Blue Garden is Dedicated," *Newport Herald*, 16 August 1913; "Newport's Loveliest Fete," *The World Magazine*, 14 September 1913; several clippings from unidentified and/or undated sources in the Scrapbook: "A Fifteenth-Century Spectacle …;" "The Week in Society."

6. Handwritten notes by Joseph Lindon Smith found in the Scrapbook.

7. "Miss Florence Noyes In Water Dance at Newport," *New York Sun*, 31 August 1913; "Blue Garden is Dedicated," *Newport Herald* (undated) and "The Week in Society" (clippings from unidentified and/or undated sources in the Scrapbook).

8. "Rich Masque Opens the James Garden …," *New York Times*, 16 August 1913; "Society in Newport Enjoys Real Novelty: 'Masque of the Blue Garden,'" *New York Tribune*, 16 August 1913; "Newport Sees 'Blue Garden' Dedicated," *Pawtucket Times*, 16 August 1913.

9. "Saunterings," clipping found in the Scrapbook, unidentified as to source or date.

10. Undated clipping from *The Club Fellow & Washington Mirror*, found in the Scrapbook. The leaders of Newport Society referred to were Mamie (Mrs. Stuyvesant) Fish, Tessie (Mrs. Hermann) Oelrichs and Alva (Mrs. Oliver H.P.) Belmont.

11. These comments were extracted from various letters found in the Scrapbook. The handwritten notes are difficult to read, and many, clearly from close friends, signed with only first names.

12. "All the Smiths" to Mrs. James, 24 August 1913, found in the Scrapbook.

13. "Newport Celebrates Day," *New York Times*, 5 July 1914; "At Newport," *New York Tribune*, 5 July 1914; "Society Women Start War Relief Fund," *New York Times*, 16 August 1914.

14. For two of these properties, the so-called Artist's Lot on Brenton Road (to become Zee Rust) and the Villa lot on Hammersmith Road (to become Vedimar), both purchased secretly for Arthur Curtiss James by J. K. Sullivan, the initial planning was done by the Olmsted firm between 1915 and 1916, Jobs #06313 and #06315. Vedimar was demolished in 1975, while Zee Rust remains as part of the Cluny school.

15. "Newport will be Gay …," *New York Times*, 30 May 1915; "Will Build Newport Villas," *Washington Post*, 2 January 1916; "Newport Looking Forward to Arrival of Atlantic Fleet," *New York Times*, 20 June 1915; "Prominent Citizens Aid Preparedness," *New York Times*, 5 November 1916; "Many Yachts and their Owners in Service of the Govt," *Miami Herald*, 29 April 1917.

16. "Garden Association Elects in Newport …," *New York Tribune*, 3 August 1915; "Newport Ball in Aid of Guardsman," *New York Times*, 16 July 1916; "Humane Side

of War American Red Cross," *Miami Herald*, 20 March 1917.

17. This poem, read by poet Gertrude Moore Richards, glorified the intrinsic rewards of simple gardening tasks in a bygone England of the pre-war era. The choice of Kipling's poem was particularly evocative at this benefit for wartime relief held in such a notable garden and especially poignant since Kipling's son was killed in 1915 at the battle of Loos. See Watters, 28 and 342, note 82.

18. "Newport Attends Unique Pageant for Red Cross ...," *New York Tribune*, 11 July 1917; "Patriotic Pageant Given in Newport," *New York Times*, 11 July 1917.

19. "Society Women Volunteer as Dance Partners," *Chicago Daily Tribune*, 9 September 1917; "$27,546 for Poet's War Aid," *New York Tribune*, 14 September 1917.

20. "Will Be Great Harvard Outing," *Boston Herald*, 10 July 1921; photographs and a map in the Frances Loeb Library collection, Harvard Graduate School of Design.

21. "Newport Gardens," *Bulletin of the Garden Club of America*, No. 12 (July 1923), 48–49.

22. "Prince Spends Day in 'Seeing Newport,'" *New York Times*, 17 June 1926. This royal visit was covered by other newspapers, such as the *Washington Post*, the *Springfield [MA] Republican* and the *Watertown (NY) Daily Times*, the latter two, in particular, because of their city's Swedish population and their connection to Harriet James. "Capital Society," *Washington Post*, 16 June 1926; "Crown Prince Visits James's at Newport," *Springfield (MA) Republican*, 16 June 1926; "Crown Prince at A.C. James Home," *Watertown (NY) Daily Times*, 15 June 1926.

23. "The Gay Sun-Kissed Gardens of Newport," *New York Times*, 29 July 1928.

24. Frederick Law Olmsted, Jr. (hereinafter FLO) to Arthur Curtiss James (hereinafter ACJ), 21 February 1921, OAR; Olmsted Photographs #03558-ph 339, 340, Album #3, FLONHS.

25. There remains an intriguing cluster of questions associated with the insertion of this exedra into the northeastern pergola: What or who influenced Harriet James to make this change? What was the origin and background of this structure? Was it a European purchase? This was a period when so many wealthy Americans were reaping the treasures from noble families impoverished after the Great War. Or was it a copy from some Italian garden? Was it marble or some other material? Finally, what happened to this structure at the garden's demise? There has been speculation among local historians that some of the columns and other elements have been resurrected in other gardens.

26. Harriet Jackson Phelps, *Newport in Flower: A History of Newport's Horticultural Heritage* (Newport: The Preservation Society of Newport County, 1979), 103, Plate 49. The ultimate fate of the four marble columns which once surrounded the wellhead in the Blue Garden is yet another unknown.

27. Aiglon Photo Image #68-30 and #68-35 FLONHS. Financial records from the Olmsted office indicate that aerials were purchased from Aiglon Aerial Photos of New York between 1924 and 1928. Bank Records, Box 35, FLONHS.

28. Harriet Jackson Phelps, *Newport in Flower*, 111; "Garden Archaeology," *The Garden Club of America Bulletin*, Vol. 74, No. 4 (February 1986), 23–24.

29. FLO to Mrs. Arthur Curtiss James (hereinafter Mrs. ACJ), 22 December 1920, OAR.

30. Photographs from the Olmsted collection taken in September 1916 (Photographs #03558-298-304, Album #3) show many of the rustic elements, the paths, surrounding planting and wooden shelter. The Rose Garden of this time at Beacon Hill House was significant enough to be mentioned in the article by Frances Benjamin Johnston entitled "Rose Gardens of America" in which she discussed rose plantings on estates from coast to coast. *Art & Life*, Vol. 10, No. 6 (June 1919), 303–307. In January 1921, Koehler's photos reveal the weedier conditions in many of the same areas photographed earlier. His images also show how close this garden was to the enormous boulder south of the garage. (Olmsted photographs #03558-341; 343; 345; 350; 353; 361–362, Album #3).

31. FLO to Mrs. ACJ, 22 December 1920, OAR; Olmsted Brothers (hereinafter OB) to Mrs. ACJ, 10 February 1921, OAR; Mrs. ACJ to OB, 14 February 1921; Olmsted Plan #3558-471, FLONHS.

32. "Newport Watches Brilliant Pageant on the James Estate," *New York Tribune*, 1 August 1925; "A. C. James Gives Newport Pageant," *New York Times*, 1 August 1925.

33. "Newport Gardens," *Bulletin of the Garden Club of America*, No. 12 (July 1923), 49–50; Aiglon aerial photograph #68-30, FLONHS; Harriet Jackson Phelps, *Newport in Flower*, 103, Plate 49.

34. "Newport Gardens," *Bulletin of the Garden Club of America*, No. 12 (July 1923), 49–50; "Mrs. James Gives Rose Pageant with Dinner at Newport," *New York Tribune*, 29 June 1923.

35. "A. C. James Gives Newport Pageant," *New York Times*, 1 August 1925.

36. "Recital to be Staged in Newport Garden," *New York Times*, 5 September 1930.

37. "$250,000 Rose Garden," *Canton (OH) Repository*, 19 September 1929; "Finest Gardens in World Is Aim," *Cleveland Plain Dealer*, 20 September 1929.

38. Julie Khuen, "Kellaway, Herbert J.," in Charles A. Birnbaum and Stephanie S. Foell, eds., *Shaping the American Landscape* (Charlottesville: University of Virginia Press, 2009), 162–66.

39. Virginia Lopez Begg, "Foote, Harriet Risley," in Charles A. Birnbaum and Robin Karson, eds., *Pioneers of American Landscape Design* (New York: McGraw-Hill, 2000), 123–25; Harriet Risley Foote, "Acres of Roses," *The Smith Alumnae Quarterly*, May 1931, 290. Foote was in the class of 1886 at Smith. In her article, she mentions Amanda Parsons Ferry, Smith 1885, (Harriet Parsons James' older sister, whom she may have known at college.)

40. Foote, "Acres of Roses," 290.

41. "Garden Gossip," *Boston Herald*, 13 February 1934; J. Horace McFarland, "A Rose for Every Community," *Mt. Vernon (NY) Daily Argus*, 1934; J. Horace McFarland, *Roses of the World in Color* (Boston: Houghton Mifflin Company, 1947), 168–69.

42. "A Sea Side Rose Garden," *Horticulture Magazine*, July 1933, 226–27.

CHAPTER 7

1. "Polish Midshipmen Feted by Society at Newport Villas," *New York Tribune*, 8 August 1930; "Mr. and Mrs. James Newport Hosts for Sir Ronald Lindsay," *New York Tribune*, 18 September 1930; "Mrs. A.C. James Hostess," *New York Times*, 5 October 1931; "Rail Importance Cited by James," *Wall Street Journal*, 18 May 1931.

2. "Just a Rail Magnate–Reputed World's Greatest Holder of Stocks Travels Unobtrusively, Alone," *Omaha World News*, 21 November 1931.

3. Minutes, Board of Directors Records, Series I, Box 8, Christodora House, Columbia University Archives.

4. "Flower Exhibition Opens at Newport– Mr. and Mrs. A. C. James of New York Win Medal for Garden Effect at the Pool," *New York Times*, 7 July 1932; "Plans Daily Music in Newport Again," *New York Times*, 24 June 1935; "Garden Display Cup Is Awarded in Westchester," *New York Tribune*, 11 June 1936; "Flower Show Sets Mark for Entries," *New York Tribune*, 10 June 1937; "Music Week at Newport," *New York Times*, 12 July 1936.

5. Frederick Law Olmsted, Jr., to Mrs. Arthur Curtiss James, 8 October 1920, File #3558, Olmsted Associates Records, Manuscript Division, Library of Congress (hereinafter OAR). No record has yet been discovered to indicate the name of the general estate manager at this time, nor the number in staff. The Olmsted record does indicate that in 1929 James had hired Percy Wilkinson, formerly of the J. P. Morgan estate, to replace John Greatorex. Arthur Curtiss James to Olmsted Brothers, 11 December 1929, OAR.

6. [Vera Scott Cushman], "A Massachusetts Puritan in New York: Resolution of the National Board on the death of Mrs. Arthur Curtiss James, May 15, 1941," *The Woman's Press*, Vol. 35 (Minneapolis: University of Minnesota Press, 1941), 322.

7. "Mrs. A. C. James Wife of Financier," *New York Times*, 16 May 1941; "Mrs. James Left Fund for Charity," *New York Times*, 22 May 1941.

8. "The Last Railroad Mogul," *New York Sun*, [June] 1941; "Arthur C. James, 74, Rail Titan, is Dead," *New York Times*, 5 June 1941; "Arthur C. James, Prominent Railroad Leader, Dies at 74," *Wall Street Journal*, 5 June 1941; "Rail Empire Builder Dies," *Los Angeles Times*, 5 June 1941; "Rail Magnate Dies in the East," *The (Portland) Oregonian*, 5 June 1941; "No. 1 Owner of Rails Dies," *Omaha World Herald*, 5 June 1941; "Trains to Stop as Tribute to James," *San Francisco Chronicle*, 7 June 1941.

9. "Notables at Rites for Arthur James," *New York Times*, 8 June 1941; "Prayer by the Reverend Henry Sloane Coffin, D.D., at the funeral of Mr. Arthur Curtiss James on June 7, 1941," Arthur Curtiss James files, Amherst College Archives.

10. "James Left Fund for a Foundation," *New York Times*, 10 June 1941; "$35,525,652 Estate Left by A. C. James," *New York Times*, 24 July 1942; "Arthur C. James Left $34,771,702," *New York Times*, 26 June 1943. It is interesting to note that among the specific bequests was one for $125,000 to Robina Greatorex, the widow of his faithful former estate manager.

11. *Amherst Capital Program Newsletter*, No. 15, 14 August 1964; "Fund Is Dissolved; Gave $144 Million," *New York Times*, 17 June 1965.

12. "Service Club Here Marks First Year," *New York Times*, 1 May 1944; Maurice Foley, "Apartments Due on Mansion Site," *New York Times*, 20 October 1958; "James Fund gets Eight-Year Lease," *New York Times*, 23 May 1959; "Treasure Hunters Find a Prize in James Mansion," *New York Times*, 12 May 1959.

13. "Notice–Sale at Beacon Hill House on June 27–29," *Boston Herald*, 25 June 1944. Harriet Jackson Phelps, "Garden Archaeology," *Garden Club of America Bulletin* Vol. 74, No. 4 (February 1986), 23–25. Records for this sale have not been uncovered. It would be interesting to see what of the garden artifacts, furniture and other decorative elements were sold at this time and to whom.

14. "Estate Given to Church," *New York Times*, 6 December 1951. The Sisters of Cluny retained Zee Rust until 2007, when it was sold. *Newport Daily News*, 1 December 2007.

15. Unidentified newspaper clipping, dated 23 September 1953, found in a book of clippings at the Newport Historical Society Archives.

16. "Dame Newport Taking its Tiara Out of Hock," *Boston Traveler Features*, 30 July 1957; "Vacant James Mansion in Newport Razed by Fire," *New York Times*, 8 May 1967. Interestingly, the story of the fire was picked up by newspapers as far removed as Baton Rouge, LA. "Mysterious Fire Razes Mansion in Newport," *Baton Rouge Advocate*, 7 May 1967.

17. "Interliving Corp.," *Boston Herald*, 14 June 1970; "The Real Estate Mart; 70 acre Newport estate to be developed," *Boston Globe*, 21 June 1970.

18. Watters, 30 and passim.

19. Helen Rollins, a founding member of the Archive of American Gardens at the Smithsonian, and Eleanor Weller were instrumental in the cataloguing of these images. Harriet Jackson Phelps to Eleanor Weller, 20 September 1984, Eleanor Weller Collection, Garden Reference files, Archives of American Gardens, Smithsonian Institution; Eleanor Weller Reade, "Savaing [sic] The Glass Slides," *Horticulture*, 1 May 2007. The subsequent volume which emerged from these slide identification efforts, Mac Griswold and Eleanor Weller, *The Golden Age of American Gardens: Proud Owners, Private Estates 1890–1940* (New York: Harry N. Abrams, 1991) furthered our understanding of what this photographic resource reveals, with its prodigious research into the intricate histories of the people associated with these places.

20. There are about 24,000 items in the F. L. Olmsted, Sr. Papers in the Manuscript Reading Room of the Library of Congress, mostly given by F. L. Olmsted, Jr. over many years. There are another 170,000 items in the Olmsted Associates Records, given in 1967 and 1971 by Artemas Richardson.

21. David Grayson Allen, *The Olmsted National Historic Site and the Growth of Historic Landscape Preservation* (Boston: Northeastern University Press, 2007) 3–57 and passim.

22. As a result of years of inventory work, the

archival collections held by Fairsted now account for nearly 140,000 plans and drawings, some of very large size; 60,000 photographic prints and 30,000 negatives; nearly 3,000 lithographs; 70,000 pages of planting lists; and financial records, correspondence, records and reports, and models for more than 5,000 design projects, in addition to uncounted study and reference materials regarding urban design, landscape architecture and fine arts. www.nps.gov/frla/olmstedar-chives.htm and www.nps.gov/frla/olmsted-archives-collections.htm.

23. The following images are all from the Garden Club of America Collection, Archives of American Gardens, Smithsonian Institution (hereinafter GCA Collection): Images #RI0350033-34, #RI035021-22, #RI035020, #RI035026, and #RI035018.

24. Additionally, this volume, which indeed advanced public recognition of Newport's important historic landscape treasures, mixed fact with some myths in its descriptions. At that time, before major databases and the Internet, there were fewer known resources to consult.

25. GCA Collection, Image #RI035037. No information has been found as to what happened to the remnants of the exedra, its columns and other parts of this pergola.

26. [Harriet Jackson Phelps] to Eleanor Weller, 30 August 1984, Eleanor Weller Collection, Garden Reference files, Archives of American Gardens, Smithsonian Institution; Harriet Jackson Phelps, "Garden Archaeology," *Garden Club of America Bulletin*, Vol. 74, No. 4 (February 1986); GCA Collection, Images #RI035017 and #RI034019.

27. Nancy Knowles Parker, "Enchanted Gardens in Newport," *Garden Club of America Bulletin*, Vol. 81, No. 1 (August 1992). At some point, work on the tiles resulted in the removal of decorative tile features which had been at both ends of the long pool. They were still in evidence in 1999, as recorded by slides in the GCA Collection, taken by Jennifer Radford.

CHAPTER 8

1. See the periodicals list in the Bibliography.

2. As an indication of how Harriet James and her famous garden remained in the public consciousness, the 2011 theme for the Newport Flower Show of the Preservation Society of Newport County was "Entertaining Newport Style." To reference the 1913 "Masque of the Blue Garden," Bartlett Tree Experts and landscape designer Catherine Weaver "faithfully recreated ... one of the most celebrated creations of the Golden Age of American gardens," basing their work upon Harriet Jackson Phelps' descriptions. While far from being faithful to the original in either form or flower, this enjoyable event was an acknowledgement of the garden's importance in Newport's cultural continuum. www.newportmansions.org/press/press-releases/bartlett-tree-experts-to-recreate-newports-legendary-blue-garden-for-newport-flower-show; www.newportseen.com/archived-news/toasting-the-recreated-blue-garden-at-newport-flower-show.

3. Video interview between Andrea Campbell and Mrs. Hamilton, Newport, 12 June 2013; Interview between Mrs. Hamilton and Arleyn Levee, May 2014.

4. Philly Mag, "The Last Great Lady," *Philadelphia*, 21 October 2008. www.phillymag.com/articles/the-last-great-lady.

5. These properties had been in the ownership of the Manice family, descendants of Harriet Parsons James' niece, Harriet de Forest Manice, who had initially inherited or purchased the parcels. For a time, this family had continued to reside at Edgehill, and the Farm continued to serve its agricultural purpose with an occasional diversion. In 1973, after some needed restoration, it was opened especially to benefit the Newport Music Festival, for a staging of Adolph Adam's French comic opera, "Le Chalet Suisse" [a play on the familiar name for this farm as the "Swiss Village"]. In the fashion of Harriet James, the singers for this event came from the Metropolitan Opera with involvement from Sarah Caldwell, Boston Opera Company's impresario. "Boston Group Does Things in a Big Way ...," *Boston Herald*, 7 August 1973. However, the property was sold c. 1975, and a 220-bed rehabilitation facility was constructed at Edgehill to treat substance abuse, often for celebrity clients. Susan Brink, "Kitty's treatment center called 'one of the best,'" *Boston Herald*, 7 February 1989. By the end of the 1990s, the property was at auction; Mrs. Hamilton purchased it in 1998.

6. SVF Foundation, www.svffoundation.org.

7. Correspondence files for Olmsted Jobs #02221 and #02261, OAR, Manuscript Room, Library of Congress.

8. At FLONHS, in the records for Job #00681 there are 76 plans; for Job #03558, there remain 159 plans of the original 521; more than 200 photographs including early aerials; 3 folders of planting lists; articles and miscellaneous ephemera. At the Manuscript Room of the Library of Congress, for Job #00681 there are 2 file folders of correspondence and numerous loose letters; for Job #03558 there are 5 folders of correspondence and other ephemera. The Prints and Photographs Room has a remarkable collection of the Frances Benjamin Johnston garden images, of which many are for the Jameses' properties, as well as numerous images for this site from other sources. The Archives of American Gardens of the Smithsonian Institution contains numerous glass slides, 35mm slides, correspondence and ephemera for the various Jameses' properties. Additionally, the Archives at Historic New England and various Newport repositories contain photographs, books, newspaper collections and other ephemera relating to the Jameses and their various properties.

9. Letter from Dana Corson, Preservation Planner for the Newport Historic District Commission, to Barbara Cobb, 18 July 2012, containing the demolition permission; Tom Shevlin, "HDC Approves Restoration of Historic 'Blue Garden,'" *Newport This Week*, Vol. 40, 12 July 2012.

10. Olmsted Plan #03558-284, 14 February 1912, entitled Sketch for Formal Garden.

11. Charles R. Wait, Report of Visit, 14 April 1912, OAR.

12. Newport Zoning Board of Review, "Findings and Decision" in re: *Petition of Barbara Cobb, et al., Trustees*, filed with the Newport City Clerk on 6 November 2014, in Book 2434 at page 54.

13. Andrea Gilmore of Building Conservation Associates, New England office, evaluated the architectural remnants on the site, the stucco walls and columns; the concrete, tiles and decorative elements inlaid in the pool copings, in order to ascertain the nature of these materials. She directed methods to clean the pool structures so that the original color would be revealed in order to make repairs and replacements.

14. Since no extant plan detailed this structure, the small fountain had to be recreated mostly from photographic evidence in consultation between Reed Hilderbrand and Robert Shure of Skylight Studios, Inc. in Woburn, Massachusetts, who constructed it from fiberglass with a patina which appeared like aged clay.

15. The hand-colored glass slides from the Frances Benjamin Johnston Collection at the Library of Congress, so beautifully reproduced in *Gardens for a Beautiful America 1895–1935* by Sam Watters, were more reliable for color, since the photographer herself had directed the painstaking color work. Many of the glass slide images from the Smithsonian collection were colored years after the original slides were produced and tended to be less subtle in hue.

16. Memorandum from Joe James of Reed Hilderbrand to Arleyn Levee, 30 August 2014. Joe notes that Tim Craul of Craul Land Scientists from Pennsylvania wrote the specifications for these horticultural soils.

17. Fountain Craft Manufacturing of Baltimore, MD, a company with extensive experience in bringing state-of-the-art technology to historic water features, was selected to collaborate with Parker Construction Company to engineer the water system. A & L Plumbing from Rhode Island installed and set up the finished system.

18. The straight beds along the walls at the northern end were originally planted with a repeated series of concentrated groupings of several *Campanula* varieties (*lactiflora, pyramidalis, persifolia*), mixed with *Baptisia australis, Veronica longifolia* and *Aconitum autumnale*. At the apse ends, this palette changed to concentrations of *Delphinium* varieties mixed with *Lupinus polyphyllus*. Olmsted Plan #03558-398 from October 1912 contains a list of 83 items, giving total number of plants required for the whole garden and in some cases planting instructions as to the spacing of plants. Also extant in the archives at FLONHS is the Plan Order list for this plan which provides additional information, such as whether the desired plants were available or whether substitutions were made; the nursery from which the material was purchased, and how much was paid.

19. This planting originally contained repeated groupings of several cultivars of German and Japanese iris in blues and white, their vertical foliage softened by various phlox ("Miss Lingard," "F.G. Van Lassburg") and *Platycodon grandiflorum*. Olmsted Plan #03558-398 and Plant Order list for Plan 398.

20. Most of the material chosen for these beds surrounding the lily pool were low growing: *Plumbago larpentae*; varied *Viola cornuta* in blue and white; *Iberis sempervirens*; *Campanula carpatica*; *Nepeta mussini; Ruella ciliosa*, intermingled with various annuals: *Papaver Miss Sherwood* and sweet alyssum. In the semi-circular beds *Iris germanica, pallida* and *kaempferi* were mixed with annuals, *Agapanthus umbellatus*, white *Antirrhinum* and blue gladioli. Olmsted Plan #03558-398 and Plant Order list for Plan 398.

21. For example, in a space where the Olmsted plan had called for 24 German iris, 21 Japanese iris and 151 larkspur, all bordered by pansies, candytuft and alyssum, the Reed Hilderbrand plan suggested 27 *Aster* "Blue Autumn," 17 *Aster x frikarti* 'Monch,' 16 *Lavender x intermedia* 'Phenominal,' greatly changing the effect while retaining a display of essential blue by using reliable plants.

22. Daune Peckham, Little Compton, RI, and Suzanne Thatcher from Russell's Garden Center, Sudbury, MA, advised on certain plant selections regarding sustainability and color. Arlene Murphy, Plant Material Manager of R. P. Marzilli Landscape Contractors, Medway, MA, contractors for the entire garden, was responsible for locating all the plants, from the large evergreen trees in the frame to the annuals and perennials in the garden. She worked closely with Reed Hilderbrand to make substitutions if required to meet sufficient quantities called out on the plant lists, and commissioned Tina Bemis of Bemis Farms Nursery, Spencer, MA to grow several of the annuals for the project.

23. Conversations and correspondence between Arleyn Levee and Sarah Vance, summer 2014.

24. Consultations with Doug Reed and Joe James of Reed Hilderbrand from fall 2013 to spring 2014; Draft principles for "Rehabilitation Planting" from Joe James, 28 March 2014; correspondence between Arleyn Levee and Sarah Vance, 25 August and 31 August 2014; correspondence between Joe James and Arleyn Levee, 30 August 2014.

25. Correspondence between Arleyn Levee and Sarah Vance, 25 and 31 August 2014.

26. Remarks made by Doug Reed at the ceremonies to celebrate the renewal of the Blue Garden, 20 August 2014.

BIBLIOGRAPHY

BOOKS

Amherst College Biographical Record: 1973. Amherst: Trustees of Amherst College, 1973.

Amory, Cleveland. *The Last Resorts.* New York: Harper & Brothers, 1948.

Annual Report of the President of Smith College 1912-1913. Series 8, No. 2. Northampton, MA: Smith College, 1913.

Anonymous. *The House Beautiful Gardening Manual.* Boston: The Atlantic Monthly Company, 1926.

Begg, Virginia Lopez. "Foote, Harriet Risley." In *Pioneers of American Landscape Design,* eds. Charles A. Birnbaum and Robin Karson, 123–25. New York: McGraw-Hill, 2000.

Boston Architectural Club. *Current Architecture.* Boston: Boston Architectural Club, 1916.

Broderick, Mosette. *Triumvirate: McKim, Mead and White: Art, Architecture, Scandal and Class in America's Gilded Age.* New York: Alfred A. Knopf, 2010.

Chicago Architectural Club. *The Thirtieth Annual Architectural Exhibition.* Chicago: Chicago Architectural Club, 1917.

Chicago Architectural Club. *Year Book: The Thirty-sixth Annual Chicago Architectural Exhibition.* Chicago: Chicago Architectural Club, 1923.

Cleland, Robert Glass. *A History of Phelps Dodge: 1834–1950.* New York: Alfred A. Knopf, 1952.

Coronet Memories: Log of Schooner-Yacht Coronet on her Off-Shore Cruises from 1893 to 1899. New York: F. Tennyson Neeley, 1899.

Cran, Marion. *Gardens in America.* New York: The MacMillan Company, 1932.

[Cushman, Vera Scott]. "A Massachusetts Puritan in New York: Resolution of the National Board on the death of Mrs. Arthur Curtiss James, May 15, 1941." *The Woman's Press.* Vol. 35. Minneapolis: University of Minnesota Press, 1941.

Davis, Deborah. *Gilded: How Newport Became America's Richest Resort.* Hoboken, New Jersey: John Wiley & Sons, 2009.

Dolkart, Andrew S. *Morningside Heights: A History of its Architecture and Development.* New York: Columbia University Press, 1998.

Downing, Antoinette F., and Vincent J. Scully, Jr. *The Architectural Heritage of Newport, Rhode Island: 1640–1915.* 2nd ed. New York: Bramhall House, 1967.

Elwood, P. H., Jr. "Olmsted Brothers, Landscape Architects." Chap. in *American Landscape Architecture.* New York: The Architectural Book Publishing Co., 1924.

Eudenbach, Harry J. *Estate Gardeners of Newport: A Horticultural Legacy.* Privately printed, 2010.

Evans, Paul. "Durant Kilns" and "Volkmar Kilns." Chaps. in *Art Pottery of the United States.* New York: Feingold & Lewis, 1988.

Frelinghuysen, Alice Cooney. "Louis Comfort Tiffany's Country Residences." Chap. in *Louis Comfort Tiffany and Laurelton Hall: An Artist's Country Estate.* New York: The Metropolitan Museum of Art, 2006.

Gothein, Marie Louise. *A History of Garden Art.* Vol. 1. London: J.M. Dent & Sons, 1928.

Griswold, Mac, and Eleanor Weller. *The Golden Age of American Gardens: Proud Owners, Private Estates 1890–1940.* New York: Harry N. Abrams, 1991.

Jekyll, Gertrude. *Colour Schemes for the Flower Garden.* With a preface by T.H.D. Turner. Reprint ed. Woodbridge, Suffolk: Antique Collectors' Club, 1983.

Kathrens, Michael C. "Beacon Hill House." Chap. in *Newport Villas: The Revival Styles, 1885–1935.* New York: W.W. Norton, 2009.

Khuen, Julie. "Kellaway, Herbert J." In *Shaping the American Landscape,* eds. Charles A. Birnbaum and Stephanie S. Foell, 162–66. Charlottesville: University of Virginia Press, 2009.

Klaus, Susan L. *A Modern Arcadia: Frederick Law Olmsted Jr. and the Plan for Forest Hills Gardens.* Amherst: University of Massachusetts Press, 2002.

————. "Olmsted, Frederick Law, Jr." In *Pioneers of American Landscape Design,* eds. Charles A. Birnbaum and Robin Karson, 273–76. New York: McGraw-Hill, 2000.

Levee, Arleyn A. "Blossom, Harold Hill." In *Shaping the American Landscape,* eds. Charles A. Birnbaum and Stephanie S. Foell, 22–25. Charlottesville: University of Virginia Press, 2009.

————. "An Enduring Design Legacy: Frederick Law Olmsted Jr. in the Nation's Capital." In *Civic Art: A Centennial History of the U.S. Commission of Fine Arts,* ed. Thomas E. Luebke, 38–55. Washington: U.S. Commission of Fine Arts, 2013.

McFarland, J. Horace. *Roses of the World in Color.* Boston: Houghton Mifflin Company, 1947.

Miller, Paul F. *Lost Newport: Vanished Cottages of the Resort Era.* Carlisle, MA: Applewood Books, 2009.

The New York Botanical Garden. *Ground-breakers: Great American Gardens and the Women Who Designed Them.* New York: The New York Botanical Garden, 2014.

Newport Art Museum. *Newportraits.* Hanover and London: University Press of New England, 2000.

Olmsted, Frederick Law. "Report to the Chicago South Park Commission." In *The Papers of Frederick Law Olmsted, Supplementary Series Volume I: Writings on Public Parks, Parkways and Park Systems,* eds. Charles E. Beveridge and Carolyn F. Hoffman, 206–38. Baltimore: The Johns Hopkins University Press, 1997.

Olmsted, Frederick Law, Jr. *Proposed Improvements for Newport.* Cambridge, MA: The University Press, 1913.

Page, Max. *The Creative Destruction of Manhattan, 1900–1940.* Chicago: University of Chicago Press, 1999.

Parsons, Henry. *Parsons Family: Descendants of Cornet Joseph Parsons: Springfield, 1636–Northampton, 1655.* New York: Frank Allaben Genealogical Company, 1912.

Pennoyer, Peter, and Anne Walker. *The Architecture of Grosvenor Atterbury.* New York: W.W. Norton, 2009.

Phelps, Harriet Jackson. *Newport in Flower: A History of Newport's Horticultural Heritage.* Newport: The Preservation Society of Newport County, 1979.

Schuyler, David. *Apostle of Taste: Andrew Jackson Downing, 1815–1852.* Baltimore: The Johns Hopkins University Press, 1996.

Scully, Vincent J., Jr. *The Shingle Style and the Stick Style.* Rev. ed. New Haven: Yale University Press, 1971.

Shelton, Louise. *Beautiful Gardens in America.* New York: Charles Scribner's Sons, 1924.

Todd, Mabel Loomis. *Corona and Coronet.* Boston: Houghton, Mifflin and Company, 1898.

V.A. and A.P.A. [Dr. Vanderpoel Adriance and Andrew Peter Alvord]. *The Maiden Cruise of the Aloha: Spring and Summer of 1900.* New York: William C. Martin Printing House, 1900.

Vogel, [Dr.] Karl. *Aloha Around the World.* New York: G. P. Putnam's Sons, 1922.

Warner, Charles F. *Representative Families of Northampton: A Demonstration of What High Character, Good Ancestry and Heredity have Accomplished in a New England Town.* Vol. 1. Northampton: Picturesque Publishing Co., 1917.

Watters, Sam, ed. *American Gardens: 1890–1930.* New York: Acanthus Press, 2006.

Watters, Sam. *Gardens for a Beautiful America 1895–1935: Photographs by Frances Benjamin Johnston.* New York: Acanthus Press, 2012.

Wilder, Louise Beebe. *Color in My Garden: An American Gardener's Palette.* Reprint ed. New York: Atlantic Monthly Press, 1990.

Withey, Henry F., and Elsie Rathburn Withey. "Stokes, I. N. Phelps." *Biographical Dictionary of American Architects (Deceased).* Los Angeles: Hennessey & Ingalls, 1970.

PERIODICALS

Gardens:

Anonymous. "A Blue Garden." *The Garden Magazine* 46 (No. 1) (1927): 41. 1 photograph: entrance to the Blue Garden.

Anonymous. "The Great Gardens of America: With Illustrations from Some of the Most Famous Estates in this Country." *The Touchstone* 2 (No. 6) (March 1918): 612. 3 photographs of the Blue Garden: 2 of the southwest pergola and 1 of lattice and gate.

Anonymous. "A Newport Garden: A Color Symphony in Blue." *Vogue* (15 June 1915): 42. 4 photographs of the Blue Garden: 2 of entrance gate, 1 of the long pool and 1 of the southwest pergola.

Anonymous. "Newport Gardens." *Bulletin of the Garden Club of America* 12 (New Series) (July 1923): 42.

Anonymous. "One of the Two Garden Gates at Beacon Hill House." *The House Beautiful* 46 (No. 4) (October 1919): 212. 1 photograph: entrance gate to the Blue Garden.

Anonymous. [Photograph of Blue Garden]. *Arts and Decoration* 17 (No. 3) (July 1922): 164. 1 photograph: lattice and entrance gate.

Anonymous. "A Sea Side Rose Garden." *Horticulture* (July 1933): 226. 4 photographs of the Rose Garden: steps to pergola, terrace in front of pergola, long view to pergola and rustic steps above lily pool.

Boyd, John Taylor, Jr. "The Work of Olmsted Brothers, Part II." *Architectural Record* 44 (No. 6) (December 1918): 502. General Plan and 6 photographs of the Blue Garden: 2 general views, 1 of entrance gate and 3 of the southwest pergola.

Colton, Arthur W. "Walls and Hedges to Frame the Garden." *The Garden Magazine* 38 (No. 2) (October 1923): 79. 1 photograph of the Blue Garden: lattice and entrance gate.

Fitz-Gibbons, Costen. "The Garden Pool and the Average Garden." *Arts and Decoration* 21 (No. 3) (July 1924): 27. 1 photograph of the Blue Garden: the long pool.

Foote, Harriet Risley. "Acres of Roses." *The Smith Alumnae Quarterly* (May 1931): 290.

Hewett, Mattie Edwards (photographer). "The Mrs. Arthur Curtiss James Garden at Newport, Rhode Island." *Arts and Decoration* 13 (No. 5) (October 1920): 310. 7 photographs and 2 renderings of the Blue Garden: 1 photograph of entrance gates, 1 of sculpture and lattice, 1 of long pool, 1 of square pool and 3 of pool details; the 2 renderings show the wellhead and an urn.

Johnston, Frances Benjamin (photographer). "Garden Photography as a Fine Art." *The Touchstone* 2 (No. 3) (December 1917): 278. 1 photograph of the Blue Garden showing sculpture and lattice.

Johnston, Frances Benjamin. "Rose Gardens of America." *Art and Life* 10 (No. 6) (June 1919): 303.

Kenworthy, Richard G. "Published Records of Italianate Gardens in America." *Journal of Garden History* 10 (No. 1) (January–March 1990): 68.

Parker, Nancy Knowles. "Enchanted Gardens in Newport." *Garden Club of America Bulletin* 81 (No. 1) (August 1992): 32. 3 photographs of the Blue Garden: 1 of the square pool and 2 of the long pool.

Phelps, Harriet Jackson. "Garden Archaeology." *Garden Club of America Bulletin* 74 (No. 4) (February 1986): 23. 3 photographs of the Blue Garden: 1 general view when garden was extant, 1 general view of remains of garden and 1 of remains of pergola.

Toombs, Elizabeth. "Mr. Arthur Curtiss James' Newport Home." *Town and Country* (10 August 1912): 17. 4 photographs: 2 of exterior of house, 1 of mantel and 1 of entrance road.

Walker, Lydia Le Baron. "Garden Decoration." *The House Beautiful* 50 (No. 2) (August 1921): 118. 1 photograph: general view along main axis of the Blue Garden.

Surprise Valley Farm:

Anonymous. [Photograph of Surprise Valley Farm buildings]. *Architectural League of New York Yearbook; 1925.* Unpaginated. 1 photograph: detail of farm building.

Anonymous. [Photographs of Surprise Valley Farm]. *Architectural League of New York Yearbook; 1925.* Unpaginated. 2 photographs: 1 of entrance gate to farm and 1 of farm buildings.

Bagley, Alfred J. (compiler). "Comparative Details Group 10: Stone Textures." *Pencil Points* 14 (No. 7) (1933): 313. 2 photographs of Surprise Valley Farm showing details of the stonework of the farm buildings.

Gottscho, Samuel H. (photographer). "Farm Group, Estate of Arthur Curtis [sic] James." *The Architect* 9 (No. 6) (1928): 713. 2 photographs of exteriors of outbuildings.

Gulliver, Harold G. "Paddock, Ringside and Byre." *Country Life in America* 44 (No. 6) (1923): 18. 1 photograph of exterior of Surprise Valley Farm buildings.

McCabe, Lida Rose. "Surprise Valley Farm on the Estate of Arthur Curtiss James, Esq., at Newport, R.I." *Country Life in America* 45 (No. 6) (April 1924): 50. 15 photographs: exteriors of the farm buildings.

UNPUBLISHED MATERIALS

The Frederick Law Olmsted National Historic Site, National Park Service, Brookline, Massachusetts, is the repository for plans, planting lists, photographs and other documentary materials relating to Olmsted Job #03558, the Arthur Curtiss James estate at Newport, and for similar materials relating to other Olmsted firm commissions in Newport which have been referenced in this book.

"The Masque of the Blue Garden." A scrapbook preserved at the Redwood Library and Athenaeum, Newport, RI, contains a compilation of photographs, "thank you" letters and newspaper clippings (some unidentified) relating to the Blue Garden's opening spectacle.

Olmsted Associates Records, Manuscript Division, Library of Congress. File #03558 contains the correspondence and reports relating to the Arthur Curtiss James estate

in Newport. Also referenced in this book are numerous other files for Olmsted firm commissions in Newport which are relevant to the story of the James property. Files for these projects are also found in the Olmsted Associates Records.

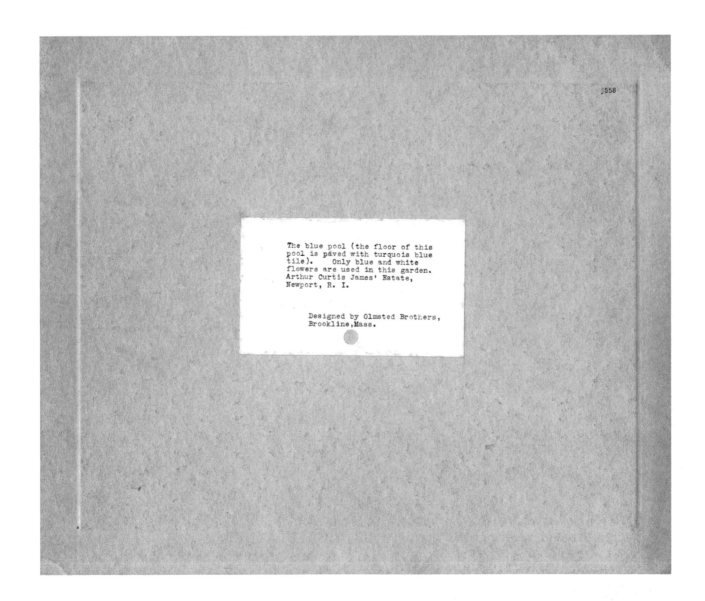

LIST OF ILLUSTRATIONS

pergola. Date and photographer unknown, private collection.

Page 110: Glass lantern slide of the vegetable garden, date and photographer unknown. Smithsonian Institution, Archives of American Gardens, Garden Club of America Collection

Page 111: Glass lantern slide of the Amphi-theater, date and photographer unknown. Smithsonian Institution, Archives of American Gardens, Garden Club of America Collection

Page 113: Glass lantern slide of the Rose Garden, date and photographer unknown. Smithsonian Institution, Archives of American Gardens, Garden Club of America Collection

CHAPTER 7

Page 114: View of garden and house, from John Taylor Boyd, Jr., "The Work of Olmsted Brothers," Architectural Record, 44 (Dec. 1918): p. 509, top. Original image #37400, from Library of Congress, Prints & Photograph Division.

Page 116: Image of ruined mansion, c. 1966. Courtesy, the Smithsonian Institution, Archives of American Gardens, Garden Club of America Collection.

Page 117: Photograph, c. 1966. Courtesy, Newport Historical Society, Newport, Rhode Island (P9747).

Page 118: Olmsted plan No.188 overlaid with contemporary subdivision property lines, c. 1980. Private collection.

Page 119 left: Frances Benjamin Johnston, c. 1911. Photograph #37463. FBJ Collection.

Page 119 right: Mattie Edwards Hewitt, after 1911. Photograph #37455. FBJ Collection.

Page 121 left: Exterior view of Frederick Law Olmsted Estate showing the firm's offices, Brookline, Massachusetts, c. 1895. Courtesy of Historic New England.

Page 121 right: Fairsted Vault, 1972, photograph by Richard Cheek. FLONHS.

Page 122 upper: Courtesy, the Smithsonian Institution, Archives of American Gardens, Garden Club of America Collection.

Page 122 lower: Courtesy, the Smithsonian Institution, Archives of American Gardens, Garden Club of America Collection.

Page 123 left: Courtesy, the Smithsonian Institution, Archives of American Gardens, Garden Club of America Collection.

Page 123 right: Courtesy, the Smithsonian Institution, Archives of American Gardens, Garden Club of America Collection,

CHAPTER 8

Page 125 upper & lower: Surprise Valley Farm. © Millicent Harvey, 2015.

Page 127 upper & lower: Wildacre. © Karen Bussolini, 2011.

Page128: Aerial photograph. © Marianne Lee, 2012.

Pages 130–131: Blue Garden prior to rehabilitation. © Marianne Lee, 2012.

Pages 132–133: Blue Garden construction. © Parker Construction Company, 2014.

Page 134: Three plans and elevations of alternative planting schemes. © ReedHilderbrand Landscape Architecture, LLC, 2014.

Page 135 left: Detail of Olmsted Plan No. 03558-398. FLONHS

Page 135 right: Detail of Revised Planting Scheme. © Reed Hilderbrand Landscape Architecture, LLC, 2014.

Page 136: Four schematic planting plans. © Reed Hilderbrand Landscape Architecture, LLC, 2014.

Page 137: Two elevations of Greenhouse and Carriage House. © Reed Hilderbrand Landscape Architecture, LLC, 2014.

Page 139: Site Plan for rehabilitated Blue Garden. © Reed Hilderbrand Landscape Architecture, LLC, 2014.

Page 140: Mrs. Hamilton and Louis in the garden. © Marianne Lee, September 2014.

PHOTOGRAPHIC ESSAY

Page 142–143 © Marianne Lee, 2015.
Page 144–145 © Marianne Lee, 2015.
Page 146–147 © Marianne Lee, 2015.
Page 148–149 © Millicent Harvey, 2015.
Page 150–151 © Millicent Harvey, 2015.
Page 152–153 © Marianne Lee, 2015.
Page 154–155 © Marianne Lee, 2015.
Page 156 © Marianne Lee, 2015.
Page 157 © Marianne Lee, 2015.
Page 158 © Millicent Harvey, 2015.
Page 159 © Marianne Lee, 2015.
Page 160 © Marianne Lee, 2015.
Page 161 © Marianne Lee, 2015.
Page 162 © Marianne Lee, 2015.
Page 163 © Marianne Lee, 2015.
Page 164 © Millicent Harvey, 2014.
Page 165–166 © Millicent Harvey, 2015.
Page 168 © Marianne Lee, 2015
Page 169 © Marianne Lee, 2015.
Page 170 © Marianne Lee, 2015.
Page 171 © Marianne Lee, 2015.
Page 172–173 © Marianne Lee, 2015.
Page 174–175 © Millicent Harvey, 2015.
Page 176–178 © Millicent Harvey, 2015.
Page 178–179 © Millicent Harvey, 2015.
Page 180–181 © Millicent Harvey, 2015.
Page 182–183 © Millicent Harvey, 2015.
Page 203: Photo Album 03558-06-ph04b. Undated. FLONHS
Page 204 © Marianne Lee, 2015.
Page 212 © Millicent Harvey, 2015.